Corporate Audit Theory

U

2

The Chapman & Hall Series in Accounting and Finance

Consulting editors

John Perrin, Emeritus Professor of the University of Warwick and Price Waterhouse Fellow in Public Sector Accounting at the University of Exeter; Richard M.S. Wilson, Professor of Management and Accounting at the University of Keele; and L.C.L. Skerratt, Professor of Financial Accounting at the University of Manchester.

E. Clark, M. Levasseur and P. Rousseau
International Finance

H.M. Coombs and D.E. Jenkins
Public Sector Financial Management

J.C. Drury
Management and Cost Accounting (3rd edn)
(Also available: Students' Manual, Teachers' Manual, Spreadsheet Applications Manual, OHP Masters, Dutch Students' Manual*, see also Gazely)

C.R. Emmanuel, D.T. Otley and K. Merchant
Accounting for Management Control (2nd edn)
(Also available: Teachers' Guide)

C.R. Emmanuel, D.T. Otley and K. Merchant (editors)
Readings in Accounting for Management Control

M. Ezzamel and D. Heathfield (editors)
Perspectives on Financial Control: Essays in memory of Kenneth Hilton

A.M. Gazeley
Management and Cost Accounting Spreadsheet Applications Manual

D. Henley, A. Likierman, J. Perrin, M. Evans, I. Lapsley and J.E.H. Whiteoak
Public Sector Accounting and Financial Control (4th edn)

B.W. Koch
European Financial Reporting Practices

R.C. Laughlin and R.H. Gray
Financial Accounting: method and meaning
(Also available: Teachers' Guide)

G.A. Lee
Modern Financial Accounting (4th edn)

T.A. Lee
Income and Value Measurement (3rd edn)

T.A. Lee
Company Financial Reporting (2nd edn)

T.A. Lee
Cash Flow Accounting

T.A. Lee
Corporate Audit Theory

S.P. Lumby
Investment Appraisal and Financial Decisions (4th edn)
(Also available: Students' Manual)

R.W. Perks
Accounting and Society

A.G. Puxty and J.C. Dodds
Financial Management: Method and meaning (2nd edn)
(Also available: Teachers' Guide)

J.M. Samuels, F.M. Wilkes and R.E. Brayshaw
Management of Company Finance (5th edn)
(Also available: Students' Manual)

J.M. Samuels, R.E. Brayshaw and J.M. Craner
European Financial Statement Analysis

C.M.S. Sutcliffe
Stock Index Futures

B.C. Williams and B.J. Spaul
IT and Accounting: The impact of information technology

R.M.S. Wilson and Wai Fong Chua
Managerial Accounting: Method and meaning (2nd edn)
(Also available: Teachers' Guide)

* The Dutch Students' Manual to accompany the third edition of Management and Cost Accounting by Colin Drury, is not published by Chapman & Hall, but is available from Interfaas, Onderzoek en Advies, Postbus 76618, 1070HE, Amsterdam. Tel. (020) 6 76 27 06.

Corporate Audit Theory

Tom Lee
Hugh Culverhouse Professor of Accounting
and Director of the Accounting PhD Program

University of Alabama

CHAPMAN & HALL
University and Professional Division
London · Glasgow · New York · Tokyo · Melbourne · Madras

Published by Chapman & Hall, 2-6 Boundary Row, London SE1 8HN, UK

Chapman & Hall, 2-6 Boundary Row, London SE1 8HN, UK

Blackie Academic & Professional, Wester Cleddens Road, Bishopbriggs, Glasgow G64 2NZ, UK

Chapman & Hall Inc., One Penn Plaza, 41st Floor, New York NY 10119, USA

Chapman & Hall Japan, Thomson Publishing Japan, Hirakawacho Nemoto Building, 6F, 1-7-11 Hirakawa-cho, Chiyoda-ku, Tokyo 102, Japan

Chapman & Hall Australia, Thomas Nelson Australia, 102 Dodds Street, South Melbourne, Victoria 3205, Australia

Chapman & Hall India, R. Seshadri, 32 Second Main Road, CIT East, Madras 600 035, India

First edition 1993
Reprinted 1994
Reprinted by International Thomson Business Press 1996

© 1993 Tom Lee

Typeset in 10/12 Plantin by Photoprint, Torquay, Devon
Printed in England by Clays Ltd, St Ives plc

ISBN 0 412 45220 0

A catalogue record for this book is available from the British Library

Library of Congress Cataloging-in-Publication Data
Lee, T.A. (Thomas Alexander)
   Corporate audit theory / Tom Lee.-1st ed.
      p.   cm.
   Includes bibliographical references and index.
   ISBN 0-412-45220-0
   1. Corporations-Auditing. I Title.
HF5667.L3873 1993   92-36202
657'.45-dc20   CIP

This book is lovingly dedicated to Katy who brings sunshine into my world and keeps auditing out of it – at least for a while!

Contents

Preface

When I entered university employment in 1966 my main teaching and research interest, almost inevitably, was corporate auditing. I had spent the years 1959 to 1966 exclusively as a corporate auditor, and I knew little else about the world of professional accountancy. I was asked to teach corporate auditing, and quickly (and gratefully) discovered the classic 1961 audit theory text written by Mautz and Sharaf, *The Philosophy of Auditing*. This book proved to be a lasting influence on my audit thinking as an academic.

Then, in 1969, when Eddie Stamp asked me to move to the University of Edinburgh, a further lasting influence occurred. Eddie was about to enter his infamous confrontation with the accountancy profession regarding accounting and auditing standards, and I and my colleagues lived through the various ups and downs of this stormy period. This experience made me acutely aware of the far-reaching economic and social consequences of audit failure, and of the related need for accounting students to be adequately taught about the strengths and weaknesses of auditing. Mautz and Sharaf's book was useful in this respect, but there was also an obvious requirement for a UK auditing text which combined concept with practice.

Eddie Stamp encouraged me in 1969 to write my initial auditing text, *Company Auditing: Concepts and Practices*. Indeed, he helped to find a publisher, and a contract was signed in 1970. I wrote the text with a background of the effects of the GEC–AEI debacle, the Leasco–Pergamon affair (and Robert Maxwell!), and the setting up of the Accounting Standards Steering Committee. However, on receipt of the draft manuscript, the publisher took fright, saying the text was too critical, and several years ahead of its time. The contract was cancelled. Fortunately, The Institute of Chartered Accountants of Scotland, and (particularly) Peter McMonnies, its Research Director, was not so risk aversive. A less critical version was published in 1972 by ICAS.

By then, however, Eddie Stamp had convinced me to get out of auditing as he felt it was not an area in which to develop an academic career! I moved into financial accounting, and became known for cash flow accounting, report user studies, accounting history, etc. *Company Auditing* was well received, and was the main 'theory' text in the UK and elsewhere for nearly two decades. But my involvement in the study of corporate auditing was largely limited to periodic revisions for new editions. Meantime, the accountancy profession continued its persistent battle against criticisms of perceived audit failure. The only major change in the 1970s and 1980s was that the issue was given a label – 'the audit expectations gap'.

But the issue is not just a convenient label for discussion. The public criticism of corporate auditing and auditors has now reached crisis proportions, and the audit profession appears unable to respond positively. Indeed, it seems unaware of the need to avoid its usual stance of denial of responsibility. In particular, in conversations with auditors (particularly those who have progressed their careers in the 1980s), I perceive a fundamental lack of understanding of what corporate auditing is (or is not) achieving. There may be many reasons why this is so. But, in my view, part of the problem is the relative lack of conceptual study of auditing at university and beyond. Indeed, despite the fact that many accounting students proceed to audit employment, auditing typically represents a small part of the university curriculum.

And, even when it does form a measurable proportion of accountancy studies, students are usually fed a diet of conventional and uncritical theory – including that contained in my previous text, *Company Auditing*. They are not typically expected to study auditing from an unconventional perspective and, sadly, few auditing courses are challenging (in the sense of critically observing corporate auditing and auditors). Meantime, the press continues to expose situations such as Polly Peck, Bank of Commerce and Credit International, and Maxwell Communications.

With these things in mind, I found that revising a fourth edition of *Company Auditing* was not a task that was either relevant or satisfying. Thus this manuscript was born, in which the framework of the previous text is retained but the explanation and analysis is completely changed. The approach remains normative and prescriptive but contains, where relevant, critical analyses. I have attempted to retain some balance in this approach, remembering the reality of existing practice and the unreality of some of its criticism. This may not satisfy the fiercest critics, but at least their published work is discussed. I may also annoy some conventionalists, but they too are given sufficient to represent their viewpoint.

The text has been written in such a way that its content should not date too rapidly, and it retains only a minimum necessary reference to the specifics of audit regulation. In this respect, it ought to travel reasonably well across frontiers. One matter, however, has been exceedingly difficult to deal with, and that is the detail of various recent corporate failures which may (or may not) involve audit failure. Because of the focus of the text, it would have been relevant to use these situations in detail to emphasize more general points. Unfortunately, very few involve completed court cases in which it is possible to determine exactly what was the standard of audit achieved. I believe it is wrong and potentially misleading to make textual judgments on these matters solely on the basis of press comment – no matter how expertly journalists investigate. Thus, the text is relatively brief on the specifics of individual cases, although they are discussed in a generic sense as part of the prevalent audit crisis.

The text is written in such a way that teachers and students can discuss the various issues sensibly and to the depth which is relevant in the particular course. Additional readings and discussion and essay topics are provided for this purpose. Hopefully, it is a book which can be enjoyed in the classroom as a means of putting corporate auditing and its problems into focus. Finally, I must record my thanks to a number of people who have directly or indirectly impacted this book. The first is George Dewar, a former Big 8 (6) partner who taught me what a profession should be about. His guidance more than any other gave me a benchmark with which to judge the auditing behaviour of present-day auditors. The second person is Bob Sterling, a leading US academic who has spent a lifetime challenging this behaviour. Bob's role as a critical academic is one which is presently and sadly neglected by most of accounting academe. The third and fourth persons are David Cooper and Tony Tinker who, by editing *Critical Perspectives on Accounting*, provide a journal forum of quality on these issues. And, finally and primarily, my thanks go to my wife, Ann who has had to endure yet another book, with yet another deadline, and yet another outbreak of anti-social behaviour. None of the above are in any way to blame for what follows in this text. But each has made it possible in what is a very peculiar and unwitting partnership. *Roll Tide!*

Tom Lee
Tuscaloosa
Alabama

1

The what and why of corporate audit theory

The purpose of this text is to provide theoretical explanations and analyses of the practice of corporate auditing. Such a study is presented within the context of a state-regulated function which is primarily intended to protect the financial interests of corporate funding groups such as investors and lenders. However, the text also provides commentaries on the subject sufficient to extend the analyses to other economic, political and social interpretations of the role of the corporate auditor.

Corporate auditing has been selected as the focus for this study, partly because it is so widely practised as an intended part of corporate governance, and partly because it is the subject of so much public scrutiny and criticism in times of major corporate failure.

The need for theory in human affairs

The text identifies and discusses corporate auditing from a theoretical perspective. It is therefore concerned with aspects of fundamental thinking which underlie corporate audit practice. Consequently, textual explanations and discussions of detailed practical aspects of corporate auditing are limited to those which relate to theoretical arguments, propositions and positions on the subject. In other words, this is not a text describing and explaining corporate audit practice. Instead, it is a review and critical analysis of the rationale on which that practice is perceived to be based.

The term 'theory' used throughout this text is defined as a framework of logically connected statements which assist in organizing, explaining and predicting observations of the so-called real world (Sterling, 1970a, pp. 444–5).[1] Its purpose is to improve understanding of elements of that real world, and assist in their management. A theory of corporate auditing comprises statements which are perceived to be the

1

main roles and objectives, underlying postulates, and primary concepts which explain and help to predict its practice. The need to provide such a conceptual overview is justified in terms of a belief that an explicit statement of theory has a number of major educational and practical roles to play.

The roles which theory plays

A theory permits apparently separate ideas to be organized into connected sets forming a body of knowledge. The existence of such knowledge is usually stated to be one of the main traits of a professionalized activity (Johnson, 1972, p.23; and Bledstein, 1976, p.88). As Hines (1989b, p.89) argues, by explicitly claiming possession of a formal body of knowledge, a profession can advance its professionalization process. But without theory, knowledge connections and relationships in a professionalized practice are difficult to observe and explain. Specific practices are reduced to rules adhered to more by custom and habit than by reference to any logical rationale. Theory is therefore intended to make sense of practice.

But the existence of a stated theory is not without its problems. In particular, the organization of relevant ideas into an apparently coherent theoretical structure is subject to limitations introduced by the theorist. Personal attitudes, knowledge constraints and cultural background tend to bias the propositions and prescriptions which attempt to observe, explain and predict the specific phenomena being studied. Theories are therefore rarely definitive statements. They are usually open to challenge, debate and amendment.

A theory is constructed to explain observable phenomena in the real world. Things which can be seen, touched and otherwise sensed may have little meaning until an attempt is made to explain them by means of the construction of propositions concerning their nature and behaviour. Empirical observations of the phenomena are then matched with the constructed theory to determine if there is a significant and explainable association. Such explanations are intended to expand knowledge and understanding of elements of the real world. This does not mean, of course, that such knowledge or understanding is necessarily either complete or correct. It is merely one view of that world.

A theory can also be used to provide normative views of behaviour in the real world, and to challenge the credibility of the existing state of affairs. Not everything in the real world is either acceptable or maintainable, and a stated theory is one mechanism by which alternative ideas and potential practices can be formulated for consideration as replacements of the existing state. This is not to say that a particular theory will be acceptable or that change is inevitable once the alternative theory is formulated. It merely indicates one role for theory as a catalyst for discussion about possible change.

A theory also provides guidance on issues in the real world for those individuals responsible for their management and control. In particular, being able to predict aspects of observable reality helps individuals and organizations to cope with their effects. Theory assists in anticipating behaviour related to real-world events and objects; thus enabling their management to be more effective because they can be forecast. But it must also be stated that a theory only provides the potential to predict. It does not guarantee either an accurate prediction or effective management.

The need for corporate audit theory

The various aspects of corporate auditing which are discussed in this text attempt to comply with the educational and practical objectives of theorizing commented on in the previous section. The need for such theorizing is well summarized by Mautz and Sharaf (1961, p.17):

> We have a strong tendency in auditing to adopt a pragmatic approach. Whatever works well is adopted and strongly advocated; what has not yet been found applicable has little appeal. To some extent this is a natural tendency, yet we must keep it in bounds. We must continually test our practices and procedures, not only in actual practice, but against the theory which underlies auditing. And we should continually search theory for possible approaches for new and old problems. If we forget the theoretical foundation of auditing and let it dwindle to a mere collection of rote procedures and practices reminiscent of its early history, it will not only lose stature in the eyes of the world, but will forfeit the best method of solving its most perplexing problems.

Of particular theoretical concern in this text are the effects which corporate auditors have in the real world, and the effects which the real world has on them. The principal object of study is a complex technical function conducted in practice by professional experts skilled in accounting matters. Such a function is broadly interpretable as a crucial means of operationalizing corporate governance and accountability – that is, of controlling corporate behaviour generally, and holding corporate managers accountable particularly. It is presently structured in the specific context of a series of audit practices designed to verify and report on the quality of the accounting content of annual financial statements which corporate organizations produce for the benefit of their owners directly, and a variety of other interested groups less directly.

The text aims to assist its reader to be aware of each of the roles for theory outlined above as they apply to corporate auditing. In particular, it attempts to provide a basis for understanding and questioning the current financial accounting orientation of the corporate audit function, and for beginning to consider potential changes in this emphasis. The text therefore helps its reader to understand the reasons why corporate auditing exists in its current form, as well as the benefits and disbenefits which can be associated with such an existence.

Where relevant, the explanations and discussions in the text examine corporate auditing in relation to aspects of economics, politics and sociology. Expanding the accounting argument of Burchell *et al.* (1980) to the role of corporate auditing, the latter activity should not be regarded merely as a technical and neutral function, designed to check the calculational veracity and appropriateness of reported accounting figures for the benefit of a privileged few investors. Instead, its existence can also be argued to have economic, political and sociological implications in the various communities in which it operates. In particular, it has a role to play in the formulation and consequences of economic decisions, modes of organizational control, and interplay between state and business.

The basic argument thus presented in this text is that corporate auditing is used in practice to satisfy various individual and organizational needs and, in so doing, is a major component in organizational change. For example, in compliance with legislation, the corporate auditor seeks to confirm the quality of reported financial information which is frequently argued to be potentially useful in a variety of economic decision-making situations. His work is therefore perceived to have the potential to impact decisions which will inevitably lead to organizational change. The corporate audit can also be seen to constitute an important part of the politically-driven state mechanism for governing corporate entities and, more specifically, for holding corporate managers accountable to both owners of capital and other interested parties. It can therefore be argued to have the potential to assist in regulating and modifying corporate behaviour – that is, as a societal device to protect the financial and non-financial interests of different groups from the consequences of otherwise damaging corporate activity.

In other words, the corporate audit can be perceived in the very broad social context of regulating human activity within an organized economic structure. It is a vital part of such regulation, and its success or failure is conditioned by the various, often conflicting self-interests of the participants concerned – a complex mix of financial information producers, regulators, users and auditors. The theory explained in this text involves each of these constituent groups.

However, as with all theoretical commentaries, the corporate auditing ideas outlined in this text should not be assumed to be a unique set. There are many possible theories of corporate auditing, each dependent and constructed on the basis of a series of normative prescriptions for corporate organizational behaviour. It is therefore important to state at the outset that the primary theoretical position adopted in this text is one in which the corporate audit is regarded, as indicated above, as a major component of corporate governance and accountability in society, and a vital part of corporate financial stewardship in the economy.

Corporate organizations and their managerial agents are entrusted by their owner principals with the use and maintenance of scarce economic resources. Such a trust also impacts on the well-being of other groups of vested interests, as well as the community in which the corporate entity is located. Consequently, it is important that the behaviour of the corporate organization and its managers is monitored and capable of being disciplined if necessary.[2] In particular, there is a perceived need to hold corporate managers accountable for their actions, and the audit function is an important means of providing such governance. As Flint (1988, p.15) argues:

> The social concept of audit is a special kind of examination by a person other than the parties involved which compares performance with expectation and reports the result: it is part of the public and private control mechanism of monitoring and securing accountability.

Stated in more detail, the most fundamental theoretical argument in this text is that the present form of corporate audit is a complex and technical function in which the auditor verifies and reports on the quality of the financial messages which corporate management discloses publicly to external constituents as part of its financial accountability to the latter. This argument further suggests that, if successfully completed, such a function provides sufficient assurance about the quality of the disclosed financial messages to allow their content to be relied on by those individuals and organizations to whom they are directed, and also others who may benefit from them more indirectly. In turn, this is presumed to give corporate financial report users comfort in the political and sociological terms of protection from unacceptable behaviour, as well as confidence in the economic context of using credible reported financial information as a basis for their decisions and related actions.

A financial focus for corporate audit theory

The financial nature and role of corporate auditing has been the predominant focus of writers on the subject throughout its long history. The beginnings of this tradition can be seen in the approaches adopted in early audit texts such as Pixley (1881) and Dicksee (1892) in the UK, and Montgomery (1912) in the US. The explanations of auditing provided in these writings are predominantly concerned with verifying calculational matters related to the production of financial statements and the accurate maintenance of the underlying bookkeeping system. This financial accounting orientation is also to be evidenced in contemporary audit theory texts such as Mautz and Sharaf (1961), Sherer and Kent (1983), Wolnizer (1987), Flint (1988), and Ruud (1989). As Flint (1988, p.49) comments:

> Auditing and accounting tend to be associated. This is because almost universally in diverse organisations accountability is exacted for the custody and stewardship of financial resources, and in many organisations and especially in business firms accountability is demonstrated by the preparation of periodic accounts reporting on the custody, stewardship and management of these resources.

The relevance of a primary audit focus on financial accounting for accountability purposes can be challenged, however, by normative prescriptions of a more socio-economic and political nature. These proposals require radically different expositions and interpretations of the nature and role of auditing with respect to corporate organizational and managerial behaviour generally, and corporate ownership and stewardship particularly. That is, they envisage the corporate auditor examining matters somewhat distant from reported accounting data, and for purposes other than complying with financial regulations to protect shareholders.

Sherer and Kent (1983, p.93), for example, propose audits to test the efficiency of operations, the quality of management information systems, and the social behaviour of organizations. Tinker (1985, p.205) argues that the auditor should be involved in adjudicating social conflicts involving corporate organizations and the communities in which they operate. Gray (1990, pp.134–5) suggests a need to amend traditional reporting practice to incorporate environmental issues. Willmott (1991, p.119) identifies a public much broader than the conventional ownership group as the potential beneficiary of audit action. Byington and Sutton (1991, p.327) conclude that auditors act as a monopoly profession likely to create welfare losses for audit beneficiaries. Briloff (1990, p.5) demonstrates, on evidence of recent corporate failures, how the audit profession desecrates its covenant to protect the public interest. Sikka, Willmott and Lowe (1989, p.65) criticize accountants and auditors for regulating their practices to maintain an accounting flexibility desired by corporate managerial reporters. And Mills and Bettner (1992, pp.193–5) state that auditing is ritualistic, creating a reality of stability and order but, simultaneously, masking social conflict and maintaining the status quo.

Whilst acknowledging the importance of studying these alternative views of corporate reporting and auditing, the decision taken in this text is to restrict its content mainly to a focus on matters of a financial accounting nature. The rationale for this is based on a perceived need to explain and discuss corporate audit theory in relation to the current practice which the reader will experience. The commentaries and discussions which follow are consequently not intended to be academic exercises without recourse to what is or is not happening in current audit practice. But nor are they devoid of critical analyses of that practice. Where appropriate, contemporary corporate auditing is examined and discussed from a critical perspective. However, such commentaries should not be taken to represent the only sets of alternative views or values which can be expressed concerning the potential utility of the corporate audit function and its roles in society today. As indicated above, there are many ways in which corporate auditing can be perceived to be or not to be of potential use.

Contributions to audit theory

There are few texts available in the area of corporate audit theory. The subject of auditing in the classroom over the years has usually been treated by accounting educators as a formal exercise in training for the practice of auditing – of teaching auditors to audit by recalculating the calculations of the producers of reported accounting information. Thus, teaching texts on the subject have tended to focus on the minutiae of audit practice, rather than the current state of its underlying conceptual framework (Sikka, 1987). The few exceptions to this general rule are cited throughout the text where appropriate in order to provide its reader with alternative reading on the topics concerned. The writers involved include Mautz and Sharaf (1961), AAA (1973), Schandl (1978), Sherer and Kent (1983), Wallace (1985), Lee (1986), Wolnizer (1987), Flint (1988) and Ruud (1989).

Normative and positive audit theory

Normative theorizing, when defined in the sense of emphasizing 'what should be' rather than 'what is' in the real world, has assumed a secondary position in recent times to other forms of theorizing in the accounting and auditing literatures. It has been particularly overtaken by what is labelled as 'positive accounting theory'. The proponents of the latter subject are explicitly concerned with the ability of accounting and auditing research to make so-called scientific observations of the real world (Watts and Zimmerman, 1986, pp.355–6). These observations are argued to assist accounting and auditing policy-makers and practitioners to explain and predict the use of accounting and auditing practices in given organizational situations. Positive theorists are not necessarily concerned to use the results of such research to recommend, challenge or change existing financial reporting and auditing practice (Watts and Zimmerman, 1986, p.7). Indeed, they are not particularly interested in normative theorizing.

This text, however, takes a somewhat different view of the value of normative theory by arguing that such prescriptions in corporate auditing are necessary to any search for understanding, change and perceived improvement in the practices of the function. As Mautz and Sharaf (1961, p.17) argue, unless such alternative ideas exist, and are proposed and discussed, no fundamental change in existing practice can be contemplated. This point has also been made in more recent times by Sterling (1990) in a critique of positive accounting theory. In particular, he argues (p.131) that normative theory provides necessary knowledge and understanding, and has the capacity to assess existing practices.

In addition, and when relevant, the text also contains a critical perspective on corporate auditing, in which comment is made on the social and political roles of the function, and what it is or is not achieving. In this aspect, it particularly broadens the focus on auditing beyond the conventional economic rationale, and explores what Cooper and Hopper (1990, p.2) describe as the 'silences' of the subject – that is, the interpretations of corporate auditing which are not normally stated.

Corporate financial reporting and audit theory

The main reason for taking a pronounced normative stance in this text is the significance of the prescriptive emphasis of the conceptual frameworks recently constructed by accounting policy-makers for corporate financial reporting. These frameworks include explicit and defined prescriptions for the quality of reported accounting information in relation to both user decisions and managerial account-ability (specifically in relation to informational relevance and reliability). Such prescriptions are distinguishable from the over-riding and undefined qualities which have been traditionally and consistently imposed by state regulators of corporate financial reporting and auditing (such as 'present fairly' in the US and 'a true and fair view' in the UK).

In this respect, the specific issue is which reporting qualities should the corporate auditor look for and attest in relation to reported financial statements? In particular, to what extent is the corporate auditor responsible for attesting the prescribed reporting qualities contained outside state regulation in the provisions of the conceptual frameworks of accounting policy-makers? Given the long-lived and apparently generally accepted historical view that an independent audit function is a necessary part of corporate accountability and reporting (Lee, 1968), the substantial argument underlying this text is that it is imperative that corporate audit action is reasonably compatible with prescribed corporate reporting requirements. Unless such compatibility is aimed for and achieved, there is a danger that the qualities specified for and expected of corporate financial reports by their regulators will not be the same as those verified and reported on by their auditors. In other words, an expectations gap will be created, resulting in potential doubt and uncertainty about the benefits of the corporate audit.

In addition, as with the issue of detailed audit practices, the text attempts to minimize its descriptions of what are typically transitory and geographically-dependent detailed regulations for corporate auditing. In a fast-changing world, and with increasing intervention by the state in corporate business affairs by means of complex regulations, it is impossible to ensure that a text on corporate auditing is kept up to date for any reasonable length of time. One solution to this problem, therefore, is to construct the textual material in such a way that the basic and relatively unchanging roles, objectives, postulates and concepts of the subject are studied – leaving the detail of specific regulations and related provisions to more practice-orientated aspects of accountancy education, literature and training. Hopefully, by taking this approach, the text will be relevant to its reader over a relatively sustained period, and potentially usable in a variety of locations.

The fundamental structure of this text

The text is primarily concerned with the nature and role of auditing in contemporary society generally and corporate business activity particularly. The explanations and discussions are concerned with perceptions of what such an audit function is trying to achieve in practice, how it is attempting to meet these objectives, who is benefiting from their achievement and the main problems which are associated with such activity. This textual mission is accomplished by means of explanations and discussions of a number of related subjects which, when taken together, constitute a normative framework of corporate audit theory – in the sense that the prescriptions offered are directed from a statement of aims towards a series of basic principles perceived as being capable of achieving the intended objectives.

In other words, the content flow logically commences with perceptions and descriptions of the main roles for and objectives of corporate auditing. These matters are explained within a context of the function's subject-matter and environment. This context includes definable aspects of corporate business which are representable in financial accounting terms, as well as the financial statements containing those representations which are to be verified and reported on by the corporate auditor. Also included contextually are the producers and beneficiaries of such verification and reporting – that is, respectively, those individuals and organizations responsible for the production of the reported financial information, as well as those to whom it is directed.

In addition to the above introduction, the history of corporate auditing is studied in general terms in order to observe significant changes in audit roles, objectives, subject-matters and beneficiaries, and to assist in providing a contextualized understanding of the state of the contemporary function. Such a historical view provides a perspective to current issues and proposed solutions.

The next step in the analysis explores the basic postulates or self-evident propositions of corporate auditing. By definition, these assumptions about the prescribed function stem from its stated roles and aims, and provide theoretical support for the main concepts to be derived from the latter. Stating corporate audit postulates in a theoretical structure is argued to be necessary to the validity and credibility of the theory. If the stated postulates cannot be seen to be valid, the basic aims of corporate auditing cannot be expected to be met. In other words, postulates are a useful way of judging the reasonableness and validity of conceptual prescriptions for corporate auditing.

The final elements in the theoretical analysis discussed in the text concern the key concepts of corporate auditing which flow from the defined objectives and related postulates. These concepts are relatively few but constitute the heart of the theory. They are the links between the objectives which are prescribed for the corporate auditor, and the practical means by which he or she attempts to achieve them. Without the specification and acceptance of these key concepts, corporate audit practice is reduced to a series of detailed audit techniques without any apparent or explicit purpose.

The following paragraphs briefly discuss each of these basic elements. The purpose is to provide an early appreciation of each prior to more detailed studies in appropriate chapters.

The nature and roles of corporate auditing

The fundamental nature and roles for corporate auditing are explained in the context of doubts and uncertainties which exist with regard to the quality of reported financial information. As a precursor to this explanation, the role of verification in society generally is discussed. In particular, the economic consequences associated with verification, the potential role it plays in monitoring behaviour, and the social effects it has in providing comfort and assurance are emphasized.

Corporate auditing is specifically discussed as a social mechanism to assist in monitoring and controlling corporate managerial behaviour, and as a political tool of the state which attempts to explicitly signal its desire to provide a means of corporate governance. Economically, the corporate auditor is observed as an agent in an agency situation, acting as an adjudicator in contractual relationships involving potential conflict and moral hazard. In other words, this text takes the view that the corporate auditor acts out a number of mutually reinforcing roles, and cannot be perceived as fulfilling one function.

Corporate auditing objectives

As introduced above, the main objectives of corporate auditing are stated in the form of normative prescriptions derived from designated qualities currently prescribed by accounting policy-makers for corporate financial statements. The consequence of this approach is that the corporate auditor's principal task is primarily perceived as one which assists in corporate governance and managerial accountability. But, more specifically, he or she is concerned with verifying and reporting on the 'relevance' and 'reliability' of the financial information disclosed annually by corporate entities to their shareholders and other interested parties.[3] Following a number of years of prescription in the academic literature, these financial reporting qualities or characteristics now regularly appear in the contemporary financial reporting policy literature as the principle foundations for the production of corporate financial statements. They are contained in recent conceptual provisions to regulate or guide corporate financial reporting practice – as, for example, in the FASB (1980) statement on qualitative criteria for US financial reporting, and a proposed ASB (1991b) statement of accounting principles in the UK. They are adapted to the audit task in this text, and defined in detail in Chapter 3.

Such a normative approach to corporate auditing, however, has to be stated in the context of specific accountability-driven regulations for corporate financial reporting which specify the ultimate quality expected of disclosed accounting information in undefined but over-riding legal terms – for example, 'present fairly' in the USA (AICPA, 1992, para.1), a 'true and fair view' in the UK (Companies Act, 1985, s236). Despite the undoubted primary nature of these undefined terms, and without in any way attempting to define them by direct comparison with the criteria of relevance and reliability, this text takes the position that, unless the latter qualities exist in relation to the accounting content of reported corporate financial statements, it is reasonably certain that the over-riding accountability criterion will not be satisfied. In other words, and assuming the UK proposal, in order to give 'a true and fair view', the financial statements require to be at least relevant and reliable – a position consistent with that of the ASB (1991b, para.43) in the UK.

This specification of corporate audit objectives differs somewhat from that prescribed by the founding fathers of modern audit theory. Mautz and Sharaf (1961, pp.158–203) saw the audit concerned with compliance with generally accepted accounting principles and disclosure regulations – that is, essentially an audit centred on the technical propriety and presentation of accounting calculations. Such a position is consistent with that currently maintained in US audit practice. The AICPA (1992, para.3) states that the 'fairness' of financial statements should be judged within the framework of 'generally accepted accounting principles', a technical term covering currently accepted accounting practice (para.2). The audit aims prescribed in this text, however, are more in line with recent writers such as Wolnizer (1987, pp.1–2) who argues that the audit should provide assurance that the verified financial statements are an independently authenticated representation of financial position and progress, and therefore reliable; and Ruud (1989, p.153) who recommends auditing's purpose as verification of the reported information's correspondence with economic reality.[4]

Thus, as previously stated, the argument in this text with respect to the financial reporting criteria of relevance and reliability is that, if they are prescribed by accounting policy-makers for external financial reporting purposes, it is logical to assume that they should be verified and reported on by the corporate auditor to comply with state-prescribed reporting qualities. It would be illogical and confusing to have the producers of published financial statements adhere to one set of reporting criteria, and the auditor commenting on a different set (Lee, 1992a).

A history of corporate auditing

The history of auditing reveals the function's gradual progression from essentially a voluntary, individual, and amateur activity, towards a role which is usually state-required and professionally organized and regulated. The audit function has also evolved from one which was initially concerned with the verification of predominantly physical events and objects, as in the Roman tax collection system or in the administration of the English Exchequer (Lee, 1971), to assurance of reporting compliance with generally accepted accounting rules of procedure and disclosure (Lee, 1988). The main aim of this study of audit history is therefore to demonstrate that contemporary ideas in corporate auditing have their origins in much earlier times. And, in particular, that the corporate audit of today is the culmination of many hundreds of years of layering of ideas, customs and habits. Corporate auditing should not be regarded as the natural consequence of activities and thoughts in recent times. Instead, it exists and changes because of generations of audit activities and attitudes passed on from one time period to the next. As Hopwood (1987, p.230) concludes (adapting to auditing):

> From such a perspective accounting (auditing) can be conceived of as creating residues of organisational consequences that can change the preconditions for subsequent organisational change. It is as if organisational transformations deposit sediments which not only interact with the organisational past but also modify the possibilities for the organisational present, and its future.

Some postulates of corporate auditing

The audit postulates supporting corporate financial report verification are those which assume that the conduct of such a function is both necessary and feasible. To make sense of the stated objectives of the function, for example, it is assumed that the corporate auditor needs to verify the relevance and reliability of corporate financial statements to determine their fair presentation, or truth and fairness, because this will be of primary benefit to individuals and organizations receiving such statements as part of corporate governance and managerial accountability; and that it is possible for him or her to do this meaningfully (in terms of access to evidence, available technical skills, and costs not exceeding benefits). If these conditions are unreasonable, in the sense that financial statement users are not concerned with informational relevance and reliability, or that the corporate auditor does not or cannot reasonably be expected to verify financial statements in these terms, then the stated aims of corporate auditing are not feasible, and should not be prescribed as the main purposes of the corporate audit function in practice.

The detail of these assumptions will be specified in Chapter 6. But, meantime, it is important to heed the appeal made by Mautz and Sharaf (1961, p.41) for an explicit statement of the postulates of auditing. Their text provides an original statement of assumptions, and argues that these should be stated in order that they can be examined, criticized and validated. Only if this is done will there be assurance that the foundations of auditing are sound.

Corporate auditing concepts

The concepts of corporate auditing form the major part of this text. Mautz and Sharaf (1961, pp.53–4) describe the importance of concepts in the structure of audit theory. They identify them as the abstract generalizations which are formulated from observations and experiences, and which constitute the basic elements of the theoretical structure. They take the form of simplistic descriptions and formal statements, and provide understanding of the structure. They are the principal focus in any theoretical study of corporate auditing. For example, the concepts statement of the American Accounting Association (AAA, 1973) provides an illustration of an attempt to institutionally provide such a focus.

Corporate auditing concepts are categorized in two ways. The first group includes certain distinctive notions pertaining to the behaviour of the corporate auditor. These are partially clustered by Flint (1988, p.48) under the generic label of 'auditor competence' – that is, the corporate auditor has sufficient knowledge, training, skills and experience to successfully complete the corporate audit. The behavioural category also includes the general concept of auditor independence specified by most theorists as a main part of the overall audit prescription (for example, Mautz and Sharaf, 1961, p.204; Sherer and Kent, 1983, p.24; Wolnizer, 1987, p.1; and Flint, 1988, p.54). What these writers agree is that the corporate auditor must be sufficiently independent in mind and action to objectively conduct and report on the corporate audit.

The final part of the behavioural category of corporate audit concepts is that of auditor responsibility or audit care. This aspect of audit theory argues that corporate auditors are capable of being held accountable for the quality of their work and the degree of care they have exercised in the completion of that work. For example, Mautz and Sharaf (1961, p.139) write of the corporate auditor exercising due care in terms of a prudent practitioner acting reasonably with average knowledge and judgment in specific circumstances. Flint (1988, p.150), on the other hand, describes the concept by reference to whether the practices of individual auditors satisfy standards expected of them at the time of the audit.

The second broad category of corporate audit concepts relates to the technical aspects of the function. In fact, two separable but related concepts can be described. The first deals with the reporting qualities expected and specified for the financial information on which the auditor is required to report. The second covers the requirement to obtain suitable and sufficient audit evidence to allow the prescribed qualities of the reported information to be verified and reported by the auditor.

As previously indicated, the quality expected of reported financial information which is subject to examination by the corporate auditor is expressed in this text in the general over-riding but undefined legal terms such as 'present fairly' or 'a true and fair view', and in the regulatory terms of its relevance and reliability. Put more specifically, this means that the information is expected to be capable of influencing specific decision models to which it may be applied by financial report users; and faithfully represent or correspond to the economic events and objects it is intended to describe.

The concept of corporate auditing dealing with verifiable informational quality has been expressed over the years by writers in different yet connected ways. For example, Mautz and Sharaf (1961, p.158) describe it as fair presentation, and explain it in terms of compliance with generally accepted accounting principles and minimum disclosure requirements. Other writers, however, have been less specific and obvious in their recognition of such a concept. Flint (1988, p.34), for example, only briefly mentions standards of financial reporting within the context of an audit postulate which states that such standards must be assumed to be sufficiently understood to be operationally viable. Ruud (1989, p.121) fails to state any such concept directly or explicitly. And Wolnizer (1987, p.89) follows a similar approach to Ruud when he specifies the 'technical ophelimity' of financial reports – that is, their fitness for use in terms of their correspondence with the actual financial state of affairs of the reporting corporate organization.

The second technical concept of adequate audit evidence, on the other hand, is more obviously identified in the auditing literature. In this text, it describes the notion that the successful completion of the corporate audit requires the identification, gathering and evaluation of sufficient and suitable evidence to support the auditor's opinion on the relevance and reliability of the reported information. This is a view compatible in broad principle with that of Mautz and Sharaf (1961, p.68) who describe the audit need for competent evidential material; Wolnizer (1987, p.27) who advocates the audit need for independent evidence to authenticate the correspondence between statements and facts; and Flint (1988, p.102) who states that without evidence there can be no audit.

Corporate audit theory and audit issues

When outlining the nature of corporate audit theory, a number of major problems inherent in such a function are identifiable. These are categorized in terms of certain explicit and implicit expectations of the corporate auditor and the audit function. Such expectations are held by external interests in corporate organizations, as well as by the state and its political practitioners. The general issue in this respect is that various individuals and organizations in society expect certain outcomes and benefits from the existence and operation of the corporate audit function – what Sikka *et al.* (1992, p.2) describe as a difference in orientation between the buyer and seller of audit services. In particular the corporate auditor is not capable or willing as the seller to meet the audit goals expected by the buyer. The result is a mismatch of expectation and achievement which puts the credibility and value of the corporate audit in doubt.

Particular issues can be divided into two broad headings. The first is concerned with 'what' the corporate auditor is expected to achieve in the audit function. And the second deals with expectations of 'how' the corporate auditor behaves with respect to audit activities. All issues can be encapsulated in the single term of 'audit pressure' – that is, the nature and role of corporate auditors in society places them in a position where, as professional people, they are under pressure to achieve and behave in ways which may conflict both with how they perceive their role and how they can satisfactorily complete it. The particular issues which create such pressure, and which are discussed in various sections of this text, are briefly explained in the following section. Specific writings which have recently concentrated on corporate auditing issues include Bromwich, Hopwood and Shaw (1982); Tweedie (1987); ICAS/ICAEW (1989); and Sherer and Turley (1991).

Specific corporate audit issues and expectations

There is a variety of expectations held with respect to the nature and role of the corporate audit function, and each seems to create problems for the auditor.

- What is **relevant accounting information** with respect to user decision models, and how is the corporate auditor to determine this? Accounting policy-makers recently prescribed relevance as a primary quality expected of reported financial information, and defined it in terms of the latter making a difference to or influencing an economic decision (for example, FASB, 1980, para.47; and ASB, 1991b, para.23). But little is known of the nature of such decisions. All that is presently available to corporate auditors are broadly-based theoretical models constructed for purposes of suggesting normative proposals for accounting and reporting reform (for example, Sterling, 1970b, pp.21–37; and Sterling, 1972).

- With respect to the quality of reliability, how does the corporate auditor authenticate whether or not reported information **faithfully represents** the underlying economic events and objects being reported? The expectation to report in terms of faithful representation has been made by accounting policy-makers (for example, FASB, 1980, paras. 59 and 63; and ASB, 1991b, para.28). But there is no clear indication of how it should be interpreted in practice by auditors and others (for example, Lee, 1992a).

- Should the corporate auditor be concerned more with the **legal and technical form** of accounting and reporting (as reflected in generally accepted accounting principles) than with its **economic substance** (as implied in current reporting policy criteria)? There is an increasing concern about the dominance in financial accounting of procedures which reflect legal or technical propriety but which fail to ensure the reporting of the substance of economic events and objects (for example, Rutherford, 1988).

- To what extent should corporate auditors be held responsible for **fraud detection**, and for reporting either illegal and anti-social acts by the reporting corporate organization? And to whom should they report such matters? Public expectations are stated to be held that the corporate auditor should be responsible for these issues, despite consistent denials of total responsibility by the accountancy profession (for example, Connor, 1986).

- If the corporate organization being audited is in **financial or operational difficulty**, should its auditor have a duty to investigate and report on this? The corporate auditor is currently expected to assess whether or not the organization is a going concern prior to issuing an opinion on its financial statements, and to qualify the report accordingly if it is not (for example, AICPA, 1991, p.197 in the US; and APC, 1985 in the UK). The problem in this context centres on the economic and financial consequences for the reporting organization of such a qualification, and the pressure on the auditor not to qualify because of this effect (for example, Peel, 1989).

- Should the corporate auditor require to undertake a 'standard' audit irrespective of the size of the corporate organization concerned? When compared with large corporate organizations, smaller entities have different characteristics of control, management and ownership which suggest a simplified and restricted audit and audit reporting (for example, Page, 1991a).

- There is also a variety of issues associated with corporate auditor behaviour. For example, what is meant by **auditor independence** in given circumstances, and how does the auditor effectively maintain an independent position? He or she must be independent in fact and appearance, but establishing this duality in practice is one of the longest-standing problems in auditing (for example, Moizer, 1991).

- To whom is the corporate auditor **responsible** beyond the well-established situation of a contractual liability to corporate ownership? There have been numerous court cases over the years attempting to resolve the issue of auditor responsibility to contracted and non-contracted parties, but the position continues to be unclear in practice (for example, Gwilliam, 1991).

- How should corporate auditors assess the degree of **risk** they are undertaking in their audit? The practice of corporate auditing is concerned with the estimation and evaluation of risk by auditors – in the sense that they cannot verify every single detail relating to the reported financial information and, instead, rely on a sampling basis (for example, Adams, 1991).
- Can the corporate auditor distinguish between two separate risks? The first concerns **judgmental risk** in making audit decisions relating to the collection, evaluation and reporting of audit evidence. The second deals with **business risk**, in the sense of considering the economic consequences of audit judgments in terms of potential law suits (for example, Johnson, 1992).
- Should corporate auditors report in detail or briefly on the results of their audit investigations? The problem of **comprehensive reporting** by corporate auditors is long-standing – particularly whether their reports on the verified financial information should be in long or short form (for example, Hatherly and Skuse, 1991).
- Should the corporate auditor have a wider **societal role** than the present situation of attesting the quality of reported financial information? Corporate auditors' perceptions of their exposure to litigation, and the considerable financial penalties associated with this, may act as a constraint on expansion of their role. More specifically, the question is whether their duty of care should deal with other corporate issues of relevance to a range of external interests extending beyond shareholders (for example, Willmott, 1991).
- Given the number of large corporate failures in recent years which have invited suspicions of audit failure, to what extent are corporate auditors failing to meet their **societal contract** to protect the public interest with respect to matters such as managerial fraud and maintaining independence (for example, Briloff, 1990; and Mitchell *et al.*, 1991)?

None of these issues presently has a clear solution. Many of them have been discussed over several decades. And several are still at the stage of early recognition as problems for the corporate auditor. Nevertheless, what is argued at appropriate parts of this text is that it is essential to an understanding of the corporate audit function, and particularly its theoretical structure, at least to be aware of these issues as potential hurdles to the successful completion of the defined corporate audit engagement.

Concluding comments

Each of the following chapters in the text deals with the topics discussed in this chapter in the order suggested. The explanations and discussions are made as simply as possible, and assume no previous knowledge of corporate auditing. However, knowledge of accounting, generally, and corporate financial reporting, particularly, is thought to be beneficial. The issues affecting corporate auditing are introduced at appropriate stages in the text. Hopefully, this provides its reader with an appreciation of the context and reasons for each of the issues concerned. To remove them from their context is to black-box them, and to create an impression that they should and can be easily separated.

Notes

1. The term 'real world' is used throughout this text to denote the physically observable and verifiable environment in which human beings are located. The existence and nature of reality is one which has puzzled philosophers and scientists of all ages (see, for example, Gregory, 1988). This uncertainty makes defining the 'real world' satisfactorily an almost impossible task. The writer therefore leaves the reader to interpret the term in the way in which it is done most frequently – that is, intuitively.
2. Armstrong (1991, pp.19–21) argues that, in addition to the traditional view of agency theory involving monitoring incentives, there is a more radical explanation involving the cost to the principal of cultivating trust in an agent. Using a further trusted agent (such as an external auditor) to monitor the agent may be less expensive to the principal than incurring the cost of establishing the loyalty of the agent.
3. The issues concerned with the verification and reporting of relevance and reliability are discussed fully at appropriate stages in the text. Meantime, at this point in the development of corporate auditing, it should not be assumed that such a task is easily attainable.
4. The problems associated with defining terms such as 'economic reality' are discussed particularly in Chapter 9.

Further reading

R.R. Sterling (1970) On theory construction and verification, *The Accounting Review*, July, pp.444–57 (an explanation and discussion of the nature of theories and their value to accountants).

R.R. Sterling (1990) Positive accounting: an assessment, *Abacus*, September, pp. 97–135 (an analysis of the positive approach to accounting research, and a rationale for the normative approach).

R.K. Mautz and H.A. Sharaf (1961) *The Philosophy of Auditing*, American Accounting Association, pp.1–17 (a detailed attempt to explain and discuss the need to determine and explore the theoretical foundations of auditing based on a study of auditing method).

C. Humphrey (1991) Audit expectations, in M. Sherer and S. Turley (eds), *Current Issues in Auditing*, Paul Chapman Publishing, pp.3–21 (a general review of the audit expectations gap and the main issues associated with it).

Discussion and essay topics

1. Describe and explain the nature and role of theory. Relate these thoughts to Mautz and Sharaf's advocation of the need for audit theory.

2. Corporate auditing is essentially a practical activity, and corporate auditors have managed for many years without an explicit statement of audit theory. Discuss.
3. Explain the concept of corporate accountability, and discuss the role of audited financial information in its practical operationalizing.
4. Discuss the denials of positive accounting theorists with respect to the utility of normative prescriptions for accounting and auditing.
5. After reading this chapter, prepare a review of the fundamental aspects of corporate audit theory.
6. Prepare a critique of the major issues currently affecting the corporate audit function, particularly emphasizing any pattern to be observed.

2

Doubt, verification and corporate auditing

The intention of this and the following chapter is to provide a broad review of corporate auditing before proceeding to a statement of its objectives. This is done in the first instance by looking at the topic of auditing generally, and then developing various explanations and discussions within the specific context of corporate organizations. Chapter 3 will deal particularly with the complementary topic of the role of corporate auditing in society. The specific objective of Chapters 2 and 3 is to ensure that their reader is provided with a broad overview of the contemporary place of the corporate audit in society generally and business particularly. Unless this overview is given, the corporate audit function cannot be put into any meaningful context; and its practices remain only as a set of apparently connected and complex technical exercises to complete a task required by state corporate regulators. Under these circumstances, the function would appear devoid of any obvious and coherent role.

Doubts, uncertainties, verifications and auditing

In order to comprehend the nature and purpose of the specific practices of corporate auditing, it is necessary to appreciate two relatively simple and connected propositions. First, certain identifiable but not necessarily observable factors in human activity appear to trigger doubts and uncertainties in the minds of individuals affected by them. Second, these doubts appear to create a need for some form of verification function to either reduce or remove them. Evidence to support these propositions can be observed in everyday human activity, and examples are explained later in this chapter. Meantime, it is sufficient to say that verification of 'things' in the real world is a common human practice. When it is formalized within a framework of connected ideas and practices, it can be said to assume the basic structure of an audit.

It is not unreasonable to suggest also that a regular and consistent feature of human activity is people performing actions, or providing information about actions, which influence the thoughts and behaviour of other individuals. Because of the consequences of these influences impacting the conduct of human affairs, there is an inevitable and often automatic questioning of the credibility of the actions or information concerned. In other words, doubts about 'things' in the real world are created, and the resultant uncertainties require to be determined. This necessitates some form of verification process to establish or disprove the credibility of the 'things' concerned.

Depending on the nature of the doubt and the circumstances, verification takes place intuitively or by instruction; instantly or over time; expertly or crudely; explicitly or implicitly; and formal or informal. Whatever the mechanism, however, verification can be described as a form of audit which is conducted with the objective of establishing the degree of correspondence between the object of doubt and some acceptable criteria by which it can be judged. The greater the correspondence or agreement between the object and its criteria, the greater the probability of removing or reducing the doubt and consequent uncertainty about it.

The human need to reduce or remove doubt is what shapes in practice the nature of the verification process generally, and the audit function particularly. This need also determines the general social, economic and psychic roles which verification or audit is perceived to serve within the community. By attempting to alleviate human anxiety created by uncertainty surrounding specific phenomena, verification or auditing acts as a stabilizing factor in the management of human behaviour. As Murphy (1943, p.25) observes:

> The capacity to secure relevant information, to judge the reliability of its authenticity, and to use it intelligently in further inquiry is essential to the right of reason in human affairs.

More specifically in relation to the subject of this text, the existence of corporate auditing is perceived to be due to a need for a function designed to reduce or remove doubts held by shareholders and other constituents about the quality of corporate financial information reported to them. Achievement of this purpose is believed to encourage the intelligent use of that information, and to provide stability in the human relationships relating to such use.

Examples of doubt, uncertainty and verification

The nature of verification generally and auditing particularly is determined by individual circumstances. However, despite variations in these circumstances, all verification processes have certain characteristics in common, and these are explained and illustrated in the following sections. Examples of verifiable doubt and uncertainty in human affairs are used to illustrate this section, and range from everyday situations to more complex and less usual cases. For example:

- A medical second opinion is given, in which a patient seeks an additional expert diagnosis of his condition and the treatment prescribed by his original doctor. What is in doubt in this situation is, at least in the first instance, the first medical diagnosis and prescription.
- A manuscript review is provided for a firm of literary publishers looking for an expert basis with which to reject or accept a manuscript submitted for publication. The marketability and salcability of the manuscript provide the initial subjects for doubt held by the publishers.
- A slow-motion action replay is called for with respect to a particular action in a ball game. The subject of doubt in this case is an umpiring or refereeing decision put into question by the players and, possibly, also by the coaches and spectators concerned.
- An external assessment of a doctoral programme in a university is undertaken, following several years of student evaluations of poor teacher performance. In this case, the relevance and quality of the syllabuses and instruction are in doubt in the minds of the university administrators responsible for the programme.
- A property survey is sought by an individual prior to making a monetary offer to purchase a building. The condition of the property, as stated in the brochure of the estate agent, is the subject of uncertainty by the potential purchaser.

In each of these cases, there is a relatively obvious doubt and consequent uncertainty about an observed or observable phenomenon in the real world. Such a phenomenon can be in the form of a physical object which has a tangible quality and does not change substantially in the short-term – such as the manuscript submitted to the publisher. Or it can comprise a past event which involves tangible actions which are observed and recorded, but which do not have a current existence – such as action in the ball game. It can also relate indirectly to more intangible and less easily observable phenomena which change rapidly and materially over time – such as in the case of the patient's health.

What is clear from these examples is that the situation which creates the demand for some form of verification varies considerably. All cases cited relate to some form of real-world phenomenon which requires to be observed in order to achieve a measure of verification. However, some phenomena can be observed, and therefore verified, more easily than others. This variation is partly to do with the nature of the individual phenomenon (particularly whether it is tangible or intangible, or whether it is a physical aspect of the real world or a description of the latter), the effect of time on it (changes in form over time can mean verification is possible only in terms of its current rather than its past state), and the availability of suitable evidence with which to verify (sometimes the situation is rich with evidence, on other occasions it is not).

The above examples also reveal that situations of doubt, uncertainty and verification typically involve a triangle of human relationships. First, there is the relationship between the doubter and the originator of the doubt – that is, one person (or persons) is uncertain about the state, quality or condition of the phenomenon which is the responsibility of a second person (or group of persons). For example, the potential purchaser of property is uneasy about the claims made by the vendor and his agent concerning the condition of the building. The verification triangle is completed by a third person who is instructed by the first person to provide a (usually) expert and objective view or opinion concerning the doubt or uncertainty which has arisen with respect to the relationship persisting with the second person(s). This opinion is made at the end of a verification process which is applied to the specific phenomenon in doubt. Provision of the opinion is intended to clarify the situation for the first person, and to allow him or her to make a rational and confident decision and/or action in connection with the phenomenon and his or her relationship with the second person. For example, the publisher can read the independent review to compare with his or her reading of the manuscript, and then make a publishing decision with respect to the author.

The conclusion to be drawn from the above analyses, therefore, is that, in all cases, the third person involved is performing a verification function which can be used by the individual in doubt prior to making decisions and taking action. Verification is therefore not just intended to remove or reduce human doubt and uncertainty. Its ultimate utility is judged in terms of its potential to allow human beings to make rational decisions with respect to other human beings, and to take appropriate actions. Its major role in human activity is seen as a form of control or regulator of human affairs, with a particular emphasis on its stabilizing effect – that is, when assisting in the introduction of rationality and the removal of anxiety caused by uncertainty.

Verification and the audit function

Each of the examples used in this chapter to illustrate the need for verification has the characteristics of an audit, and therefore justifies the use of that term. There is a subject-matter whose condition is in doubt. There is an individual or individuals made responsible for verifying and reporting on its condition to the person(s) harbouring an uncertainty about it. Verification takes place through observable and reportable procedures. And usually the uncertainty is reduced or removed as a result. In practice, however, these situations are rarely given the label of audit. Such a term is normally atrributed to activities which are explicitly of an audit nature – that is, involving someone described as an auditor. In addition, in those situations most obviously suitable for description as an audit, the identity of individuals as auditors is apparent because they are employed to conduct an activity which is specifically termed auditing.

The most familiar example of this activity in the general area of accountancy is the use of an expert professional accountant with the explicit remit of providing an opinion on the quality of published financial statements to an identifiable user. The doubt and uncertainty associated with this situation relates to the accounting content of the financial statements and, specifically, the various accounting processes by which they have been constructed. The particular concern is whether these processes have been sufficient to provide the designated recipients with financial information meeting the quality standards specified for it. Such an audit is defined in the following terms (APC, 1980a, para.2):

> An audit is an independent examination of, and expression of opinion on, the financial statements of an enterprise by an appointed auditor in pursuance of that appointment and in compliance with any relevant statutory obligation.

Thus, as an American Accounting Association committee (AAA, 1973, p.8) comments, the audit is a critical process designed to provide useful economic information of a judgmental nature. The committee further describes the audit function in the following terms (p.2):

> Auditing is a systematic process of objectively obtaining and evaluating evidence regarding assertions about economic actions and events to ascertain the degree of correspondence between these assertions and established criteria and communicating the results to interested parties.

Establishing and reporting on such correspondence appears to be the main aim of an audit function concerned with providing assurance to doubting individuals about the quality of reported accounting messages.

The audit of financial statements can therefore be viewed as an agency function and cost in situations where an agent (for example, the board of directors of a company) is entrusted by a principal (for example, its shareholders) to manage its resources and operations, and to report thereon (Wallace, 1985, p.18). In particular, the auditor can be viewed as an arbiter to determine the consistency of the agent's financial statements with specified accounting procedures (Ball, 1989, p.39). Generally, if the perceived economic benefits associated with such a task exceed the costs of undertaking it, a demand for it should exist (Ng, 1978). This demand will be a function of the ability of the principal to specify the accounting procedures in contracting – the less ability he or she has in that respect (because of the difficulty of providing for a variety of different situations), the greater will be the need for an audit (Ball, 1989, pp.38–9). In other words, the audit of financial statements can be interpreted as an economic cost of monitoring the behaviour of agents in the context of business activity, and in circumstances where the accounting procedures cannot be pre-specified. It is part of the governance of agents in contracting situations.

An alternative interpretation of the audit as part of economic agency is to regard the relationship of owner–principal and managerial agent as one which operates on the basis of trust and loyalty (Armstrong, 1991). The cultivation of such trust and loyalty, and the consequent creation of reasonable freedom of action for the agent, involves costs being incurred by the principal which may reach a level at which it is less expensive to employ an alternative trusted agent (such as the auditor) to monitor the managerial agent (pp.20–1). In other words, the auditor is an agent verifying the actions of other agents in a situation of minimizing the costs to the principal of cultivating agency trust.

Financial statements and verification

The idea of verification of disclosed financial information is an old one. It has been recognized and put into practice in almost every civilization involving economic activity – a point which has been demonstrated by accounting historians as far apart as Brown (1905, pp.74–92) and Littleton and Zimmerman (1962, pp.102–35). However, the more specific function of verification of published financial statements has a shorter but consistent history. For example, in both the UK and the US, auditing has been observed in corporate organizations continuously since the mid-nineteenth century (see, for example, Lee, 1970a, re the UK, and Boockholdt, 1983, re the US). Indeed, the notion of verification in financial reporting is so strong, it has institutionalized itself in the form of explicit specifications of verifiability as a primary quality expected of externally reported financial information.

For example, in a study for the American Accounting Association, Paton and Littleton (1947, pp.18–21) stipulate 'verifiable, objective evidence' as one of the key concepts of accounting. A committee of the American Accounting Association (AAA, 1966, p.10–11) advocates verifiability as one of four main standards of accounting. A further committee of the American Accounting Association (AAA, 1973, p.3) explicitly relates its prescriptions of audit concepts to the above 1966 accounting advocation of verifiability. And a committee of the Accounting Standards Committee in the UK (ASC, 1975, p.29) argues that the credibility of reported financial information is enhanced if it is 'independently verified'.

More recently, the Financial Accounting Standards Board (FASB, 1980, para.59) states verifiability as a qualitative characteristics of accounting information, and a sub-concept of the over-riding prescribed criterion of reliability. FASB (1980, para.81) describes such verifiability in terms which summarize the way in which the concept is currently interpreted by accounting policy-makers:

> The quality of verifiability contributes to the usefulness of accounting information because the purpose of verification is to provide a significant degree of assurance that accounting measures represent what they purport to represent.

And Solomons (1989, pp.34–5), in guidance on accounting standards for the Institute of Chartered Accountants in England and Wales, provides a similar reasoning (p.34):

> The foregoing definition of reliability in an accounting context requires not only that financial statements should faithfully represent what they purport to represent, but also that users of the statements should have reasonable assurance that they do so.

The connection between reliable and verifiable financial information is also made by leading financial accounting theorists such as Chambers (1966, p.164) and Sterling (1985, p.22). Their fundamental argument is that, in order to be reliable (in the sense of adequate correspondence between reported figures and the phenomena they purport to represent), financial statements must also be verifiable to provide assurance of such correspondence.

Relevance, reliability and verification

Understanding this last point is essential to coping with the rationale prescribed for corporate auditing in this text. In particular, as mentioned in the previous chapter and within the context of regulations demanding fair presentation or truth and fairness, the two main qualities prescribed in this text as the focus of operational attention for the corporate auditor are, first, the relevance of reported financial statements as inputs to and influences on the decision models of their potential users; and, second, their reliability in terms of a faithful representation of economic phenomena. In other words, the doubts and uncertainties presumed to exist with respect to the accounting content of published financial statements of corporate organizations are as follows: First, that the disclosed financial statements contain knowledge in an accounting form which is appropriate as an input to the decision models of their intended recipients, and that they are therefore capable of making a difference to the decisions inferred in these models, second, that the financial information containing potentially relevant knowledge for decision models also faithfully represents those economic events and objects it purports to describe. And, third, in so doing, such information meets the regulator's accountability standard of fair presentation or truth and fairness.

Thus, what is argued in this text is that the role of the corporate auditor is centred on a detailed verification process designed to report on the adherence of published financial statements to specified quality criteria, and thereby remove prior doubts and uncertainties about these statements as part of the process of corporate governance and managerial accountability. This argument is made in more detail in Chapter 3.

Further reading

See Chapter 3, pp.42–3.

Discussion and essay topics

1. Think through and discuss any areas of doubt with which you are familiar, and with which there is some form of verification process associated (other than those mentioned in this chapter).
2. Why is verification such a normal feature of human affairs?
3. Define and explain the verification process usually described as audit.
4. What is the concept of verifiability in accounting thought, and what is its connection to the concept of reliability?
5. Discuss in broad terms the connection between verifiability and the corporate audit function.

3

Economic and social roles for corporate auditing

The discussions and explanations in the previous chapter provide a preliminary basis for comprehending the role of verification generally and auditing particularly. However, to study auditing only at the level of general introductory statements limits such an enquiry to an examination of the broad justifications to be made for the function in practice. It ignores auditing's strategic value. The latter topic can be expressed in terms of the role of verification in human affairs generally, and auditing (including corporate auditing) particularly. This role can be observed and discussed at various distinct levels, none of which are mutually exclusive. These extend from a very broad societal view of auditing to a much narrower focus on the economic needs of the individual for audit services.

In particular, the following explanations and analyses enable the reader to contrast the economic view of corporate auditing with its societal counterpart. The economic approach assumes that corporate auditing assists in the efficiency of rational economic exchanges by corporate organizations (Wallace, 1985, p.19). The societal approach, on the other hand, perceives the corporate audit function either as assisting in corporate governance and managerial accountability (Flint, 1988, p.15) or, more critically, as a means of establishing and maintaining unequal power relations which exist in society, and which may not be rational, efficient or fair (Clegg, 1989, p.193).

A general societal role for verification and auditing

From a review of the verification and audit situations outlined in the previous chapter, it can be argued that the major role for these processes of monitoring and control is societal. They provide a useful service in the community to individuals and organizations in need of assurance and comfort because of prior doubts and uncertainties about the state of 'things' in the real world in which they have an interest. Not only is such assurance and comfort provided by verification, but protection is also given by preventing or identifying any human carelessness or deceit which could damage individuals and organizations with an interest in the 'things' concerned.

In other words, verification and auditing assist in the accountability and control of the conduct of human affairs generally, and economic activity particularly. Whenever an individual or organization is invited, implicitly or explicitly, by another individual or organization to accept the state, quality or condition of a defined object or event, there is an almost inevitable need to create conditions which allow the latter individual or organization to be held to account should the state, quality or condition of the phenomenon concerned be potentially sub-standard. Verification is a function which sets out to evidence and report on this state, quality or condition, and assists in the achievement of accountability. It therefore constitutes a governance mechanism within a relationship in which there is a need to monitor behaviour.

Holding individuals or organizations in society accountable for their actions by means of verification or auditing by a third party is a form of societal control mechanism. It assists in stabilizing human relationships. As Flint (1988, pp.14–15) has commented:

> Audit is a social phenomenon. It has no purpose or value except in its practical usefulness. It is wholly utilitarian. The function has evolved in response to a perceived need of individuals or groups in society who seek information or reassurance about the conduct or performance of others in which they have an acknowledged and legitimate interest: it exists because the interested individuals or groups are unable for one or more reasons to obtain for themselves the information or reassurance they require.

The existence of these connections are seen in the various non-accounting situations described in the previous chapter. The predominant message in each is that verification has a strong relationship with accountability, and that this acts to provide comfort and stability in human affairs. For example, medical experts diagnosing a patient's health and prescribing a treatment know, when they do so, they assume a professional risk that the eventual outcome may not be as they prescribed, and that the patient may hold them accountable in a court of law for their opinions and actions – particularly if the patient is damaged by such opinions or subsequent medical actions. Also knowing that the patient could seek or has sought a second professional opinion as a verification of the original opinion, should have the effect of strengthening both the care with which the doctors undertake their examinations and treatment of the patient, and their awareness of their potential accountability to the latter. The second opinion provides assurance and comfort to the patient about the quality of the first opinion. Verification and report therefore provides a measure of peace of mind that decisions or actions have not been taken on the basis of unknown conditions or qualities; and that accountability is enhanced as a consequence.

A specific societal role for auditing

The same general principle applies in situations involving the reporting of financial information by organized entities to their external constituents. The need for assurance and comfort by means of verification is particularly evident in situations where the organizational structure involves a distinct separation of the funding and management of organizational resources. External constituents, who have funded at least part of the resourcing concerned, or who are in various ways affected by the use of funded resources, need to know how well or badly management is discharging its responsibility for the resources entrusted to it.

This 'need to know' is satisfied generally in the form of a stewardship function – that is, an activity in which the managers of resources account to those individuals and organizations with a legitimate interest in the resources and their use. These activities form part of a contracted agency relationship in which it is difficult to pre-specify the detailed procedures of such accounting (Ball, 1989, p.38). However, at least part of it is completed in financial information form, and is made credible by the existence of a verification function called an audit to report on the accounting quality expected of the information disclosed. In other words, the managerial agents of the organization are accountable for their actions, and attempt to comply in part with this duty by reporting formally in accounting terms to the organization's external constituents. The audit of such reports enhances the credibility of the reported information, and is a means of strengthening the process of accountability taking place. The consistency of this role through time is commented on by Mautz and Sharaf (1961, p.243):

> . . . the purpose of an audit still seems to be to provide certain interested parties with an attestation of the reliability of certain information supplied by those entrusted with the property of others.

A specific societal role for corporate auditing

In the specific context of this text, the information reported as part of managerial stewardship is of a mainly financial nature, and the accountability is that of corporate managers to the shareholder–owners of the corporate organization. In most developed countries, such stewardship and accountability is mandated by regulatory or legislative provisions stipulating at least an annual reporting of financial results. These provisions also typically require an audit by an independent professional accountant to verify the informational quality expected.

Such verification in the corporate sector is argued to be of benefit to both the individual shareholder and society at large. With respect to all but the smallest corporate organization, reported information can be regarded as a public good. It is available not only to the individual shareholders to whom it is usually addressed, but also to the community at large as a matter of public record. In many individual situations, therefore, reported financial information is available for use by any member of the public, and can result in a variety of economic and social decisions and actions by individuals who rely on it for such purposes, but who are not directly specified in the regulations concerned. The existence of the corporate audit, although perhaps not legally intended as such, thus provides public assurance and comfort with respect to the quality expected of publicly-available information. In so doing, it consolidates the societal role of such information in terms of the accountability of corporate organizations to the community at large.

This argument, however, should not be construed to mean the traditional financial reporting by companies to their shareholders is sufficient to hold these entities and their managements fully accountable for all aspects of their behaviour and actions. Indeed, as writers such as Chen (1975, p.542) argue, corporate financial reporting is directed narrowly at financial stewardship. It has little or nothing to say with respect to the issue of accountability in terms of broader social objectives. Tinker (1985), for example, provides a coherent argument on the need for social accountability – presumably also involving a suitable audit function. And Flint (1971, pp.291–2) states the need for auditors to be aware of changing public expectations and perceptions with respect to a widening social role for auditing.

The social role for corporate auditing also has to be put in the broader context of the general issue of corporate governance – that is, the various organizational mechanisms which exist externally and internally to monitor and control the corporate entity and its management (see, for example, Alkhafaji, 1989). Such monitoring and control is complex and multi-layered. It includes both internal and external audit, the use of audit committees, the appointment and role of non-executive (or outside) directors, shareholder voting rights, including proxy voting, and institutional investor involvement in corporate affairs.

Power and the societal role of auditing

Clegg (1989, p.193) argues that organizations as collections of contractual relations are never fully controllable because of the existence of agency in these relations. That is, control can be eroded by agents (such as managers) with the power to erode. Agency involves pre-specified rules as part of the contractual process, but rules require implementational discretion by the agents, and discretion necessitates a process of potential disciplining if rules are broken (p.201). Put differently, the managerial agent requires sufficient freedom to conduct satisfactorily the management function. He or she therefore has to be trusted with this freedom by the principal owner. But cultivating such trust is difficult and expensive, and may involve different levels of agency activity (Armstrong, 1991, pp.20–1).

Taking these general thoughts into the context of the agency situation concerning corporate financial reporting, it is possible to interpret the audit function in terms of trust, power and discipline. More specifically, trusted corporate managers are in a powerful position, in the absence of audit, to use their agency situation to determine the rules of reporting to their principals – that is, they have a considerable amount of accounting discretion as to how and what to report *vis-à-vis* their performance and actions. Corporate auditors, on the other hand, can be seen as the introduction of a trusted disciplinary device to minimize such agency discretion. Not only can they attest the contractual propriety and consistency of the accounting procedures used in reporting (thus exercising a direct discipline on the managerial agents), but their presence as auditors also acts as a more subtle disciplining (in the sense of having the potential to prevent managerial abuse of the quality of the reported financial information). Thus, the corporate auditor acts as an important societal device in restricting the power of corporate managerial agents in contractual relations.

However, as trusted agents for corporate ownership, auditors are also in a powerful position to act with discretion (with respect to the rules of auditing). Consequently, they too must be subject to a disciplining – that is, by means of the professional standards of conduct expected of them, which will be discussed later, particularly in Chapters 7 and 8.

A general economic role for verification and auditing

What the previous sections explain and discuss is a series of linkages which can be made when observing human and organizational behaviour. First, a specific phenomenon exists in the real world which is central to the relationship of the participants in the situation concerned. Second, a doubt is raised concerning the condition or quality of this phenomenon. Third, such doubt creates uncertainty for at least one of the participants. Fourth, this uncertainty provides a need for verification of the phenomenon to reduce or remove the uncertainty and the doubt. Fifth, verification of the condition or quality of the phenomenon gives sufficient assurance and comfort to the participants to remove or reduce the doubt and uncertainty. And sixth, in the context of their various decisions, the participants are able to relate more rationally with respect to one another and to the phenomenon.

Rational relations in this respect usually involve the making of a sensible decision concerning a choice between available alternatives, and the taking of a sensible action which is compatible with that decision. Such decisions and actions have been discussed to this point solely within a societal context. That is, they have been observed only at a very general level of communal human interaction, and specifically with respect to their effects on individuals and groups within the community. They have not been examined in the economic context of the use of scarce resources. Human relationships resulting in economic decisions and actions, however, involve the same sequence of doubt, uncertainty, verification, assurance and comfort demonstrated in a social context.

Much of human activity in a developed society has observable economic consequences. The relationships which humans establish at an individual or organizational level typically result in an identifiable effect in the form of measurable economic benefits and associated costs. When such a relationship results in a sequence of doubt, uncertainty, verification, assurance and comfort, and decision and action, the specific process involving verification usually has economic implications. In particular, the economic role of verification is concerned with the function's ability to permit the making of rational economic decisions, and the taking of rational economic action in contractual relationships. From this perspective, verification is capable of assisting in the management and control of economic risk – that is, in helping in situations where doubts and uncertainties exist about the economic outcomes of contractual decisions and actions because of a largely unknown future, but where such outcomes can be estimated with a degree of probability. Verification of the condition or quality of the suspect phenomenon relating to an economic decision or action is therefore intended to assist in reducing uncertainty, estimating probability, and minimizing attendant risk. It is undertaken in a rational world when its perceived benefits are greater than its anticipated costs.

This economic process can be illustrated by using one of the non-financial situations from the previous chapter, before proceeding to the case of financial information in organized activity generally and corporate activity particularly. For example, purchasing the building without the benefit of verification by independent survey has an obvious economic implication – particularly if after purchase the property proves to require significant repair in order to maintain its market price. A report from an independent surveyor on the state of the property at the time of purchase can prevent an economically damaging decision being made. The potential purchaser is aware of possible repair costs, and can make an offer accordingly. In other words, the cost of the survey is exceeded by the potential financial savings. Put more generally, completion of the verification process by means of suitable reporting to the participants concerned assists in bounding economic uncertainties. In turn, this permits decisions to be made and outcomes to be realized more rationally and knowledgeably than might have been the case otherwise.

A specific economic role for auditing

The same conclusion can be arrived at in the more specific organizational setting of an entity reporting to its external constituents on its financial progress and position. The information at doubt is typically the responsibility of the reporting entity's management acting as agent for its owner–principals. And the doubt and uncertainty created is that which arises from a situation in which management is reporting on its achievements. Such self-assessment is a condition of moral hazard which does not engender confidence in the minds of external constituents who are potentially relying on the reported information for credible knowledge of the entity's financial progress and position. And it could inhibit the proper fulfilment of contracts between the entity and these constituents (Wallace, 1985, p.34).

Such potential reliance in contractual relations can be illustrated in a number of ways. For example, existing owners require reported information in order to take economic decisions concerning the status of their investment and the retention of entity management. Potential investors base their investment decisions on reported information to assess entity performance. Bankers and other lenders use reported information to make loan and credit decisions regarding the reporting entity's funding needs. Suppliers access reported information with respect to decisions connected with the granting of credit and the continuation of trading with the entity. Customers and employees, similarly, can use reported information to decide on the continuation of their economic relationships with the reporting entity.

The doubt and uncertainty which exists in each of these situations can be assumed to increase in inverse proportion to the degree of closeness between the external constituent and the reporting entity. The closer the former is physically to the latter, the less uncertainty there should be concerning the credibility of the reported financial information. Alternatively, the more difficult it is to pre-specify con-tractually accounting and reporting procedures, the more uncertainty there is likely to be about the quality of the financial information (Ball, 1989, p.39). Thus, the verification function is designed to remove or reduce underlying doubt or uncertainty which persists in constituent–entity contractual relationships with respect to reported financial information. In doing so, its economic role is the removal or reduction of doubts and uncertainties which inhibit or restrict the use of such information in rational decisions with probable economic outcomes. By improving the quality of reported information, it can be argued to improve the rationality of the decisions it impacts, and assist in the successful completion of contracts to which these decisions relate (Wallace, 1985, p.41).

However, as mentioned in relation to verification, the demand for audit services is a function of their perceived benefits exceeding their costs (Ng, 1978, *passim*; and Wallace, 1985, pp.34–43). The auditor can be observed in a contractual agency situation, involving entity owners as principals, managers as agents, and other groups in contractual relationships with the entity. The economic role of the auditor is to act as a further agent for the owners (and, possibly, these other groups) in a situation where there are contractual incentives to complete such an audit (Antle, 1982). That is, the audit exists to assist in avoiding potential contractual conflicts between entity management and its owners and other external interests which could be economically damaging. By signalling the quality of the audited financial information to the entity's external constituents, the auditor assists in reducing the potential moral hazard to the latter of management taking advantage of its given function to report on its actions, and thereby prevents a decline in the amount and quality of contracting activity (Wallace, 1985, pp.41–2).

This economic argument for auditing thus suggests that, if the economic consequences of potential conflicts in contractual relations (such as investment in an entity) exceed the costs of audit, it is in everyone's interest to have an audit (Wallace, 1985, p.55). Auditing has the potential to improve the quality of financial reporting, and better financial reporting has the potential to reduce contractual conflicts. However, this argument is made in the absence of regulation for accounting and audit services. It can be argued that, in an unregulated environment, the market for reported information could be distorted by the reporting entity acting as a monopoly supplier of information to the highest bidder (Wallace, 1985, p.53). In turn, this distortion in the availability of information for decision-making and action could result in market failures concerning a suboptimal allocation of resources and, consequently, a need to mandate the publication of financial information and require its audit.

As previously mentioned, the necessity to audit publicly available financial information results from its existence as a public good, available for relatively free and unrestricted public access (rather than private use), and therefore requiring a minimum quality standard to protect the public consumer. In other words, the basic economic role of the auditor in a regulated environment can be perceived as an agency one for owners (and, indirectly, others), in which there is a public source of information from and about a private entity source, and with the potential to economically damage its consumer unless it is subject to a minimum quality control process such as auditing. However, it should also be noted that this creates the free-rider effect, in which entity owners are effectively paying a tax in the form of the cost of audit monitoring, and the benefits from this tax are being shared by the community at large (Wallace, 1985, p.51). In other words, the economic arguments for regulated as against voluntary audits are a continuing issue for accounting and auditing policy-makers (Wallace, 1985, p.53).[1]

A specific economic role for corporate auditing

The above review and conclusions are particularly apposite to corporate organizations. Typically, the management of a company is in an agency situation, separated from its shareholders as well as from its other external constituent groupings such as lenders and creditors. This remoteness, which is accentuated as the corporate organization grows, creates a natural dependency among its external constituents for formal and credible sources of information which provide pre-decision knowledge of its financial progress, position and prospects. This dependency tends to vary from situation to situation. It is influenced not only by the size of the corporate organization, and the degree of remoteness of the individual constituents from it, but also by the ability of these constituents to read and use financial information, and the variety of other sources of information about the corporate organization which are available and accessible to them. However, irrespective of these variations, reported financial information from such entities triggers doubts and uncertainties in the minds of its recipients regarding its credibility generally and veracity particularly. Potential conflicts therefore exist in the contractual relations between the company and its management, and external interests such as shareholders, lenders and creditors. A process of verification in the form of a corporate audit is designed to remove or reduce these doubts, uncertainties and potential conflicts, at least to the extent that the information concerned has the potential to influence or make a difference to the decisions and actions of its recipients.

More specifically, financial information from corporate organizations, which is not identified as irrelevant and/or unreliable, can cause economic disbenefits to shareholders and other corporate constituents if reliance on it results in inappropriate decisions – that is, if the information provides wrong or misleading signals concerning the company's financial progress, position or prospects, and if these signals have been acted upon by means of decisions on alternative courses of economic action. For example, if shareholders decide to increase their investment on the basis of reported but unaudited accounting messages of increasing profitability (when, in fact, profitability is decreasing), they will lose economically if the value of their investment falls following their acquisition. In these circumstances, the existence of a corporate audit at least provides an expectation that the lack of truth in the reporting of income by the company would have been either observed and reported on by the auditor, or caused by the auditor to be removed by management prior to reporting. It would not, on the other hand, have guaranteed a wise investment decision. The latter is dependent on factors other than the expert verification of reported accounting numbers.

Literature prescriptions for an economic role for auditing

The importance of audited financial information with respect to rational economic decision-making in corporate activity can be demonstrated by reference to the broader literature of financial reporting theory and practice. This literature contains consistent prescriptions by accounting policy-makers and theorists concerning the primary need in external financial reporting for accounting information with the capacity to influence, or make a difference to, the specified decisions of individuals and organizations. This link between corporate reporting and economic decisions will be explored in greater depth throughout the text. But, meantime, it is relevant to suggest that, if such a connection is made, it is on the premise that the reporting is subject to a formal process of auditing. In other words, the connection is between rational economic decision-making and audited financial information.

This view of the role of auditing is supported in a variety of writings on external financial reporting over the last fifty years. Each of these writings advocates a role for financial reporting in terms of assisting in economic decision-making, and also argues the need for a process of verification to be applied to the information concerned. One of the first institutional statements of the need for auditing in the provision of useful financial information for economic decisions is in a committee report of the American Accounting Association (AAA, 1966). It specifies the main aim of accounting as providing information for making decisions concerning the use of limited resources (p.4), and prescribes the adoption by reporting accountants of the standard of verifiability (pp.10–11). A similar approach is taken by a committee of the American Institute of Certified Public Accountants (AICPA, 1973) which outlines an economic decision-making aim for external financial reporting (p.13), and specifies the criterion of reliability for reported information (p.58). Although not mentioning verifiability, the AICPA committee's supporting volume of papers includes such a concept as a defined sub-set of the overall reliability criterion (Ronen, 1974, p.87).

This approach to corporate financial reporting objectives was expanded in 1978 by the Financial Accounting Standards Board (FASB, 1978). In its objectives statement, FASB states the main reporting aim as follows (para.34):

> Financial reporting should provide information that is useful to present and potential investors and creditors and other users in making rational investment, credit, and similar decisions.

FASB later states that such an objective supports the argument for its prescribed reporting qualities (FASB, 1980, para.21), and specifically advocates verifiability as one of these expected qualities (para.81). Such conceptual linkages are repeated by Solomons (1989) in his guidelines for UK accounting standard-setters – specifically, the aim of assisting economic decision-making (pp.12–13), and the companion reporting quality of verifiability (pp.34–5).

The US accounting policy-making approach of linking auditing with the economic decision basis of financial reporting is compatible with that of the UK. For example, in 1975, the Accounting Standards Committee issued a discussion paper in which the basic aim of corporate financial reports is stated as the communication of useful economic information (ASC, 1975, p.28). This prescription is based on an *a priori* analysis of the information needs of various report user groups, with user decisions as a recurrent theme (pp.19–27). The ASC implicitly prescribes the reporting quality of reliability, defining this in large part on the basis of independent verification (p.29).

There has been a similar consistency in the advocacy of verified accounting information for economic decision-making by individual writers. For example, Paton and Littlejohn (1947, pp.14–18) focus on the need for 'test readings' to compare managerial efforts and accomplishments for purposes of internal and external decisions (p.14). They argue for accounting to be based on verifiable, objective evidence (pp.18–21). Moonitz (1961) makes similar observations in his prescriptions for the role of reported financial information. He states (p.21) that quantified data are helpful in making rational economic decisions, and that financial reports provide part of the required data (p.27). Moonitz goes on to argue that measurements of such data should be objective (p.41), and that objectivity should be interpreted as subject to independent verification (p.42).

Other writers can be seen to provide similar normative statements. Chambers (1966, p.102) describes accounting's role as a continuous source of financial information to guide future actions in markets. He further argues that such information is objective in the sense of having been corroborated (p.164). Staubus (1977) is even more direct when he defines accounting in the following terms (p.29):

> The primary objective of accounting is to provide financial information about the economic affairs of an entity for use in making decisions.

He proceeds (p.44) to prescribe reliability as a primary criterion for reported information, and suggests that this should include verifiability (p.71).

Sterling also develops relevant theoretical arguments. His original reporting focus is on verity (Sterling, 1970b, p.353) – that is, to be useful, reported information should correspond in some way with reality, and this correspondence should be tested by agreement among qualified observers. However, by 1979, Sterling (1979, p.85) appears more concerned with identifying the economic atrributes for reporting purposes which are relevant to a defined decision model. And, by 1985, he is arguing (Sterling, 1985, p. 76) for accounting information useful for economic decisions, and prescribing verification of the faithful representation of decision-relevant attributes of the reporting entity as a necessary quality of such accounting.

It is therefore evident from the above comments that there is a general consensus on this issue among financial reporting writers and policy-makers over many years. In particular, there is agreement that the annual reporting of financial information should be made only on completion of its verification. The consistent view is that the corporate audit has a significant role with respect to economic decisions because of its provision of an expert verification of reported financial accounting information which is intended to impact such decisions.

This general conclusion about the economic role of auditing is one articulated by Wallace (1985) in the context of agency theory in unregulated and regulated environments. She describes the audit function as an economic service (p.1), and argues its historical importance on the basis of observations of its existence over time in unregulated economic environments (p.3). Wallace's arguments are concerned with the economic role of auditing from the perspective of the self-interests of participants in organized economic behaviour. She also articulates statements relating to more general economic issues and the role of auditing. First, she sees auditing enhancing the reliability of financial information, thus assisting in reducing the risks associated with economic decision making (p.32). And second, she envisages a variety of other economic benefits from audit activity – for example, the prevention of fraud and other abuses, and compliance with regulations (p.32); improved systems of control and information, and operating efficiency (p.32); assistance in assessing organizational and managerial performance (pp.32 and 41); and accessing the reporting entity's customer base, and the provision of other services (p.32).

Wallace is suggesting that the very existence of an audit function not only has the capacity to determine the quality of reported financial information, but also has the capability of improving that quality and providing significant economic benefits to the reporting entity and its external constituents. She particularly argues that perceptions of the value of these benefits, if they exceed the costs of auditing, provide an explanation of the consistent demand for audit services through time – even in unregulated environments (p.16). These arguments are consistent with the more formal agency models of Ng (1978) and Antle (1982).

Economic self-interest and verification

The above discussion of the relationship between economics and auditing highlights a further dimension to the argument for verification generally and auditing particularly. It is rooted in the familiar behavioural concept of self-interest mentioned above – that is, individuals and organizations have selfish reasons for permitting verification to take place because they can benefit from this happening. In this respect, the role of verification generally and auditing particularly is observed from the position of the individual or organization being verified, rather than from that of the beneficiary for whom the function is taking place. Traditional audit theory tends to focus on the benefits of auditing to the user of financial statements. Alternatively, this section is concerned to examine the producer rather than the consumer of these informational products. The basic proposition is that there are benefits to be derived from verification or auditing for the individuals being verified or audited.

In the case of non-accounting verification, the self-interest argument is an obviously economic one. As stated previously, the starting proposition is that verification activity is desired if the economic benefits expected from it exceed the costs of putting it into practice. This is also true of accounting-based audits, and Wallace's (1985) monograph is largely concerned with this issue. It is therefore used in the next section as the main source of comment. However, before proceeding to examine the professionalized practice of auditing, it is useful to initially consider one of the less formal situations used throughout this chapter. For example, the umpire in the ball game has an identifiable self-interest with respect to play-backs of actions on which he makes decisions. To have such a device to hold him accountable provides an explicit expression of his potential 'stewardship'. It is also an information source available to enable his original decision to be confirmed or altered, and it is an insurance against both a right or wrong decision.

This situation identifies several key aspects of the self-interest role of verification. First, it provides explicit messages to interested parties that the individual being verified is willing to be verified. This enhances the image of stewardship in the conduct of human affairs, adds to the credibility and status of the individual being monitored, and has the potential to consequently enhance his or her economic well-being (by being rewarded for being open). Second, verification provides an additional information source in a situation in which debatable decisions are taken. It can improve the potential quality of these decisions and improve prospective economic positions. Third, the verification function can be seen as a form of quality control or insurance by means of protecting everyone involved in the original decision, and by preventing consequential economic disadvantages.

Economic self-interest and auditing

These features form the basic self-interest argument which Wallace (1985) applies to the economic role of auditing. In situations involving the production and disclosure of financial information, it is observed that self-interest has a large part to play in the desire for and implementation of an audit function to verify the quality of reported financial information. Wallace (1985, p.14) states the self-interest argument in three hypotheses which predict a demand for auditing, each of which are consistent with evidence of observed individual and organizational behaviour. She describes these propositions as the stewardship, information and insurance hypotheses, thus bringing together the economic (decision) role of auditing with its social (accountability) emphasis.

The **stewardship** hypothesis is stated (p.20) as:

> . . . when one party is delegated decision making power, he has an incentive to agree to be checked if the benefits from such monitoring activities exceed the related costs.

Then, in relation to the **information** hypothesis (p.26):

> [it] predicts a demand for audited information as a means of reducing the risk of investments, improving internal and external decision making, enhancing gains from trade, and improving the portfolio investment position of individuals.

And, with respect to **insurance**, Wallace identifies a number of different perspectives – for example, reporting managers look to the auditor as a form of insurance policy should something go wrong with the use of the information concerned (p.27); managers respond to societal expectations that they act professionally by having an audit of the information (p.31); the auditor assists in improving the quality of information disclosure for management (p.31); the auditor represents a form of protection for an otherwise uninsurable business risk (p.31); and the auditor protects politicians from public criticism of failure to act against business abuses (p.32).

The role of the audit function is therefore not argued solely in terms of its economic and social assistance to individuals and organizations with doubts and uncertainties about the quality of reported financial information. It should also be seen from the perspective of the producers of information who are able to satisfy a self-interest by having an audit take place. In other words, such individuals need an audit as much as do the consumers of audit services.

A psychic role for auditing and verification

What is argued in previous sections is that the verification process generally, and the audit function particularly, has the capacity to fulfil three distinct but somewhat related roles. The first role concerns assistance in providing needed stability in societal relationships by giving assurance and comfort to doubting individuals and organizations. The second role involves enhancing the rationality of individual and organizational decisions and actions with economic consequences. And the third role serves the social and economic self-interests of individuals and organizations. However, this is not the end of the discussion on the roles of verification and auditing.

There is a further role, much less tangible than the others discussed, and only indirectly commented on by observers of accounting behaviour. This relates to the psychic nature of verification or auditing – that is, the capacity of the latter processes to benefit the 'psyche' of individuals forming organizational structures. Put differently, in addition to the socio-economic roles for verification or auditing, these activities provide personalized psychological benefits of assurance and comfort to individuals attempting to cope with an organized world of increasing doubt, uncertainty and change. As such, the role of the verifier or auditor is observed directly from an individualistic rather than organizational perspective – although psychic comfort to the individual can also provide socio-economic comfort to the organization of which he or she is a part. What is of particular concern in this respect is the degree to which verification or auditing can reduce or eliminate stress created for individuals by identifiable but inaccessible factors impacting on their lives. Verification or auditing provides them with images which signal an explanation of the factors concerned. The benefits of such a role are impossible to quantify in any measurable way. But, nevertheless, their qualitative nature ought not to cause them to be forgotten in any review of the role of verification or auditing.

The basic argument in this regard is that what individuals and organizations are seeking (often implicitly or subconsciously) from the verifier or auditor is a message of assurance that the subject-matter which is in doubt is, in fact, not one over which there should be doubt – even though it may otherwise appear to be dubious. The value of this role for verification and auditing is that, irrespective of whether the inherent doubt or uncertainty can be or is clarified, such activity has the potential to prevent anxiety for individuals and, arguably, thereby assists in maintaining stability in their economic and social relationships. The mere existence of the verifier or auditor at work is sufficient to reduce doubts and uncertainties. This is because of an intangible 'faith' in them and their function, rather than because of the more tangible and explicit results of their verification or audit activities.

This argument can be extended further in relation to the specific use by corporate regulators of undefined accounting quality terms such as 'present fairly' in the US, and 'a true and fair view' in the UK; and by accounting standard-setters of defined quality terms such as 'relevance' and 'reliability'. Irrespective of the precise meaning of these terms in relation to reported accounting numbers, and the consequent difficulty of operationalizing them in practice, their existence as the explicit accounting quality controls can be argued to provide an image of the existence of a substantial body of knowledge capable of providing credible financial messages for use (Lee, 1992b). In other words, it is the perception rather than the achievement of accounting quality which provides psychic comfort and assurance to corporate financial report users.

Magic accounting and ritual

Gambling provides arguments relating to this alternative view of the role of accounting (and, more implicitly, auditing) (for example, Gambling, 1977 and 1987). The essence of his explanation is that accounting performs a 'magical' role in society, in which its utility is ritualistic as well as economic. This is not magic in the traditional sense of supernatural matters, but more a societal assenting to the need for accounting

'just to be there' irrespective of its specific operational utility. Gambling (1990a)
further argues that the usual complexity and outdatedness of reported accounting
information suggest that its potential recipients must use other less complex and more
immediate sources of information for their decisions and actions. This therefore leaves
the role of reported accounting numbers in society as something much deeper but
much less tangible than the conventional functional descriptions of it. Gambling
(1978, p.28), indeed, suggests that what people seek from accounting is not an
absolute truth but what they can come to agree on as an explanation of what happened
economically. In these circumstances, the role for accounting is a ritualistic one of
providing comfort in a given situation via an agreed interpretation of the reported
accounting message (Gambling, 1978, p.43):

> One might suppose that accounting was a matter of precision of analysis and balancing
> the books to the last penny. So it is, but viewed from a situation of a more senior
> accountant, one sees it is also a matter of assessing how far data can be pushed to
> accommodate 'political' compromises between collaborators in the enterprise – and still
> remain in some sense 'true and fair'.

What is being suggested is that accounting (and auditing) is a part of an image-making
process by corporate management, in much the same way as the architecture of the
buildings of kings and queens is judged by social historians – that is, not in terms of
the quality of the architecture or the construction processes but, instead, as explicit
symbols of the magnificence of royalty, and the power and status of kings and queens
as rulers (Thurley, 1991, p.14; and Burke, 1992, pp.25–8). As Gambling (1990b,
p.21) suggests, accounting may be no more than a statement of respect to enhance the
reputation of the reporting organization and its management – that is, it is a social
representation of its overall 'totemic' wealth which includes power and authority, as
well as the more familiar economic aspects of wealth.

A psychic role for verification

With the above thoughts in mind, it is relevant to relate them to the subject of, first,
verification, and then auditing. For example, if it is legitimate to think of reported
accounting information as a form of ritualistic image-making to convince individuals
and organizations that the reporting entity and its management are powerful and
beyond reproach, it is equally logical to suggest that the role of verification is
consolidating that image. For example, the obtaining of a second medical opinion is
unnecessary from a medical standpoint if the first specialist is professionally
competent and careful in the examination and diagnosis. Thus, the second opinion
can be interpreted as a ritualistic necessity to comfort the patient that the first expert
has, in fact, been competent and careful.

A psychic role for corporate auditing

It is therefore possible to interpret the role of verification as benefiting the psyche of
the potential beneficiary. The same can be said of the audit of accounting information

– particularly in the context of corporate organizations. The company may have considerable professional accounting expertise available to produce its financial statements, and there may be very sophisticated systems of internal control in operation with respect to such production. Therefore, the question is raised as to why an audit is required in such circumstances (particularly for larger organizations). The answer may lie in the explanation of ritual. The corporate audit function is necessary because, just by having the audit, it is sufficient to provide assurance and comfort to external constituents that all is well with the financial statements, the reporting company and its management. The corporate audit becomes a seal of approval – a label that the information is safe to use.

This perspective of auditing as a ritualistic activity is explored by Mills and Bettner (1992). They argue for its ritualistic nature on the basis that its procedures are predictable and repetitious, the auditor (priest) uses symbolism in the form of an audit report, creates a reality of credible financial statements describing economic events and objects, and promotes social order by introducing such credibility to the market process (pp.191–3). In other words, the audit fosters perceptions of balance, harmony and order but, in so doing, it can also mask the conflicts which underlie auditing with respect to differing perceptions and expectations of audit (pp.194–6). As an important component of corporate accountability, it can provide comfort to some, and discomfort to others.

A political view of corporate auditing

Before proceeding to examine the specific objectives which are prescribed for corporate auditing, it is useful to present a further alternative view of the role of that function. This adopts a fundamentally political position which has its origins in the notion of corporate auditing as a professionalized activity. The basic argument centres on corporate auditors as professionals who claim to be acting in the public interest by using an authoritative body of knowledge, whereas, in reality, they are working to serve their self-interest and, consequently, preserving the status quo of certain power relations in society (Sikka, Willmott and Lowe, 1989; and Willmott, 1990).

These power relations concern the principal–agent relationship on which corporate activity is founded, and in which the shareholder–principals entrust responsibility for the utilization of scarce resources to their managerial agents in return for a regular accounting by the latter for their actions. Corporate management, however, does this in terms of a flexible accounting practice which can be manipulated to state its performance according to how and what it wishes to report. In turn, and as argued in this text, corporate auditing exists to ensure fair play in such reporting. The corporate audit can therefore be interpreted as an important mechanism in corporate activity to protect the financial interests of the providers of funding for companies. The corporate auditor's role in this respect is legitimated and given authority by the mandatory requirements of state regulators for a professional audit, and satisfies the political role of such regulators as guardians of the public interest – they are seen to be putting mechanisms such as audit in place to monitor and control corporate behaviour. As a professional, the corporate auditor claims to serve this public interest – that is, with the express objective of protecting various user groups from poor quality financial information. And it is argued to be in corporate management's interest to be seen to be audited and held accountable by such a professional.

Alternatively, however, the position may be somewhat different. Corporate auditors are perceived to have economic and social self-interests to serve. Their audit role is interpreted in terms of skilled professionals, dependent on the economic patronage of corporate managerial agents, and tolerating a flexible accounting practice because it provides substantial economic rewards for them (Sikka, Willmott and Lowe, 1989, p.65). Under such circumstances, the corporate auditor maintains a power position in which the corporate managerial agents can determine how they are going to account to the shareholder and other principals. In other words, the role of the corporate audit may be nothing more than a complex device to maintain corporate power relations in the name of the public interest. These issues will be discussed further in later chapters when considering such matters as corporate auditor independence and reporting on informational quality. But, meantime, the thesis of Hooks (1992) should be noted. Writing in the context of the audit expectations gap(s), she argues that an analysis of the accounting profession's responses to various audit issues related to such a gap reveals that its behaviour ought not to be explained solely in terms of the public interest or self-interest (pp.129–30). Instead, such explanations should involve various theories of professional behaviour (including public-interest-based professional traits and functions (p.112), and the self-interest-based desire for market control (pp.113–14) and involvement in class conflict (p.115). In other words, acting in the public interest and self-interest may both contribute to public welfare (p.129).

Note

1. As mentioned in previous chapters, an alternative explanation of the economics of the auditor in an agency situation is that the cost of cultivating the trust of the managerial agents exceeds the cost of employing an external audit agent to monitor the latter (Armstrong, 1991, pp.20–1).

Further reading

R.K. Mautz and H.A. Sharaf (1961) *The Philosophy of Auditing*, American Accounting Association, pp.18–36 (a traditional review of the nature of the audit process, and the role of the auditor as a tester of audit hypotheses).

D. Flint (1988) *Philosophy and Principles of Auditing: An Introduction*, Macmillan, pp.3–17 (a traditional review of the nature and role of audit in the context of social accountability).

W.A. Wallace (1985) The economic role of the audit in free and regulated markets, *Auditing Monograph 1*, Macmillan (an argument for the audit function based on the economic theories of agency and information in market conditions).

S.K. Mills and M.S. Bettner (1992) Ritual and conflict in the audit profession, *Critical*

Perspectives on Accounting, **3**(2), pp.185–200 (an alternative view of the audit serving a ritualistic function to create social order and stability).

H. Willmott (1991) The auditing game: a question of ownership and control, *Critical Perspectives on Accounting*, **2**(1), pp.109–21 (an extended argument that the auditor acts to maintain the status quo of power relations in society).

Discussion and essay topics

1. Explain the general role which auditing fulfils in society, and comment on how it relates to corporate governance and accountability.
2. Discuss the connection between corporate auditing and stewardship, particularly relating your thoughts to the role of financial reporting.
3. The corporate audit function involves aspects of power and authority. Discuss.
4. Comment on the prescription that corporate auditing assists in economic decision making.
5. Discuss the role of the corporate auditor as an economic agent in contractual situations.
6. Prepare a critique of Wallace's case for auditing as an economic service, with particular reference to the idea of economic self-interest.
7. Prepare a commentary on the prescriptions of accounting policy-makers regarding the economic utility of auditing.
8. Discuss the ritualistic role of corporate auditing in society with particular reference to the writings of Gambling.
9. Critique the political role of the corporate audit with respect to maintaining power relations in society.

4

Prescribing an objective for corporate auditing

The intention of the review in the previous chapter is to identify different roles for verification and auditing. Despite the diversity of perspective provided, the analysis reveals several common features which distinguish these activities from any other in society. Each contains recurring features which, when collected under the generic label of verification or auditing, provide a useful description of such a function. These common features also provide a basis for deriving statements concerning the prescription of the main aims of auditing generally, and corporate auditing particularly. As stated previously, it is necessary in any theoretical structure and argument to prescribe a statement of objectives from which fundamental concepts governing practice can be derived.

Subject-matters and empirical phenomena

Verification and auditing can be observed in different ways from the perspective of a definable subject-matter. That is, as demonstrated in the previous chapter, each identifiable situation of verification or audit involves a subject-matter which has the potential to be observed and/or interpreted in the so-called real world. Such reality is typically described in terms of the state, quality or condition of specific phenomena, and is usually verified by reference to evidential material which exists in the real world. For example, the manuscript is a physical subject-matter available for empirical verification, and its specific contents are read by its independent reviewer in order to come to an expert judgment for the publisher as to its marketability. Alternatively, the economic events, resources and obligations of a reporting entity such as a company form the verifiable subject-matter of a corporate audit. Their content and quality are observed and examined mainly by reference to such physical evidence as reported financial statements, underlying accounting records and supporting documentation, as well as physical observations of tangible economic events, resources and obligations.

Thus, a common thread running through most situations involving verification is a subject-matter comprising real-world phenomena which typically can be empirically tested by reference to physical evidence derived from the same real world. These phenomena exist in some form of reality, although not always tangibly, and give rise to the doubts and uncertainties which verification or auditing is intended to alleviate. The verifier or auditor, therefore, is dealing with various realities which he or she attempts to observe empirically and test by reference to evidence which may also be part of the overall reality. Indeed, there would appear to be little sense or rationale in a situation in which verification is of imagined matters, using imagined evidence and alleviating imagined doubts. Thus, the function of auditing is concerned with subject-matters and evidence which are argued to be part of what is commonly described as reality – even if their tangibility in a physical sense is difficult to determine on occasion.

Corporate subject-matters and empirical phenomena

Put more specifically in relation to corporate auditing, the verifiable reality of economic activity is observable in the context of the corporate organization which is formed to transact such activity. Following the basic argument of Coase (1937) that the transaction is the basic unit of economic analysis, Williamson (1975, pp.8–10) argues generally that, in a world of uncertainty, biased exchange relations, limited information and opportunism, economic activity will be conducted within an organized firm instead of by individual market exchange when the relative costs of transacting (including contracting) make it economical to do so. He further argues (Williamson, 1981, pp.1537–40) that the organized firm which forms the corporate entity is effectively a governance structure as well as a profit-maximizing function. As a governance structure, it is designed to minimize transaction costs by means of an organized control of economic activity, and such control includes the use of audit services (Williamson, 1975, pp.29–30). Thus, the corporate auditor can be viewed as part of an overall control mechanism to monitor the subject-matter of corporate transactions. The verifiable empirical phenomena inherent in these transactions are the economic events, resources and obligations to which the transactions relate – that is, so-called economic reality.[1]

Auditing, economic reality and literature prescription

The idea of an observable and testable economic reality as the subject-matter of audit activity is one which has been commented on by various writers in recent times. In particular, there are a number of direct and indirect arguments for accountants to report on real-world events and objects, and to verify their existence with respect to real-world evidence. For example, the 1973 concepts committee of the American

Accounting Association (AAA, 1973, p.2) defines auditing in terms of a presumed reality of economic actions and events:

> Auditing is a systematic process of objectively obtaining and evaluating evidence regarding assertions about economic actions and events to ascertain the degree of correspondence between the assertions and established criteria and communicating the results to interested users.

In this respect, the committee recognizes the difference in auditing between establishing the empirical truth of accounting assertions (by relating language with experience), and validating these assertions (by checking their compliance with established rules) (p.24). Indeed, the committee further recognizes that, because of the nature of accounting, many aspects of auditing are concerned with validation rather than empirical truth (p.24).

Sterling (1979), on the other hand, has been much more normative in relation to the subject-matter of auditing. He describes his views in the context of accountants being unable to resolve the problems of accounting (p.3), and advocates the following prescription (p.13):

> Our financial statements ought to provide descriptions and explanations of empirical phenomena. We should seek laws and theories which will allow us to predict (in the scientific sense) those phenomena. In short, as 'accounting' seems to imply, the principal objective ought to be to account for empirical phenomena.

And, in relation to auditing, he states (p.18):

> Specifically, we must ask how to audit empirical phenomena.

This view has been supported by Wolnizer (1987, p.4):

> In particular, dated accounts . . . must be descriptions of empirical phenomena, the veracity of which may be ascertained by recourse to evidence which is beyond the control and influence of those who prepare them.

And Ruud (1989, p.153):

> Financial reporting should adopt an objective for describing economic reality. Auditing would be defined as a verification process to ensure the information's correspondence to economic reality.

It is also described in similar terms in recent accounting policy-making prescriptions of the Financial Accounting Standards Board (FASB, 1978, para.17; and FASB, 1980, paras. 63–70), Solomons (1989, p.32), and the Accounting Standards Board (ASB, 1991b, para.30).

In other words, there is an explicit view that accounting should be concerned with descriptions of economic reality in the form of empirically testable phenomena, and that the auditor should be undertaking the testing required. In particular, following Sterling (1985), the argument runs as follows. Financial statements are the means of communicating messages about the reality of economic events and objects pertaining to a reporting entity such as a company. What is important to the user of these statements is that, as part of the more general exercise of managerial accountability, the descriptions of these events and objects are capable of making a difference to his or her decisions (the relevance criterion); and that the descriptions faithfully represent or correspond to the designated relevant events and objects (the reliability criterion) (Sterling, 1985, p.76). The function of auditing in these circumstances is to verify that the accounting messages faithfully represent relevant economic events and objects (p.76). If this function is successfully completed, then it can be further argued that the financial statements concerned present a *prima facie* case to be described in the regulatory but undefined accountability form of 'present fairly' or 'a true and fair view' (ASB, 1991b, para.43).

Informational quality and auditing

As argued above, economic events, resources and obligations constitute the subject-matter of auditing generally and corporate auditing particularly. But the specific aspect of these real-world phenomena with which auditing is concerned is informational quality – that is, the auditor is responsible for verifying and reporting on the quality of the information which describes the economic subject-matter. Quality in this respect is defined in this text mainly in terms of the relevance and reliability of the reported information. That is, financial statement users are presumed to be concerned that the relevance and reliability of the financial statements they receive are such that they can confidently rely on them – a form of what Wolnizer (1987, p.45) describes as quality assurance, and from which he defines auditing as independent testing (p.46).

Wolnizer (1987, p.89) further argues that the quality expected of financial statements should be expressed in terms of their 'technical ophelimity' or fitness in use. He states this notion in terms of the characteristics expected of the statements concerned – that is, their relevance to all market actions (p.73), reliability defined as their correspondence with observable, real-world referents (p.87), and independent testability using publicly available evidence (p.72–3). What Wolnizer is arguing in the context of the audit function is that it is capable of being used with confidence prior to the making of decisions or the taking of action by its user. The ultimate aim of verified information is that it is credible. It should have the capacity to give its users belief in the overall quality of its accounting message content. If such belief exists, the potential exists for doubts and uncertainties to be diminished, rational use of the information to take place, and proper accountability between the reporting entity and management and its external constituents to be enhanced.

Added-value and auditing

As the 1973 concepts committee of the American Accounting Association states (AAA, 1973, p.11), the audit of financial statements adds value to the primary communication of financial information from the reporting entity to its constituent external interests. It does so by reporting to these individuals and organizations on the quality of the information reported (p.12). In other words, the audit provides added value to reported financial statements because it reports on the results of verifying the relevance and reliability of the contents of these statements. As such, it is also capable of adding value to the overall function of accountability between the reporting entity and its external constituents. Such added-value should not be confused with that which is claimed typically by auditors when they provide advice to corporate management as a consequence of their audit work. Such advice is undoubtedly valuable, but is additional to the audit and, very often, will lead to the provision of management services by the audit firm. The problems associated with auditor independence regarding these services will be discussed in Chapter 7.

The added-value of verification can also be evidenced in the situations observed throughout this and the previous chapter. For example, the second medical report not only provides basic information concerning the patient's health. It also informs its reader about the informational quality of the first report (albeit indirectly through comparison). The manuscript review contains comments on the manuscript which can be used by the author to improve its quality. The video recording provides observations of the play in the game hitherto unseen by the umpire. The doctoral programme review contains comments and suggestions with the potential to improve the programme's quality. And the surveyor's report gives additional information on the building's quality beyond that found by casual observation or in the estate agent's brochure.

An information perspective of auditing

The idea of added-value and auditing is related to a further common feature of verification and auditing activity, and this is the provision of additional information by way of report. Such reporting is intended to be the means of communicating assurance and comfort to those individuals and organizations in doubt about the particular subject-matter in question. For example, the surveyor's report is concerned specifically with the condition of the building. And, in the case of reported financial statements, the auditor's report contains an expert professional accounting opinion on the quality of the contents of the financial statements. This process is described by the 1973 concepts committee of the American Accounting Association as attestation (AAA, 1973, p.6):

> Attestation is a communicated statement of opinion (judgment), based upon convincing evidence, by an independent, competent, authoritative person, concerning the degree of correspondence in all material respects of the accounting information communicated by an entity . . . with established criteria.

In other words, what the audit report provides is an expert opinion on the quality of reported financial information, thereby providing additional information to the recipients of the verified statements. In the context of the specific function of corporate auditing, and its stated overall mission of accountability and control, the prescription of Flint (1988, p.116) is relevant:

> The responsibility of auditors is to convey to persons who do not have direct access to the relevant data and who do not have special knowledge of the peculiar technicality of auditing, the nature and extent of reassurance they can give about the information these persons already have, or to convey to them information which they wish to have with an

evaluation of it to enable them to take appropriate decisions and action on some aspects of accountability or on some failure to adhere to the standard of expectation.

It is also pertinent to note the recommendation of Mautz and Sharaf (1961, p.200) that auditors' reporting obligation to provide information goes further than the information contained in the audited financial statements. They also have a responsibility to present fairly their audit opinions on these statements – particularly with regard to preventing the users of the financial statements being misled over the extent of their examination or the nature of their opinions (p.201). Indeed, Shaw (1980, p.1) comments that the audit report is significant with respect to internal corporate control as well as to a wider societal control of corporate affairs. The messages communicated by the auditor act as a means of providing information about information with the capacity to impact both internal and external decisions. They act as an explicit informational quality control within society generally and its corporate sector particularly.

Human affairs, conflicts and auditing

The analyses and explanations of verification and auditing indicate consistently that these activities are concerned with stabilizing human relationships. Each such function comprises an explicit relationship between the subject of verification or audit (the auditee), the beneficiary of such activities, and the verifier or auditor. In the case of auditing financial statements, this relationship is between the corporate managers responsible for producing the financial statements, the individuals and organizations likely to benefit from them, and the appointed auditor. This human triangle of agency is formally recognized as the basic structure of the audit function by the 1973 committee of the American Accounting Association (AAA, 1973, pp.8–9), and by writers such as Schandl (1978, pp. 2–4) and Wolnizer (1987, pp.39–45). Indeed, Schandl defines auditing in strictly human terms (p.4):

> Auditing is a human evaluation process to establish the adherence to certain norms, resulting in an opinion (or judgment).

And Wolnizer (1987, p.45) describes the function as providing quality assurance to give customer confidence.

The reason for this human evaluation process consistently taking place is an underlying potential conflict of interest between the contractual participants in each of the triangles concerned. This general conclusion has been articulated by the auditing concepts committee of the American Accounting Association (AAA, 1973, p.10). It argues that, when the recipients of reported financial information perceive a conflict of interest between themselves and its producer, their concern is that the information is not biased in some way to their detriment. In these circumstances, the auditor (or any other expert verifier) is expected to attest the non-existence or otherwise of such informational bias. This argument is also articulated in some depth by Wolnizer (1987, pp.39–42).

Situations concerning a potential conflict of interest between the producer and consumer of information appear to be the consequence of two distinct but related factors which, when combined, create the anxiety which leads to the need for verification or audit. These factors are, respectively, the separations which exist between producer and consumer, and the economic consequences of such separations causing abuses by the producer to the detriment of the consumer.

The non-accounting situations used in this and the previous chapter suggest identifiable separations between the producer and the consumer of information. These separations occur at a physical and an intellectual level. From a physical perspective, the separation is the inability of an individual or organization to assess the quality of the information provided because of a physical remoteness from the underlying reality it is describing. An intellectual separation, on the other hand, is the consequence of the complexity of the subject-matter requiring a relevant mix of knowledge, expertise and skill which prevents the individual or organization verifying it. Different situations will contain different separations. Sometimes they will be physical, sometimes intellectual, and sometimes a combination of both. For example, the patient may be able to sense or perceive physically his medical condition but only in an inexpert way. He requires the skills of a qualified medical expert to attest the precise state of his health.

A similar situation exists with the audit of financial statements. The typical potential statement user, such as a shareholder in a company, neither is physically present in the reporting entity nor has the accounting expertise to assess the quality of the reported accounting numbers. This situation is explicitly recognized by the American Accounting Association auditing concepts committee (AAA, 1973, p.10) in terms, first, of the complexity of reported financial information making it difficult for its user to assess its quality; and, second, an acknowledgment of the physical, legal, institutional and financial separations which make the user of such information remote from its producer. These points are also commented on by Wolnizer (1987, pp.42–5) in terms of the incapacity of financial statement consumers to perform audits.

A further common feature of verification and auditing activities is that they all appear to be related to areas of doubt and uncertainty in human affairs which have economic consequences. In each of the situations examined, a potential economic loss seems to be a root cause for having verification or audit take place. This point of argument is raised by the 1973 American Accounting Association committee in relation to the identifiable causes for a demand for audit services (AAA, 1973, p.10) – that is, particularly, the creating of a need for verification as a result of a fear of economic loss due to doubts about the quality of a specified subject-matter. For example, publishing an unsaleable manuscript is costly to the publisher in terms of realized losses. And poor quality financial statements can lead to inappropriate investment or lending decisions and to consequential economic losses.

All of these common features underlying verification and audit situations are recognized by Wallace (1985, p.14) as related to each of the hypotheses for auditing which she specifies, and which are discussed earlier in the text. The ability of the audit function to assist in monitoring management and making explicit its duty of stewardship and accountability; enhancing the quality of reported financial information; and providing producers, users and auditors with insurance against claims of poor quality reporting, are suggested by her as roles for auditing stimulated by human relationships involving physical and intellectual separations with economic consequences. Such a conclusion is significant in the formulation of a normative statement of corporate audit objectives.

A statement of a corporate auditing objective

Having identified the main characteristics of situations involving verification of information provided by one person or organization to another (including auditing), it is appropriate to attempt to draw these thoughts together. This is done in the form of a normative prescription of corporate audit objectives. These are expressed in terms consistent with the basic features of verification and auditing previously identified, and with the qualitative characteristics of corporate financial reporting discussed earlier.

The general purpose of corporate auditing can be expressed as follows:

> **Within the context of a need for corporate governance and managerial accountability, to verify and report on the quality of published financial statements of companies for the benefit of individuals and organizations in some way remote from these entities but with reasonable rights of access to the information contained in the statements.**

'Remote but with reasonable rights of access' is interpreted in terms of three specific and connected factors. The first is the potential user of the published financial statements who is prevented either physically or intellectually from personally assessing the quality of their informational content (thus, the need for accountability). The second factor relates to an identifiable but potential conflict of interest between the managerial preparers of the reported financial statements and their potential users, which creates an informational need for the latter to clarify the conflict (the agency situation of potential moral hazard). And the third factor is whether the separation and conflict of interest factors are sufficient to cause potential users to be anxious about the economic consequences to them of relying on the financial statements when they may be of inadequate quality (indicating a cost–benefit relationship). In other words, individuals or organizations who are remote, affected by a conflict of interest, and could suffer economically as a result, have a reasonable right of access to information.

So far as the quality of reported financial statements is concerned, this has been explained in the text in terms of the primary financial reporting characteristics prescribed in recent times by accounting policy-makers. Specifically, these are the relevance of the reported information, in the sense of its capacity to influence or make a difference to the decisions of those individuals and organizations with reasonable rights of access to the information; and reliability, in the sense of the reported information's capacity to faithfully represent or correspond to the economic events and objects which are deemed to be decision relevant, and which the reported financial statements are intended to describe.

Summarizing therefore on the above, a more specific objective of corporate auditing can be stated:

> **Within the context of a need for corporate governance and managerial accountability, the primary concern of the corporate auditor is to attest the relevance and reliability of published financial statements on behalf of those individuals and organizations known to have reasonable rights of access to such information, and expected to rely on the existence of such qualities with respect to such statements when making use of them.**

The main inference to be drawn from this objective is that the corporate auditor is working on behalf of individuals reasonably relying on the quality of the financial statements, and that such quality is defined in two main parts. The first concerns whether or not user-appropriate financial messages are communicated in the financial statements, and the second with whether these messages are credibly produced. Both parts must be reasonably responded to by the corporate auditor if he or she is to satisfactorily meet the objective. Such an objective, as mentioned in previous chapters, is consistent with the objectives currently expected of external financial reporters. It also is a specific formalization of the over-riding regulatory but undefined mandate to report on either 'present fairly' (in the US) or 'a true and fair view' (in the UK). As previously mentioned, neither of these terms is specifically defined in regulations, but exist as the over-riding expressions of the quality of audited financial information. What is suggested in this text, however, is that information which has been found by the corporate auditor to be relevant and reliable should, in large part but not necessarily totally, satisfy the over-riding but undefined regulatory quality.

Informational quality criteria and corporate auditing

Determining whether or not corporate financial statements comply with specified quality standards implies that a mechanism exists which operationalizes these standards, and that the corporate auditor's task is to report on the consistency or compliance of the reporting with the stated operational criteria. This objective is recognized explicitly in specific auditing standards (for example, the US requirement for the auditor to report on compliance with generally accepted accounting principles: AICPA, 1991, p.7; and the UK standard requiring the auditor to be satisfied on the appropriateness, consistency and disclosure of accounting policies: APC, 1989, para.8). This suggests that an important element of the corporate auditor's task is to determine what is meant by criteria such as generally accepted accounting principles, and appropriate accounting policies. The auditor is assisted in this respect by professional guidance in the form of specific audit standards defining or interpreting such terms (as in AICPA, 1992, para.2 in the US; and, less specifically, APC, 1989, para.8). The problems associated with such guidance, however, and their impact on the overall corporate audit objective of attesting financial reporting quality, will be discussed more fully in Chapter 9.

Silent audit objectives

The above sections establish the main purpose of the corporate audit as determining the quality of reported financial statements in terms of specified criteria. Given that both the content, and the quality of the content, of such statements is dependent on the integrity of the accounting record-keeping system as a source of data for reporting purposes, the existence of strong internal controls to maintain such integrity, and the adequacy of disclosure of reported data, it would be wrong to ignore these matters in relation to corporate audit objectives. In most circumstances, these matters form the basis of silent objectives of corporate auditing. For example, in the US, the need to determine the adequacy of the underlying accounting records is mentioned indirectly in relation to the nature of evidential material (AICPA, 1991, p.123). In the UK, it is explicitly stated as a major but unreported objective of corporate auditing (Companies Act, 1985, s.237(1)). Internal control evaluation, on the other hand, is stipulated in both the US and the UK as a potentially major audit focus in relation to attesting financial statement quality (AICPA, 1991, p.7; and APC, 1980f, para.2). And the adequacy of disclosure is prescribed as a usually unreported corporate audit task in both the US (AICPA, 1991, p.245) and the UK (APC, 1980g, para.10). These matters will be discussed in further detail in Chapters 9 and 10. Meantime, the above brief remarks remind the reader that the objectives of a complex function such as corporate auditing are not always stated explicitly or directly.

Note

1. Such economic reality should not be interpreted solely in terms of physically-verifiable matters. It also includes economically-based phenomena which constitute a socially-constructed reality – that is, they do not exist in tangible form but have an 'existence' by means of a societal acceptance and assenting to their presence. These social realities include periodic income and temporal capital. A full discussion of this problem is found in Thornton (1988) and Mattessich (1991).

Further reading

T.A. Lee (1970) The nature of auditing and its objectives, *Accountancy*, April, pp.292–6 (an early attempt to research the perceived objectives of auditing).

G.W. Beck (1973) The role of the auditor in modern society: an empirical appraisal, *Accounting and Business Research*, Spring, pp.117–22 (a later study of audit expectations).

C. Humphrey, P. Moizer and S. Turley (1992) *The Audit Expectations Gap in the United Kingdom*, Institute of Chartered Accountants in England and Wales (a recent study to reveal the variety of expectations for the auditor and his function).

T.F. Ruud (1989) *Auditing as Verification of Financial Information*, Norwegian University Press, pp.141–55 (an argument for the decision utility approach to auditing, emphasizing the need to verify accounting's correspondence with economic reality).

P.W. Wolnizer (1987) *Auditing as Independent Authentication*, Sydney University Press, pp.1–46 (an argument for auditing's role as an assurance of the quality of accounting information in terms of its fitness for use).

Discussion and essay topics

1. Discuss the relationship of real-world phenomena to corporate auditing.
2. What empirical phenomena do corporate auditors typically observe in the audit process, and what matters do they verify which are difficult to test empirically?

3. The corporate audit has been described as a quality assurance function. Discuss.
4. How does the corporate audit add value to externally reported financial information?
5. Human conflict appears to be at the centre of all auditing activity. Discuss this perception in relation to the objectives of corporate auditing.
6. Read the corporate audit objectives stated in this chapter, and prepare a critique of them in comparison to those specified by other writers such as Mautz and Sharaf, Flint, and Wolnizer.

5

Towards a history of corporate auditing

The aim of this chapter is to explain and discuss the threads of consistency and points of change in the history of the corporate audit function. This is done within the context of a brief review of the nature, purpose and limitations of historical studies.

The nature of history

History is a formal study of time, and a generally accepted construct by which humans administer and discipline their lives. By distinguishing between past, present and future moments and events, humans organize and manage their existence and regulate their relationships. History is concerned with past moments and events affecting these relationships. It is the study of the temporal development of human phenomena.

More specifically, history attempts to map the inheritance of thought and transfer of skills from one generation to the next (Carr, 1987, p.114). It is therefore primarily intended to observe the minds behind the actions of the past (Collingwood, 1974, p.25). For example, in order to obtain a meaningful insight to corporate auditing at the time of its formal inception in the mid 1800s, the accounting historian should explore the function from the perspective of an auditor of these times rather than from the position of a public accountant of the 1990s. To impose contemporary thinking and standards on past practices is historically invalid, and likely to result in erroneous historical interpretations.

The historical study of the temporal transfer of thought processes is genealogical in nature – that is, it presumes a natural and evolutionary flow of ideas from generation to generation (Toynbee, 1972, p.477). It is to be contrasted with the archaeological approach to history which investigates the layering and accumulation of thought processes over time (Miller and O'Leary, 1987, p.237). The latter primarily concentrates on the stock-piling of customs and habits, and the consequent creating of tradition and precedent. For example, in the context of accounting history, several writers argue that contemporary accounting thought and practice is not just a product of its context; it is also the result of a long-term layering of ideas and practices (Sterling, 1977, p.2; Chambers, 1989, p.20; and Previts, Parker and Coffman, 1990, p.5).

Continuity of thought and action indicates that history can be described as an unending dialogue between past and present (Carr, 1987 p.30). As such, it is principally concerned with facts – that is, with actual events, actions and thoughts. But facts for historical study are not self-evident observations. They are suspended in time, waiting to be found by the historian. And discovering history does not and cannot reveal the complete truth about the past. History is partial in all cases. Historians search for the facts of history and, in doing so, identify what they regard as relevant facts, and reject what they perceive as irrelevant facts (Carr, 1987, p.15). In effect, they judgmentally and subjectively construct history according to their personal selections and interpretations of what they find (p.22).

For this reason, it is not surprising to find historians talking about history in terms of probabilities (Marwick, 1981, p.21; and Carr, 1987, p.68); and, indeed, in terms of prophecies rather than predictions (Popper, 1986, p.43) In other words, as Previts, Parker and Coffman (1990, p.9) comment in relation to the nature of accounting history, it deals with an identification and explanation of probable facts relating to a historical event rather than with a statement of its causes.

The purpose of history

Marwick (1981) is explicit but ambiguous with respect to the *raison d'être* of history. He states it as a response to a need (p.16) and as a social necessity (p.14). Carr (1987, p.55), on the other hand, is more informative when describing history as a means of providing knowledge and reason in human affairs. Popper (1986, p.20) suggests the need for intuitive understanding of social phenomena. And Marwick (1981, p.21) and Carr (1987, p.134) both write of history assisting in coping with the present.

Other writers assert alternative views. Toynbee (1972, p.477) prescribes a role for history in the discovery and classification of facts and relationships in order to make reality comprehensible. Lloyd (1986, p.8), on the other hand, expects history to explain trends and themes, and provide causal explanations through verification. He is looking to history to reveal changes in the layers of time (p.20), a thought similar to that of Hopwood and Johnston (1986, p.39), who appeal to history as a means of uncovering the mechanisms of change in accounting, and Hopwood (1987, p.230) who describes the accounting researcher of history as an archaeologist. Alternatively, Previts, Parker and Coffman (1990, p.3) assert history's purpose in terms of its ability to deal with a continuum in thought between the 'was', the 'is', and the 'ought' of time – that is, the past leading to the present leading to the future.

In other words, the objective of history is formulated in terms of prescriptions of a need for knowledge, understanding and explanation of the past generally, and past changes particularly – partly because of a natural curiosity and partly because of present problems. In the context of accounting and, specifically, corporate auditing, however, it is available as an educational support regarding the adequacy of explanations of change (Previts, Parker and Coffman, 1990, p.4); policy-making in terms of identifying the effects of policy decisions (p.5); and practice in terms of observing the suitability of practices in specific circumstances (p.7).

A history of auditing

Very little has been written on a general history of auditing. For example, contributions exist from writers as temporally apart as Brown (1905, pp.74–92) and Lee (1988, pp.xi-xxviii). The primary emphasis has been on individual aspects of auditing – that is, changing audit objectives (Brown, 1962); audits as part of corporate regulation (Hein, 1963); auditor independence (Youkins, 1983); auditor responsibilities (Davies, 1979); the auditable quality of reported financial information (Chastney, 1975, pp.4–13); the auditor and uncertainty in financial reporting (Brief, 1975); and the auditor and the emergence of a self-regulating accountancy profession (Kedslie, 1990, pp.135–71).

The purpose of the remainder of this chapter is to redress this imbalance by examining the main features of the development of corporate auditing. The predominant approach adopted is one of providing a historical study of auditing rather than a history of the function. It focuses primarily on the significant historical points of relevance to a study of the theory underlying the practice of corporate auditing. The study observes both continuity and change with respect to the corporate audit and auditor. It reveals the function as a technical and skilled mechanism which assists in enabling organizational functioning to take place, but which is also part of the shaping of organizations and society (Hopwood, 1987, pp.208–9).

A brief chronology of auditing

In order to provide a context for comments about the historical significance of corporate auditing, a brief chronological description of its historical development is given, and divided into two main periods. The first relates to pre-incorporation history – that is, from the earliest times to the mid-nineteenth century. The second specifically deals with the modern audit of corporate organizations.

Pre-incorporation audits

Auditing has been a regular feature of organized human activity from the earliest times. It has also been consistently associated with economic activity and accountability. Indeed, evidence suggests that formal audit procedures existed in the economic activities of most of the early civilizations (Brown, 1962; and Stone, 1969). Sometimes the function was undertaken by individuals whose designated single task was auditor. On other occasions, the auditors were property owners who wished to verify the activities of their managers and employees.

The context for auditing in these early times also varied (Brown, 1905, pp.74–92). Considerable audit activity existed in several early civilizations at the level of the individual property owner. These were mainly domestic audits in which it is difficult to identify a definable business entity and separate it from purely personal transactions and property. They served a stewardship function – the steward being held accountable to the property owner by means of the process of audit. The subject-matter for audit was usually some physical aspect of economic reality, such as personal possessions or commercial property, or specific trading or domestic transactions (Hain, 1966, p.701). Accounting records, where these existed, appear also to have been used as part of the process of audit – that is, as a source of verification of past events or contemporary positions.

Early auditing also existed in formally constituted organizations. These mainly related to government activity generally, and the collection of taxation revenues particularly (Brown, 1905, pp.74–92). The auditor was usually an expert individual designated to fulfil a verification function. The subject-matter of auditing typically involved accounting records and systems which demanded an expertise sufficient to successfully complete the verification task.

Whatever the audit situation, however, auditing throughout most of its long history to recent times has had a consistent objective to protect the owner of economic resources from fraud and error associated with the stewardship of these resources (Brown, 1962, p.699). Such a function was usually directed at detecting fraud or error by a steward acting as an agent for his or her principal, the property owner. It also served the complementary task of attempting to prevent the existence of these activities. This general conclusion appears to be applicable whether the transactions and resources in question were those of a governmental organization or an individual property owner.

Corporate audits

The evolution of the corporate organization to handle business activity in the early nineteenth century had the significant effect of separating ownership from management, and accentuating the historically well-established stewardship function. The need to account to the shareholder–owners of companies by means of published financial statements, and the corresponding need to verify the quality of the content of these statements, was also recognized at this time (Brown, 1962, p.698). Such a situation is a more complex example of the earlier principal–agent relationship identified in organized economic activity.

The aim of the corporate audit, however, continued to reflect the fraud theme (see, for example, Robertson, 1897, p.632; Staub, 1904, p.91; and Jenkinson, 1913–14, pp.113–17). The subject-matter of auditing was accounting records and the financial statements derived from these records. The principal reason for checking the accuracy of record-keeping was to determine whether or not the financial statements prepared from accounting records were affected by fraud or error (Brown, 1962, pp.698–701). Indeed, these audits have been described by accounting historians as bookkeeping audits (Moyer, 1951, p.4; and Littleton and Zimmerman, 1962, p.107); and, more specifically, as a function of tracing accounting voucher to accounting entry (Kitchen, 1982, pp.26–7). This type of audit necessitated the employment of auditors with an accounting expertise sufficient to cope with the increasing technical complexity of accounting record-keeping, and many of the earliest corporate auditors were bookkeepers by occupation (Boockholdt, 1983, p.73).

Over relatively recent years to the present time, however, the work of the corporate auditor has been increasingly focused on the routines and techniques associated with the production of financial statements (Brown, 1962, p.702; Kitchen, 1982, pp.31–40; and Lee, 1986, pp.21–31). In particular, the declared aim of the corporate auditor over several decades has been the verification of the compliance of financial statements with specified and generally accepted accounting rules of computation and related disclosure provisions (see, for example, Montgomery, 1912, pp.9 and 18; Waterhouse, 1934, p.121; Stewart, 1957, pp.213–14; Bevis, 1962, p.28; Bird, 1970, p.44; and Lee, 1986, p.18).

This change in audit emphasis coincided with the emergence of a self-regulating accountancy profession whose members were educated and trained sufficiently to take responsibility for the corporate audit (see Stewart, 1977; Walker, 1988; and Kedslie, 1990). In particular, professionalization saw the new accounting professionals move gradually from the audit of accounts of bankrupt estates to the verification of records and statements of live corporate entities such as railway and insurance companies (Mautz and Sharaf, 1961, p.242; and Kedslie, 1990, pp.135–71). Indeed, Kedslie (1990, p.134) comments that this switch in occupational emphasis in the UK resulted from an economic self-interest when the field of bankruptcy audit became too competitive. Competitive pressures also drove UK professional accountants to seek audit work in the US, thus transporting audit expertise and skills, and related customs and habits, from one country to another (Moyer, 1951, p.3; Brown, 1962, p.699; Littleton and Zimmerman, 1962, p.123; and Kedslie, 1990, pp.171–5).

The drive by professional accountancy bodies and their members to achieve a monopoly or near-monopoly position in corporate auditing was maintained over many decades, and was achieved eventually in both the UK and the US by the middle of the twentieth century (Hein, 1978, p.157; and Langenderfer, 1987, p.306). It required the establishment of formal education and training programmes capable of providing the expertise necessary to successfully complete the designated audit (see Langenderfer, 1987; and Kedslie, 1990, pp.179–217).

Thus, the contemporary corporate auditor emerged as a competent professional with sufficient accounting expertise to complete the designated audit task. Such a task evolved from checking and reporting on the accuracy of accounting messages about the economic effects of corporate management (as expressed and represented in accounting books and records), to verifying and reporting on the acceptability of accounting calculations and disclosures, and the latter's compliance with stated rules and regulations. In other words, the audit of modern times is largely concerned with establishing the legal propriety of reported accounting data rather than their economic substance (Zeff, 1987, p.67; Gerboth, 1987, p.97; McMonnies, 1988, p.20; and Tweedie and Whittington, 1990, p.97). The auditor therefore appears not to be concerned primarily in recent practice with whether such compliance results in a relevant and reliable reporting of the economic reality underlying accounting figures but, instead, with whether prescribed rules of accounting calculation have been applied correctly. This will be an issue returned to later in the section, and throughout the remainder of the text.

The historical dominance of the detection or prevention of fraud and error as the primary audit focus has diminished in practice in recent times to the point at which the accountancy profession explicitly limits the auditor's role and related responsibility for fraud and error to the context of providing assurance about the accounting quality of published financial statements. For example, as Tweedie (1991, p.28) comments:

> The profession, not surprisingly, agrees with the government that the primary responsibility for the prevention and detection of fraud, other irregularities and errors rests with management: in addition to its business responsibilities, management has the fiduciary roles of safeguarding assets and preparing accounts which show a true and fair view.

Thus, the current institutional perception of corporate auditors' task in practice is that their goal is to report on the rule-based accounting quality of financial statements, and that their work is directed at managing the audit in such a way that fraud and error which materially affects financial statement quality should be detected and reported (AICPA, 1991, p.56; and APC, 1990, para.9).

The above portrayal of the corporate audit function within its historical setting also needs to be examined in the context of a very recent financial reporting change which has been introduced earlier in this text. More specifically, the prescription by standard-setters (FASB, 1980, paras.46, 47, 59 and 63; and ASB, 1991b, paras. 23 and 26) of financial reports which are decision-useful (because they satisfy both relevance and reliability criteria) has serious implications for the contemporary corporate auditor – even within the context of over-riding and undefined accountability reporting qualities such as 'present fairly' and 'a true and fair view.' In particular, the focus of the auditor's attention should be directed away from purely accounting calculations for compliance purposes. Instead, and as stated previously, he or she needs to verify that, first, the published accounting data describe economic phenomena which could make a difference to the decisions of their potential users, and, second, that these data are faithfully representations of such phenomena. Such a focus brings the corporate auditor back to the long-standing historical role of judging observable aspects of the real world – that is, verifiable economic phenomena in the real world which are relevant to decision-based behaviour, and which can be reliably reported for that purpose.

Identifying change in audit history

The previous sections attempt to outline briefly a chronology of the development of auditing activity. They provide a general review of a continuum which reveals that the audit and the auditor have fulfilled a role in society over many years to provide protection to its members from the effects of unacceptable behaviour, and to counter a seemingly intuitive distrust of humans for one another in situations o agency.

However, to understand contemporary corporate auditing better, and to be able to observe and comment on its current issues, it is necessary to explore audit history further, to identify the mixture of continuity and change which appears to constitute its past existence. This is done in the first instance by reviewing layers of history for evidence of significant changes in corporate audit thinking and practice. Then, by identifying matters which have been consistently present throughout the long history of auditing, the stabilizing features in its structure are identified.

The changing nature of corporate audits

One of the most obvious changes to be found in the history of corporate auditing is the distinctive switch in emphasis in relatively recent times with respect to the nature of the audit task – from an activity directed at fraud and error detection or prevention as it relates to the accuracy of the accounting record-keeping, to one which attests the overall accounting compliance of published financial statements. Curiously, this change has occurred within the context of a consistent regulatory prescription of an undefined nature – for example, from 'true and correct' (in both the US and the UK) to 'present fairly' (in the US) and 'a true and fair view' (in the UK) (Lee, 1992b, pp.4–12). This suggests that the legal and, thus, accounting interpretation of these reporting quality over-rides can vary over time according to context and situation, and that the corporate auditor has to cope with this combination of surface stability and below-surface instability.

Functional transformation in corporate auditing over time is also the source of one of the most substantial and long-standing issues affecting it – that is, the conflict between what the auditor does and what the public presumes the auditor to do. This is part of what has come to be known as the so-called 'expectations gap' in auditing, and which is defined as follows (Humphrey, 1991, p.7):

> . . . a representation of a feeling that auditors are performing in a manner at variance with the beliefs and desires of those for whose benefit the audit is being carried out.

Early business audits inherited a long-held convention established by custom and habit that the auditor's role was to assist in the stewardship function with respect to a proper recording and accounting by an agent for the holding and use of the principal's resources and related obligations. The specific audit focus was fraud and error detection. This role appears to have been initially accepted by business auditors as part of the price of a professionalization (Sikka *et al.*, 1992, p.15). This function was gradually translated into the corporate context in the nineteenth and twentieth centuries. However, in doing so, a point seems to have been reached when corporate auditors replaced fraud and error detection or prevention with accounting and disclosure compliance as the major audit aim (Sikka *et al.*, 1992, p.16). The reasons for this change can only be speculated as a mixture of organizational change, economics, and professional self-interest – that is, respectively, management control systems improving and reducing the incidence of fraud and error; the cost of fraud and error detection exceeding the economic benefits to be derived from such monitoring; and the pressures on the corporate auditor induced by potential litigation for fraud and error failures (Humphrey, 1991, p.11).

Whatever the reason, a major change in emphasis occurred by the early 1960s (Brown, 1962, pp.701–2). But the long-standing public perception remained of the corporate audit as a 'common-sense' one of fraud and error detection (Sikka *et al.*, 1992, p.17) – thus perpetuating a persistent expectations gap (Humphrey, Moizer and Turley, 1992b, p.145). In other words, the corporate audit can be viewed historically as switching its primary operational attention away from human beings and their behaviour (as expressed in formal accounting recordings of economic events), to the records themselves and, most recently, to the written financial statements derived from these records – that is, from the observable reality of the individual human being and his or her accountable actions in stewardship, to a quantitative data base of these actions, and, finally, to summary reports of certain aspects of the content of that data base. But, also historically, the public perception of the corporate auditor's role has remained consistently focused on the human behaviour expressed in accounting terms.

The consequences of this historical process are twofold. First, the corporate audit functions as a service more concerned with the legal form of the accounting record than with the economic substance of the underlying business activity and related human behaviour. Second, the corporate audit profession increasingly has to cope with public expectations of an audit service different from that delivered in practice. In particular, the profession consistently attempts to control the debate on the audit expectations gap (Humphrey, Moizer and Turley, 1992b, p.157) – for example, by changing the focus away from audit failure to alternative services (p.153); and by arguing a need to re-educate audit beneficiaries to the 'true' purpose of the audit (Sikka *et al.*, 1992, p.8).

However, as previously mentioned in this chapter, the recent introduction by accounting policy-makers of financial reporting criteria such as decision relevance and informational reliability creates the need for the corporate audit emphasis to be further changed. In particular, the guiding conceptual framework for corporate financial reporting switches the audit emphasis from largely abstract accounting matters in auditing to topics more directly related to testable realities such as financial report users and their decisions, and observable economic activities. The extent of such a change in practice is indeterminate, despite the existence of the stated reporting criteria. It certainly has yet to be properly debated, and is discussed further in this text in Chapter 9.

The above paragraphs indicate a continuing instability in the corporate audit. Yet there remains a strong thread of continuity running through this picture of change. For example, the corporate audit has persistently existed as a societal response to human distrust in situations of economic agency. In other words, in the most general sense of the term, the corporate audit remains as a function to encourage and test for fidelity in the conduct of corporate affairs involving agents (Littleton and Zimmerman, 1962, pp.104–6). And, as for many decades previously, it continues to be concerned with the quality of the reporting of financial accounting representations (Brown, 1962, p.703). In other words, the broad purpose of corporate auditing does not appear to have changed throughout its history. What has altered are the ways and means by which that purpose is achieved and interpreted – different generations of corporate auditors have sought the same general purpose, but differing environments and interests have caused its operationalization to vary.

The audit environment and audit history

A further area of apparent change in the history of the corporate audit function concerns its economic and organizational environment or context. This is a point which is mentioned by most writers on the history of the audit function generally and its theory particularly (for example, Mautz and Sharaf, 1961, p.242; Brown, 1962, p.698; Littleton and Zimmerman, 1962, p.112; Burton and Fairfield, 1982, p.15; Kitchen, 1982, p.25; and Boockholdt, 1983, p.70). Matters such as industrialization and related technologies, capital and other markets, and improved management and controls are believed to have shaped the audit function into its present form.

Equally, however, it has to be argued that the corporate audit function has influenced the shape of its environment at specific points of time. The reason for this is that the audit not only enables organizational activity to take place; at least in part it also determines such activity (adapting Hopwood, 1987, p.211). For example, an economic argument can be made that the existence of the corporate audit has improved the quality of reported financial statements, rendered them more credible for use, consequently increased their use and the quality of decisions, and thereby improved the efficiency of the markets in which they are used (Gwilliam, 1987, pp.53–4). Auditing history appears to provide some support for this notion – the corporate audit has evolved in recent times from a function originally intended to serve the internal needs of management (Littleton and Zimmerman, 1962, p.112); to one which attempted to meet individual needs in the market place such as investors in the financing of railways (Boockholdt, 1983, p.79) and bankers in the provision of finance (Littleton and Zimmerman, 1962, p.112); to one which attempts to respond to a wide range of societal needs and expectations (Flint, 1971, p.293).

But, despite this apparent turbulence, a strong continuity is present. The corporate audit can consistently be seen as a response to an agency need. Whatever the situation, the auditor exists to bridge a gap between a principal (for example, the shareholders of a company) and an agent (the directors and managers). The auditor attempts to reduce uncertainties created by these gaps by verifying and reporting on management's financial accounting representations to shareholders. The corporate audit thus appears tightly focused on these uncertainties over time and in different economic situations. For example, in the context of the arguments made in this text about the contemporary audit, the corporate auditor appears to have emerging responsibilities to cope with the uncertainties inherent in producing financial statements by verifying the degree to which the reported accounting data, first, are capable of making a difference to specific decisions (relevance); and, second, correspond with the economic phenomena they purport to describe (reliability).

The corporate auditor and audit history

The evolution of corporate auditors as expert verifiers and reporters also appears to have followed a changing sequence. In relatively recent historical times they can be identified as shareholders – amateurs with little or no accounting expertise, often working in the context of a committee of shareholders and, in some cases, sub-contracting the actual audit work to specialist bookkeepers (Brown, 1962, p.698; and Bookholdt, 1983, pp.72–4). Gradually over several decades, however, corporate auditors have evolved to the point at which they are skilled professionals with a suitable educational and training background, and subject to the discipline of being members of a recognized professional accountancy body (Langenderfer, 1987).

This process of change in skills has also provided a consistency over several recent decades. The corporate auditor is now expected in most situations to have a substantial professional competence in a variety of related areas which impinge on the conduct of the audit. Flint (1988, p.50) outlines this change, *inter alia*, in terms of the increasing number of subjects in which the corporate auditor has to be competent – for example, accounting, statistics, computing, economics, law, management, and public policy. This is very different from the earlier expectation of a predominance in bookkeeping skills (Drummond, 1891–3; and Staub, 1904).

Accompanying the above change in the auditor as a skilled expert, and particularly relating to the emergence and establishment of a self-regulating accountancy profession, is the trend towards legitimizing the corporate audit task by means of institutional regulations which require the auditor to be a skilled and independent professional. Such a trend can be evidenced in legislative developments commencing in the mid-nineteenth century, and stabilizing with a universal provision for an independent audit and qualified auditor in the mid-twentieth century (Hein, 1978). It can also be seen in the introduction of regulatory requirements for independent audits in the first half of the twentieth century (Moyer, 1951). In this respect, corporate auditors appear historically to have acted consistently with the general aim of balancing economic and social self-interest with a stated desire to serve the public interest (Willmott, 1990, p.327; see also Hooks, 1992). Whether they have succeeded is a matter for debate and challenge (Sikka, Willmott and Lowe, 1989).

The history of auditing over the last one hundred and fifty years also highlights the changing importance of the concept and practice of auditor independence. This stipulates that the corporate auditor is physically and mentally in a position to properly exercise the role of a professional person acting in the public interest – that is, without the presence of pressures created by conflicting relationships (Lee, 1986, p.88). The historical evidence with respect to auditor independence is of gradual change – that is, from a position in which the concept in either its physical or mental mode was not deemed of relevance because the auditors were either individual or committee–shareholders (Hein, 1978, p.508; and Boockholdt, 1983, p.76); to one in which the appearance of independence is fundamental, and is demonstrated by means of specific provisions or regulations banning relationships with client companies which could jeopardize it (Lee, 1968; and Youkins, 1983). However, as Wolnizer (1987, p.121) argues, the consistency within this change has been the persistence in thinking by accountants that, ultimately, independence is a matter of the auditor's mental approach to auditing. And, as mental attitudes are hard to demonstrate tangibly, accountants have sought to convince the public over the years that they are not in positions which would pressure their independent state of mind (as in Flint, 1988, pp.61–2).

The historical quest by professional accountants for explicit public recognition of corporate auditor independence has created a recurrent problem for the audit profession. This relates to the expectation that the corporate auditor is independent, and the accompanying need to maintain public confidence that this is indeed the case in practice (Humphrey, 1991, p.14; and Moizer, 1991, pp.34 and 41). The conventional solution of the accountancy profession to this issue has been to pursue means of improving the appearance of auditor independence by prohibiting specific client–auditor relationships (Wolnizer, 1987, pp.129–46). The issue, however, persists and continues to give public concern (Wolnizer, 1987, p.160; Briloff, 1990, p.10; and Humphrey, 1991, pp.15–16). Indeed, due to the current rash of corporate failures, it has created a publicly-expressed crisis of confidence regarding the credibility of the accounting profession (Mitchell *et al.*, 1991).

The duty of care in auditing and audit history

The history of the corporate audit is as much as anything else a study of the evolution of an explicit duty of care by a professional expert. As indicated earlier in this chapter, this point was apparently less important in the early corporate audits which were undertaken by shareholders. However, with the emergence of a self-regulating accountancy profession with members acting as corporate auditors, and with the accompanying requirement by regulators to have corporate audits undertaken only by such persons, the concept of auditor responsibility has evolved, and has remained to the forefront of audit thinking.

The historical continuity in this respect over the last one hundred years or so has been to determine both the nature and the extent of this professional duty of care in the context of the corporate audit (Davies, 1979). This has been done predominantly with respect to specific court cases and responses by professional accountancy bodies to these decisions. For example, in the area of determining auditor responsibilities for fraud and error, a number of court cases over the last part of the nineteenth century and first part of the twentieth century established a basic principle that corporate auditors had a duty of care only in circumstances where it could be determined that they ought to have had their suspicions aroused, and that they failed to follow through on them in their audit actions (Lee, 1986, pp.115–17). In response to these legal decisions, the accountancy profession has consistently denied a blanket responsibility for fraud and error detection or prevention as the primary audit focus, but accepted a need to report when the auditor's suspicions are aroused (Tweedie, 1991, p.32; see also Godsell, 1991, p.113).

With respect to the issue of to whom the auditor owes a duty of care, the historical position is far from clear. As previously stated, the history of the issue reveals that the corporate audit was originally conceived in terms of an agency relationship between management and shareholders, with the auditor responsible for reporting to the latter on the (stewardship) quality of the accounting representations of the former (Davies, 1979, pp.95–9). However, gradually over several decades, the courts have attempted to erode this relatively narrow position and, alternatively, substitute a more societal duty of care in terms of third-party liability (Davies, 1979, p.102) – that is, compatible with a broader social accountability (see Godsell, 1991, pp.15–36).

The present position, however, is of a swing back towards a less open-ended duty of care (Gwilliam, 1991, p.72; and Godsell, 1991, pp.41–2). This appears again to raise a serious corporate audit issue in terms of public expectations of the auditor. Audited corporate financial statements are effectively a public good and can be used by a variety of different individuals. Poor quality auditing impacts the latter in different ways, but with the consistent effect that they are damaged. The expectation in these circumstances may be that the corporate auditor does have a duty of care which embraces all these different interests. History says that this is a real possibility. It also says that auditors will intuitively tend to deny it (Humphrey, Moizer and Turley, 1992b, p.145). The current situation involving substantial corporate failures and frauds is a case in point. There is considerable *prima facie* evidence (much of it admittedly as yet uncontested in the courts) of auditor dependence, failure to detect fraud, and improper audit reporting (see, for example, Briloff, 1990; and Mitchell *et al.*, 1991). There is as yet little sign of any significant professional response.

The denials of auditors in audit history

If there is one consistency running through the history of auditing it is the state of tension with which corporate auditors have had to cope. In effect, the corporate audit profession has been under siege for more than a hundred years. The major battle-ground has been the right to self-regulate as a profession – that is, as professionals, corporate auditors have entered into an implicit covenant with society to protect the public interest from unacceptable behaviour by corporate management in its stewardship reports. In return for a monopoly of service provided by corporate regulation, and the high financial rewards and social status which go with the latter, the auditor has accepted certain specific responsibilities – for example, to act independently and with due care.

In other words, historically, the corporate auditor as a professional has the persistent occupational challenge of coping with the conflicts associated with the occupational balancing of power, authority and responsibility (Montagna, 1974). But, in attempting to face these responsibilities, corporate auditors have also consistently tended to deny rather than accept public expectations of their role (see Humphrey, Moizer and Turley, 1992b; and Sikka *et al.*, 1992). This resistance to change is, in itself, not surprising, but it does lead in the longer term to problems – for example, the slowness to respond to the excesses of manipulatory accounting practices, thus creating the public impression of a profession lacking leadership (Kitchen, 1982, p.41); and the failure to specify rules regarding auditor independence, thus prompting governmental regulation on the matter (Youkins, 1983, p.22).

None of these aspects of the history of auditing has enhanced the reputation or credibility of corporate auditors or their profession. Indeed, the evidence suggests that the profession has had to be pushed into sudden change by the enormity of specific scandals – as with the problem of manipulatory accounting and secret reserves in the 1930s (Littleton and Zimmerman, 1962, pp.119–21; see also Byington and Sutton, 1991). This indicates a conservative profession living with a constant fear of state intervention in its affairs despite the difficulties of such interference because of the complex and technical nature of the accounting subject-matter of auditing.

For example, as Brief (1975) reveals, the basic accounting task for financial reporting purposes, and thus for auditing, is dealing with uncertainty about the future. Accounting data reported in conventional financial statements are dependent on assessments of the reporting company's future. No matter how many accounting rules and regulations are provided in the form of accounting standards, the essential reporting and auditing task is applying professional judgment on aspects of the future as these relate to the standards. Such judgments cannot be regulated and institutionalized. But, historically, in dealing with them in practice, the reporting accountant and the corporate auditor have had to interpret and report on the quality of corporate financial statements in terms of relatively vague, ambiguous and undefined terms.

For example, in the US the term 'present fairly in accordance with generally accepted accounting principles' appeared for the first time in the early 1930s (Flesher and Flesher, 1984, p.62). But since then, there has been no consensus as to its specific meaning (Chatfield, 1974, pp.298–9). Accounting principles have been interpreted in the US in terms of those procedures with substantial authoritative support as explicit accounting standards (Zeff, 1972, p.266), and there are guidelines available which attempt to assist auditors to interpret the term 'present fairly' (AICPA, 1992). But questions have been raised consistently in the past as to what constitutes general acceptance (Spacek, 1958a, p.116; Tietjen, 1963, p.65; Parker, 1964, p.272; and Garner, 1966, pp.101–4).

Interestingly, despite the lack of resolution of meaning, there appears to be some evidence suggesting that reporting accountants and users are content with the term 'generally accepted accounting principles' (McEnroe, 1991, p.160). History therefore seems to be suggesting that those individuals involved with corporate financial statements have become accustomed to using vague and difficult-to-define terminology despite its vagueness and lack of definition. This supports the recent view of Hines (1989b, p.85) that the audit profession, in order to combat government intervention and maintain a monopoly over the provision of services such as auditing, does so on the basis of an appearance or image of accounting knowledge. That is, by using these undefined terms, it lays claim to the possession of a coherent body of knowledge of accounting and auditing (see also Lee, 1992b).

This conclusion is more clearly seen in the context of the history of the UK approach to the quality of corporate financial statements. As Chastney (1975, pp.4–13) demonstrates, since the nineteenth century this approach has consistently used legally determined but undefined labels such as 'full and fair', 'true and correct', and 'true and fair'. Views on the meaning of such reporting labels vary. Chastney (1975, p.36) suggests that legislators invite a technical accounting meaning (presumably along the US lines of generally accepted accounting practice), and demonstrates (pp.38–49) that this is how accountants typically react to the problem.

The technical interpretation of reporting quality labels is an approach which has had the support of writers such as Ryan (1967, p.104) and Chambers and Wolnizer (1991, p.211). Other writers argue for specific definitions and interpretations to assist producers, auditors and users of corporate financial statements to more fully comprehend their nature and content (Chastney, 1975, p.4; and Lee, 1982). An alternative view is that phrases such as 'true and fair' are expressions of honesty, matters of ethics and morality, and therefore reflections of accountability which vary over time and are not susceptible to definition (Flint, 1971, pp.289, 291 and 293; Flint, 1982, p.30; and Flint, 1988, p.34). Indeed, a general philosophy speculated for the lack of definition is that such vagueness is a reporting strength as it allows the quality of financial information to vary over time according to societal expectations about it (Flint, 1982).

It is also consistent with the conclusions of legal philosophers concerned with the historical use of specific legal terminology as a major basis for operationalizing the law. Goodrich (1987) analyses this problem in depth. In particular, he concludes from a historical analysis that legal discourse is self-referential and impenetrable (p.55), and an instrument of social control (p.72) organized to exercise power (p.78). He further argues that each legal term is generic and offers its authorized user the greatest possible scope and power to determine its meaning (p.179). In other words, by closing off legal discourse to lawyers with an infinite number of interpretations possible depending on the circumstances, the legal profession puts itself in a position of power and authority to exercise judgment as to what is right or wrong. Given that the accounting quality labels used by auditors throughout the history of the corporate audit have a legal source and status as part of corporate governance and managerial accountability, it is relevant to interpret their audit use in the same context as legal discourse generally. They are means by which corporate auditors have historically maintained an unassailable monopoly position in which to exercise their professional judgment (Lee, 1992b).

Thus, a strong feature of the history of corporate auditing is its persistent lack of clarity in the meaning given to the explicit labels of financial reporting quality. As suggested above, this can be interpreted in terms of flexibility over time in order to accommodate changing views about such quality. Or it can be observed as a powerful profession unwilling to state explicitly its standards in order *not* to have these assessed easily – whilst, equally vehemently, holding on to its monopoly of service and right to set standards.

However, having recently specified the expected qualities of corporate financial statements in the defined terms of relevance and reliability, it is now much less possible for corporate auditors to defend their duty of audit care with the vagueness and ambiguity of the past. In particular, given the stated definitions of relevance and reliability, specifically with respect to real-world economic phenomena, the corporate auditor will find it increasingly difficult to interpret these matters solely within terms of conventional, generally accepted accounting principles and related rules. Indeed, there are already signs from the recent history of corporate reporting and auditing of explicit recognition of this point. For example, professional pronouncements have been made about the need to report on economic substance rather than legal form (AICPA, 1972, p.127; AICPA, 1973, p.57; and AICPA, 1975, para.9). And individual writers on audit-related matters have made similar points (Shaw, 1980, p.14; Sherer and Kent, 1983, p.83; and Wolnizer, 1987, p.94). The dilemma this presents to the corporate auditor is of interest here, and is discussed further in Chapter 9 – that is, the need to maintain a professional monopoly by means of an undefined legally-based discourse, and the existence of a defined accounting discourse to guide accounting and auditing practice.

Further reading

E.H. Carr (1987) *What is History?*, Penguin Books, pp.7–30 (an introduction to the nature of history and historical study).

G.J. Previts, L.D. Parker and E.N. Coffman (1990) Accounting history: definition and relevance, *Abacus*, March, pp.1–16 (a rationale for the study of accounting history, and its relationship to the study of history).

A.G. Hopwood (1987) The archaeology of accounting systems, *Accounting, Organisations and Society*, **8** (2/3), pp.207–34 (an argument for a more critical study of the history of accounting and auditing, based on an understanding of the nature of history).

T.A. Lee (1988) *The Evolution of Auditing Thought and Practice*, Garland Publishing, (an edited collection of studies of the history of auditing from the earliest times).

Discussion and essay topics

1. What is history and why is it so useful?
2. Prepare a commentary on the purpose of studying the history of corporate auditing.
3. Explain the form of auditing which took place in pre-incorporation times, and contrast this with the conventional corporate audit which has evolved in more recent years.
4. Discuss the features of corporate auditing which are unique to such an audit function.
5. Prepare a critique of the concept of fraud and error detection in corporate auditing.
6. What is meant by the expectations gap in the history of corporate auditing?
7. Describe the evolution of the corporate auditor as a competent and responsible professional.
8. Throughout the history of the modern corporate audit function, the auditor can be observed continuously denying rather than accepting responsibilities. Discuss.

6

The feasibility of corporate auditing

Before proceeding to the detail of this chapter, it is necessary to explain what is meant by the term 'postulate' in the context in which it is used throughout this text. The definition adopted is that of Mautz and Sharaf (1961, pp.37–9):

> Postulates are assumptions that do not lend themselves to direct verification. The propositions deduced from the postulates of a given system, however, can be directly verified and such verification bears evidence of the truth of the postulates themselves.
>
> They provide the basis for making inferences which are valid and useful to the extent that the postulates themselves satisfy the needs of the particular discipline. Once we accept the postulates we can draw propositions from them. They provide a basis for thinking about problems and for arriving at solutions.

In other words, using a deductive approach to the formulation of theoretical propositions, the postulates of corporate auditing, together with the function's stated roles and objectives, provide a basis from which to develop its main concepts, and then its basic principles of practice (Moonitz, 1961, p.1; Chambers, 1963, p.15; and Flint, 1988, p.20). To do this successfully, however, the stated postulates must be practically as well as theoretically sound. As Mautz and Sharaf (1961, p.39) conclude:

> . . . the postulates, once accepted as useful and valid, may at a later date be challenged and even demonstrated to be invalid. As noted earlier, postulates cannot be directly verified. Neither can they be proved untrue, or they would have no usefulness. That means that when a postulate can be proved untrue, it has lost its value as a postulate and must be discarded.

Postulates are not only theoretical means of attempting to identify and understand the foundations of corporate audit activity, they are also potentially a way of thinking about and resolving the function's inherent problems. They permit the student of corporate auditing to determine whether such activity is based on sound theoretical grounds. As Chambers (1963, p.15) argues, postulates exist:

Because a man's postulates are the substance of his understanding of the world in which he acts; if his postulates are irrelevant or inconsistent, neither he nor his practices merit the esteem of his fellows. Because to examine one's postulates is the simplest and most effective way to discover the possibility and direction of improvements and innovations in practice. Because man's reasoned judgment is his only protection against self-delusion, cant and deceit.

Postulates are the apparent and accepted truths of a subject or discipline. They are its *a priori*, the basic descriptions of things in its environment and provide an outline of the intrinsic character of such activity (Flint, 1988, p.20). In particular, postulates support all the terms and theorems of the subject concerned (Mautz and Sharaf, 1961, p.38; and Chambers, 1963, p.15). They provide means by which testable propositions can be derived (Mautz and Sharaf, 1961, p.38; and Flint, 1988, p.20). In effect, therefore, they bound both the theory and practice of a subject such as corporate auditing.

But, in providing such shape, postulates have qualities which act as constraints or controls to their specification, use and acceptance. These are outlined by both Mautz and Sharaf (1961, p.51) and Schandl (1978, pp.25–6). First, postulates should be coherent in the sense that they belong to the one body of theoretical knowledge. Second, they should contribute to that knowledge by allowing their user to deduce testable propositions, hypotheses or conclusions from them. Third, they should have an independent status which determines that each stated postulate cannot be deduced from any other postulate of the designated body of knowledge. Fourth, they should be internally consistent to the extent that each can be accepted as true. And finally, they should be susceptible to challenge and to being discarded as events and knowledge render them unacceptable as a basis for theoretical deduction.

This is not the only view possible of the utility of specifying the postulates of auditing. Gwilliam (1987, p.49), for example, concludes that such 'quasi-philosophical' underpinnings to audit theory may be less useful than an alternative of examining it through the economics lens of agency theory. In particular, he appears to be concerned that auditing postulates are not rationales for the audit process as a whole but, instead, represent no more than statements of potential feasibility (p.42). He is particularly against the uncritical acceptance of the postulates originally specified by Mautz and Sharaf (1961) (p.44).

These criticisms are not entirely appropriate when placed within the context of this text. First, the postulates specified in the following sections are additional to the descriptions, explanations and discussions of the rationale for corporate auditing in previous chapters. Second, attention should be given in any theory text to the role of postulates to test the legitimacy and potential of the specified normative prescriptions. In this case, it is not so much the feasibility of corporate audit practice which is being questioned by means of postulates (although that is an inevitable consequence). It is more the reasonableness of the expectations contained within them regarding corporate auditors and their function of verification and attestation.

The postulates of corporate auditing

There are three groups of postulates to be stated as the fundamental theoretical truths of corporate auditing. The first is concerned with justifying assumptions relating to the existence of the corporate audit. The second group is focused on the actions of the corporate auditor, and deals with the behavioural aspects of corporate auditing. The final group covers matters of corporate audit procedure, and has the title of functional postulates.

Justifying corporate audit postulates

There are a number of corporate audit postulates which provide a theoretical basis for its existence in practice. These are described as justifying assumptions, and are explained in the following paragraphs.

> **The quality of the accounting information reported in the financial statements of the generality of corporate organizations lacks sufficient credibility without formal verification and attestation to be used with complete confidence by shareholders and other report users as part of the corporate accountability process.**

In the economic agency situation described as corporate organization, the process of accountability by means of reported financial statements is founded on the notion of corporate management preparing these statements as explicit financial representations of the outcomes of its activities and efforts, and thereby communicating its financial stewardship to shareholders and other legitimate external interests. However, corporate management is responsible for and in control of the production of the accounting information which comprises the content of these financial statements. It is a process of self-assessment which lacks the appearance of impartiality on which the credibility of the reported information depends for confident use. The managerial agent group is responsible not only for reporting on its financial stewardship, but also for managing the accounting means by which such reporting takes place to ownership and other interested groups.

If this situation were different, and the production of reported financial statements could be completed independent of corporate management, there would appear to be far less reason for having an external auditor to verify and attest the quality of these statements. Under existing circumstances, however, it is reasonable to presume that a situation in which corporate managers have the power and authority to control the reporting of the financial consequences of their actions in the form of unaudited financial statements to shareholders and others does not assist meaningfully in the process of corporate governance and accountability. It is not conducive to the confident use of the accounting information contained in these statements.

Thus, unless the above postulate is stated and accepted, there is little point in having an audit of corporate financial statements. Put differently, no such audit is necessary if shareholders and other interested users of these statements are willing to use them in an unaudited state. If they were so willing, it would indicate a situation in which the benefits of external auditing were perceived not to exceed the costs of such a function.

This postulate is the most fundamental of all in corporate audit theory. If it is not acceptable, then no other is reasonable. However, it has been deliberately stated in terms of a 'generality' of companies because it also recognizes that it is difficult to support in every case. There may be situations (for example, with very small companies) when the main or sole users of financial statements are the shareholder–managers. In such cases, the absence of significant external interests may cause the postulate to be unreasonable. Indeed, there is a persistent implied concern about its legitimacy in the context of small companies (Page, 1991a).

There is also a question-mark with respect to very large corporate organizations. Williamson (1975, pp.29–30), for example, suggests that such entities internalize their markets by means of subsidiary company structures to protect or govern their competitive advantage and minimize transaction costs. Consequently, as part of this governance structure, they internalize their control mechanisms including audit. This would suggest that companies with internal audits may not have the same need for external audit as suggested in this postulate (see Vinten, 1991).

What is therefore argued in this text is that for most corporate organizations the postulate holds true. It is developed from one first stated in 1972 (Lee, 1972, p.53; and Lee, 1986, p.74). It is also used by other audit theorists (Sherer and Kent, 1983, p.19). And it is similar in nature to a justifying postulate stated by Flint (1988, p.22) that accountability is too remote, complex or significant to be discharged effectively without an audit. Mautz and Sharaf (1961), on the other hand, do not specify such a postulate in their exposition of auditing postulates, despite the main focus of their study being reported financial statements.

When using the audit function as part of the process of corporate accountability, verification and attestation of the quality of reported financial statements to shareholders and others is the most desired audit in the generality of corporate situations.

This postulate makes explicit the presumption that, of all possible audit functions which could be undertaken on behalf of shareholders and others with a legitimate interest in corporate organizations, the audit of reported financial statements is the most needed in terms of balancing the benefits to their users against the costs of reasonable audit completion. When looking at the widespread use made of corporate financial statements in a variety of decision contexts, it appears reasonable to make this assumption – again in terms of the generality of corporate situations.

The postulate, like any other, is always open to challenge if evidence concerning expectations of the corporate auditor reveals conclusively that a different form of audit is desired, and that the cost of this will be borne because its perceived benefits to report users exceed such a cost. Alternative economics-based audit functions to that specified in this postulate include fraud and error detection, attesting the effectiveness and efficiency of corporate control systems, judging the effectiveness and efficiency of corporate management, and assessing the financial soundness of the corporate organization.

There is also a variety of specific arguments for audits and accountability directly related to the social behaviour of the reporting corporate organization – that is, concerning the potential and actual impact of its operations on the community. For example, Chen (1975) and Tinker (1985) argue for a broad societal stewardship; Gray (1990) examines the specific issue of reporting on the impact of the corporate organization on its environment; and Willmott (1991) suggests the current audit is too narrowly grounded with a main objective of satisfying the financial needs of corporate ownership.

At the present time, however, despite these economic and societal arguments, and recent severe criticisms of the existing audit function (for example, Briloff, 1990; and Mitchell *et al.*, 1991), a long-standing debate about an expectations gap in relation to fraud and error detection (for example, Tweedie, 1991), and some relatively dated empirical data of a broader range of audit expectations (for example, Lee, 1970b; and Beck, 1973), there appears to be no overwhelming reason for refuting the validity of this postulate. The present situation of the state mandating a financial audit on behalf of corporate ownership is a world-wide practical reality.

The above postulate relates indirectly to the assumption of Schandl (1978, p.22) that there is a purpose to the audit, and to that of Flint (1988, p.23) that there are economic and social benefits to be derived from the audit. As with the first postulate, this assumption is developed from an earlier version (Lee, 1972, p.54; and Lee, 1986, p.75), used by other writers (Sherer and Kent, 1983, p.19), but not specified by Mautz and Sharaf (1961).

> **Verification and attestation of the quality of reported financial statements to shareholders and others is best achieved by regulation in the generality of corporate situations.**

In most economic situations involving corporate organizations, the external audit of their reported financial statements to shareholders and others with a legitimate interest in them is required by means of a specific and formal regulatory provision. This postulate assumes that the external audit of the quality of corporate financial statements is best achieved by such mandates and, consequently, that it should not be left as a voluntary function.

Once it is accepted that there is a relatively universal need for a corporate audit (as stated in the first and second postulates above), it is logical to assume that an effective way of ensuring such a need is generally satisfied is by explicit regulation. As Wallace (1985, p.53) argues, much of the relevant literature is predicated on this notion. What it stipulates is that, given the character of corporate financial information as a public good, it is necessary to provide consumer protection by the imposition of an external audit 'tax' on reporting companies. This is a predominant view, given the almost universal existence of regulated corporate audits, and is premised in this section. However, as Wallace (1985, p.53) also points out, there is a contrary assumption which suggests that the effects of the market in agency situations (including stewardship and insurance) provide incentives to both principals and agents to voluntarily provide for external audit services.

Given the typical existence of corporate auditing as a regulated activity, this alternative assumption is recognized but not utilized in this chapter. The postulate specified above was first prescribed in 1972 (Lee, 1972, p.54), is used by Sherer and Kent (1983, p.19) but not stipulated by Mautz and Sharaf (1961), Schandl (1978) or Flint (1988) – presumably because their theoretical expositions are not specifically focused on corporate organizations.

> **In the generality of corporate situations, the quality of reported financial statements to shareholders and others can be satisfactorily attested by the verification process of an external audit.**

This postulate is one which is developed from earlier versions (for example, Lee, 1972, p.55; and Lee, 1986, p.76). It is also to be found in the postulate listings of other audit theorists and, thus, there appears to be a degree of consensus on the matter. For example, Mautz and Sharaf (1961, p.42) assume financial statements and related data are verifiable. Flint (1988, p.22), on the other hand, assumes that the subject-matter of auditing, whatever its form, is susceptible to verification by evidence. The version of the assumption used in this text is also stated by Sherer and Kent (1983, pp.19–20).

What this postulate articulates is a prior acceptance that the specified informational quality of corporate financial statements is auditable. To believe otherwise would be asking the corporate auditor to attempt an impossible task. Corporate auditors implicitly accept this assumption on each occasion they carry out the audit task. There are, however, certain circumstances which are a threat to the universality of this postulate, and which have caused it to be phrased in general terms. For example, the size, volume and complexity of the largest corporate organizations may be such that, despite the use of a variety of audit procedures, there remain doubts as to whether any audit would be sufficient to satisfactorily verify and attest the quality of such an entity's financial statements. In these situations, however, the presence of internal audit may well act as a counterweight to these doubts (AICPA, 1991, pp.98–9). Equally, in certain smaller companies, inevitable weaknesses in control systems may be such that the postulate cannot be expressed in a strong form (Page, 1991a, p.217). The present consensus is relatively unclear as to what is the preferred position (pp.221–2). Meantime, therefore, the postulate is stated in the restricted form of a generality of companies.

> In the generality of corporate situations, shareholders and others with a legitimate interest are not in a position to verify and attest personally to the quality of the reported financial statements.

This assumption was originally prescribed in 1972 (Lee, 1972, p.56), developed in later versions (for example, Lee, 1986, p.77), and is used by Sherer and Kent (1983, p.20). It does not appear in the work of other audit theorists specifying postulates (for example, Mautz and Sharaf, 1961; Schandl, 1978; and Flint, 1988).

The structure of the corporate organization tends to physically divorce its shareholders and other constituent interests from its management. This is a typical agency situation in which corporate managers act as agents for shareholder–owners, and is particularly observable as a definite sequence in cases in which a small private 'family-run' company has extended into a larger public entity. In other words, as corporate organizations grow, their shareholders and other external interests increasingly tend not to be conversant with the daily operations of the reporting entity. They become both mentally and physically separate from it.

In addition, and again particularly in larger organizations, shareholders and other external constituents may only have a temporary interest in a reporting company – that is, their involvement with it extends temporarily to the point at which they cease to invest, lend or do business with it. Thus, there may be little motivation in the relationship to sustain a long-standing personal interest in the reporting entity. And, even if this personal interest does exist, the size and technical complexities of the corporate financial reporting function is beyond the competence of almost all external report users. Indeed, available empirical evidence supports this conclusion in the context of both private shareholders (Lee and Tweedie, 1977, p.177), and institutional investors (Lee and Tweedie, 1981, p.141).

Finally, even if the motivation and expertise are available to personally audit, it would place impossible administrative burdens on corporate management if individual shareholders and other report users were able to verify and attest personally accounting records and financial statements. For this reason, the normal practice (and theoretical assumption) is that corporate organizations employ suitably qualified professional accountants to act as corporate auditors on behalf of their external constituents.

Behavioural corporate audit postulates

Corporate auditing is a service function whose nature and quality is dependent to a considerable extent on the personal attributes of the corporate auditor. This aspect of corporate audit theory therefore comprises certain key assumptions about the behavioural characteristics of an auditor charged with the task of verifying and attesting the quality of the accounting information in corporate financial statements. In this respect, the term 'auditor' is used to denote those individuals responsible for the corporate audit function in practice. In reality, however, the auditor is usually a firm of suitably qualified professional accountants employing sufficient staff to complete the verification task and justify the attest opinion.

> **There is no conflict of interest between the corporate auditor and corporate management which hinders his or her verification and attestation of the quality of reported financial statements to shareholders and other interested users.**

Having presented a rationale for a corporate audit function, it is sensible to assume that, once instituted, it can be carried through to a satisfactory conclusion. The rational expectations argument in agency theory suggests that, in addition to the relatively obvious needs of shareholders and other constituents for audit monitoring, and even in the absence of regulation, it is in corporate management's best interests to demand an external audit service. Provision of such a function maximizes its compensation for good management as it will be seen to be acting in the interests of the shareholder–principals (Wallace, 1985, p.19). In other words, a corporate audit provides management with credible information for stewardship reporting, improves the informational influence on its decision-making, and provides an insurance against poor quality accounting (p.14). It is therefore postulated in this section that corporate auditors will not be in a position in which they are prevented by the actions of management from attempting to achieve their stated objectives.

The presumption is therefore that corporate auditors will be able to meet their objectives regarding verification and attestation of corporate financial statements (and supporting accounting records) because they have the fullest co-operation of and access to corporate management and its accounting systems. In particular, it is assumed that corporate auditors have access to all records, statements and other evidence they need in order to determine and report on the quality of the financial statements. In certain situations, they are given this right of access to relevant evidence by specific regulation (for example, in the UK in the Companies Act, 1985, s. 389A(1). In other cases, it is implied in auditing standards relating to the need for the corporate auditor to obtain sufficient competent evidential material to support his or her opinion (AICPA, 1991, p.7).

If this postulate is not stated and accepted then, in practice, the corporate auditor could never be certain of management's co-operation, and this could create a defensive and confrontational approach to the audit. As there is currently no argument or evidence that the interests of corporate auditor and corporate management are incompatible, the assumption appears to be valid. Indeed, available evidence is strongly in support of it if current criticism of auditors and their function is examined – that is, the closeness of corporate management and the auditor is such that the latter is no longer independent and acting on behalf of the shareholders (see, for example, Briloff, 1990, p.30). The postulate was first stated in 1972 (Lee, 1972, p.57), repeated in later editions of that text (Lee, 1986, p.78), quoted by other writers on audit theory (Sherer and Kent, 1983, p.20), but originally stated in a simpler form by Mautz and Sharaf (1961, p.42).

There are no unreasonable legal or other regulatory restrictions placed upon corporate auditors which hinder their verifying and attesting the quality of reported financial statements to shareholders and other interested users.

It is logical to presume that, in a regulated corporate environment which involves the use of an external auditor, the regulations concerned contain relevant provisions giving adequate rights, privileges and protection to conduct the audit function meaningfully. In other words, it has to be assumed that they contain no exclusions which prevent auditors exercising their right of access to either the evidence they require in situations in which corporate management is not operating in accordance with rational expectations theory; or the shareholders when management is so acting. In particular, the corporate auditor should be assumed to have the right to communicate with shareholders in situations where this is necessary for their protection as well as that of his or her own.

Unless this assumption is made, there can be no guarantee that corporate auditors will be able to discharge their function adequately, and thereby fulfil their objectives as stated. The existing evidence of corporate audit regulations throughout the corporate world is that provisions are typically in place to ensure that this postulate can be confidently stated and accepted. For example, in the UK, the Companies Act, 1985, ss. 389A–392A operationalizes the postulate. It was originally conceived in 1972 (Lee, 1972, p.58), is used by Sherer and Kent (1983, p.20), and prescribed by Flint (1988, p.22) in the alternative form of an audit being free of investigatory and reporting constraints. However, Mautz and Sharaf's (1961) list of audit postulates does not contain a similar presumption about the auditor's position.

The corporate auditor is in a suitably independent position, both mentally and physically, to verify and attest with sufficient objectivity the quality of the reported financial statements to shareholders and other interested users.

This notion is one of the most important presumptions in the theory and practice of corporate auditing. The quality of the accounting information contained in the reporting company's financial statements is presumed in the first postulate of this chapter to lack sufficient credibility without a formal audit to be used confidently by shareholders and other interested constituents. However, it is equally essential that the person given the task of financial statement verification and attestation is in a position to carry out these functions free from any potential or existing biases and pressures which could impair his or her audit judgment. If corporate auditors lack this vital neutrality, their audit work and opinions can be doubted, and this may well cause shareholders and other interested report users to have little or no confidence in either the audit opinion or the accounting information which is the subject of that opinion.

The conventional perception of the way in which the corporate auditors achieve a position of independence is focused on their ability to mentally disregard any pressures from situations which are biasing or are likely to bias their audit judgments. What is presumed of corporate auditors is that they have the honesty and integrity as professional people not to allow their audit reasoning to be swayed. However, if, as is being suggested, corporate auditor independence is basically a state of mind resulting from a combination of education, training and experience as a professional expert, it is obvious that no person other than the auditor concerned will be aware of the extent to which he or she is successful in preserving an independent state of mind in any given audit situation. And perhaps not even auditors can be fully aware of the pervasive influence of economic, social and cultural influences on their objectivity.

For this reason, it is vital to the credibility of the corporate audit opinion, and to the perceived quality of the reported accounting information, that the corporate auditor is assumed to be mentally independent and physically seen to be so independent. It is the physical appearance of corporate auditor independence which is presumed to be the initial and, perhaps, only direct means by which shareholders and other interested report users can judge the integrity of the auditor and his or her opinion. For this reason, it is unsurprising to find regulations in practice which are intended to provide this physical appearance – for example, a generalized audit standard in the US (AICPA, 1991, p.17); and more specific legal regulations in the UK (Companies Act, 1985, Chap.V).

It should be added that an economic agency argument exists to support the validity of this assumption in the absence of such regulation – that is, a failure to act independently, if eventually detected, could create reputational effects, and cause a loss of economic compensation to the corporate auditor (Antle, 1984, p.18). It should also be noted that there is an argument which suggests that the presumption of auditor independence should be made at the level of the individual auditor as well as the audit firm (Miller, 1992). In particular, it is conceivable that the relationship between the partner and the corporate client is just as critical to the independence postulate as the relationship between the latter and the audit firm – that is, it may be economically worthwhile for the partner to be client dependent despite any economic effect this may have on the firm (p.83).

This postulate was formulated in its present form in 1972 (Lee, 1972, p.58). It was developed at that time from an earlier postulate of Mautz and Sharaf (1961, p.42) which states that the auditor acts exclusively as an auditor when verifying and attesting financial data. Flint (1988, p.22) expresses independent status as an essential distinguishing feature of an audit. Sherer and Kent (1983, pp.20–1) use the 1972 Lee version prior to a detailed exposition of the primary importance of the concept of auditor independence in practice. And Wolnizer (1987, p.15) argues that the assumption should not be restricted to the behavioural characteristics of the auditor. Instead, he believes it encompasses the independent testability of the accounting information being verified and attested.

The corporate auditor is sufficiently skilled and experienced to competently conduct the audit function of verifying and attesting the quality of the reported financial statements to shareholders and other interested report users.

Corporate auditing is concerned with verifying and attesting the quality of a highly complex and technical subject-matter – the accounting information contained in reported financial information to shareholders and other external constituents. It is therefore pertinent to assume that the corporate auditor has sufficient and appropriate skills and experience to achieve the stated objectives of the corporate audit function. If these personal characteristics are lacking, or are insufficient, there appears to be little point in asking the corporate auditor to attempt to achieve them.

This is a postulated position consistent with that of US audit standard-setters when prescribing an auditor with adequate technical training and proficiency (AICPA, 1991, p.7); and UK legislators stipulating professional accounting qualifications for corporate auditors (Companies Act, 1985, s. 389). In addition, the postulate is expressed by Flint (1988, p.22) as part of the process of accountability which requires special skills. He explains the authority of the auditor at least partly in terms of competence (Flint, 1988, pp.48–53). Interestingly, Mautz and Sharaf (1961) make no mention of such an assumption. Sherer and Kent (1983, p.21), however, use it as one of their foundations for a wide-ranging exposition of auditing and its relationship to accountability. The postulate expressed in this section originated in 1972 (Lee, 1972, p.59).

The corporate auditor can be held accountable as a professional expert for the quality of his or her audit work and related opinion on the quality of the reported financial statements to shareholders and other interested report users.

The original version of this postulate appeared in 1972 (Lee, 1972, p.59), and was retained in subsequent editions of that text (for example, Lee, 1986, pp.80–1). It is used in Sherer and Kent (1983, p.21), and can be traced to an earlier assumption of Mautz and Sharaf (1961, p.42) that the professional status of independent auditor imposes commensurate professional obligations. Flint (1988), despite a lengthy exposition of the auditor's duty of care (pp.144–50), and the prescription of a postulate relating to the assumption of the existence of audit terms of reference for the auditor (p.22), does not refer to a responsibility postulate.

The work of the auditor is that of a service in which only the audit report and fee note are tangible evidence of the skill, effort and time devoted to producing the report and justifying the fee. There is little tangible proof for shareholders and other external constituents of the audit activity which has taken place in order to arrive at an audit opinion. Report users are therefore required in practice to have a great deal of confidence in the corporate auditor as a professional expert. However, as with other professional services such as medicine or law, the potential beneficiaries of the service must have reasonable assurance that the professional experts on whom they are relying can be held responsible for the quality of their work and the nature of their related opinion.

This is a fundamental and generally accepted tenet of professions – professionals enter into an implicit covenant with society to apply their skills in the service of their client; to put the needs of their client and, indeed, the public interest before their self-interest; and to adhere to a code of conduct (Johnson, 1972, p.23). Johnson (1972, p.12) further argues that professions are moral communities which provide stability in the conduct of a democratic society. If corporate auditors cannot be presumed to behave in such a way as professional experts, no one could reasonably rely on their opinion. They could conduct their audit activities as well or as badly as they wished, safe in the knowledge that they could do as they liked. It has to be presumed that, in such circumstances, they are subject to some form of effective accountability.

Evidence of this can be demonstrated in a number of ways. For example, auditor accountability can be seen in terms of a continuous stream of court cases since the mid-nineteenth century, in which the duty of care of the corporate auditor with respect to shareholders and other interested individuals has been challenged and formulated (Davies, 1979; and Godsell, 1991). It is also evident in specific auditing standards issued by professional accountancy bodies throughout the world over recent decades (AICPA, 1991 in the US; and APC, 1980a in the UK). These standards specify minimum levels of audit performance expected of the corporate auditor in given circumstances. Without these standards, there is nothing with which to compare the corporate auditor's actual performance in order to judge its adequacy. However, as well as being acceptable, these standards should also be attainable. If they are not, there is little point in having them. Auditors would have little guidance available to them with respect to the proper conduct of their audits.

Consistent with other sections in this text, in the absence of regulation, it should also be noted that corporate auditors can be observed to be in a situation of economic agency in which their self-interest is such that they will act responsibly and with due care – because of the economic consequences of loss of reputation (Antle, 1982, p.526). Recent criticism, however, of the lack of responsiveness of the auditing profession to charges of failure in its primary duty of protecting report users, indicates that it may have engineered a strategy of 'doing nothing', and thereby put itself in a position of non-accountability (Forgarty, Heian and Knutson, 1991, p.222) – that is, by pleading the impossibility of assuming a broad societal responsibility, and invoking the financial disasters of such responsibility, corporate auditors are attempting to say they cannot be held responsible for business failures and other related problems. Indeed, a further analysis of the audit profession's response to audit expectations-gap issues suggests that it can act in terms of both the public interest and self-interest in order to maintain its monopoly position in providing audit services, and contribute to social welfare (Hooks, 1991, pp. 129–31).

Functional corporate audit postulates

There is a third group of fundamental postulates which concern corporate audit activity. These are stated in this text in support of the functional and procedural aspects of corporate auditing. They relate to the nature of the quality of audited accounting information, the availability and sufficiency of audit evidence, and the need for the corporate auditor to report meaningfully.

> **The over-riding quality of reported financial statements for corporate audit purposes is interpreted mainly in terms of their relevance and reliability, and there are standards by which the corporate auditor can determine the existence of such a quality.**

As previously explained, as part of corporate governance and managerial account-ability, the expected quality of reported financial statements to shareholders and other report users is expressed in terms of their relevance for decision purposes and their reliability as faithful representations of reportable economic phenomena. If such qualitative criteria are specified for corporate financial reporting purposes, it is logical to expect them to be the basis of the corporate auditor's objectives. It is equally logical to argue a presumption that the existence or otherwise of the reporting criteria of decision relevance and informational reliability can be determined by the corporate auditor by potential access to appropriate standards providing guidance as to their interpretation in specific circumstances. Without this assumption, there is no certainty of the corporate auditor being able to attest the relevance and reliability of the reported accounting information.

The reasonableness of this postulate with reference to current corporate audit practice is presently problematic. Certainly the qualitative characteristics of relevance and reliability are specified in corporate financial reporting prescriptions with the intention of being used as the primary conceptual basis for specific financial accounting standards (FASB, 1978, para.2; and ASB, 1991b, paras. 23 and 26). And there are attempts by accounting standard-setters to operationalize them in terms of such basic matters as accounting recognition criteria (FASB, 1984) and financial reporting elements (FASB, 1985). However, the existence of specific accounting standards as norms for reporting relevance and reliability in practice is at a preliminary stage. This, of itself, does not invalidate the postulate in the long term, but it does cause concern in the short term about the effectiveness of the current corporate audit in terms of these specified objectives.

What also requires to be taken into consideration in the typical situation of a regulated system for audited corporate financial statements is the regulatory prescription of reporting quality in the undefined terms of 'present fairly' in the US and 'a true and fair view' in the UK. These terms have a legal derivation as part of corporate accountability and, following the custom and habit of legal discourse, provide their authorized users (such as corporate auditors) with the maximum scope for interpretation in terms of specific meaning (Goodrich, 1987, p.180). In other words, the potential of this postulate is in conflict with the realities of the reporting quality legal over-rides. Accounting standard-setters have recently attempted to bridge that gap by defining certain key quality criteria and relating them to the over-rides (ASB, 1991b, para.43). But, even then, operationalizing these criteria is a relatively unexplored area of policy-making and standard-setting.

This postulate is similar in very broad terms to a number of others made in recent times by audit theorists, and thus reflects a degree of unanimity on the subject. For example, Mautz and Sharaf (1961, p.47) stipulate that judging the fairness of financial statements requires the existence of a standard, and that this standard exists in the form of generally accepted accounting principles. However, this is comparable with the prescribed postulate of this text only in the sense that a reporting quality has been prescribed. In particular, it is specified in an undefined legalistic sense of fairness rather than in the more specific economic terms of relevance and reliability.

Other theorists are somewhat broader in approach and, therefore, inevitably more ambiguous. Nevertheless, they all have emphasized the presumption of prior reporting quality standards. Schandl (1978, p.24), for example, writes of a postulate of norms by which the auditor can judge accounting information; and Flint (1988, p.22) postulates standards of accountability by which the auditor can compare that which is measured in accounting terms. Thus, there is a general agreement in this area that, whatever the corporate auditor is expected to achieve in terms of his audit function, he cannot succeed without the assistance of quality standards or norms as points of comparison for the subject-matter of auditing. The problem in practice is the ill-defined nature of the existing norms.

> **There is sufficient competent and reliable evidential material available to allow the corporate auditor to properly substantiate an audit opinion on the quality of the reported financial statements to shareholders and other report users; and the corporate auditor can collect and evaluate this material within a reasonable time and at a reasonable cost.**

The accounting information contained in the financial statements reported to shareholders and others with a legitimate interest in them is the end-product of a complex technical process. The latter is a long-lived function to represent in statement form a myriad of economic events and objects in the complex and abstract language of accounting, and thereby inform a variety of individuals and organizations to whom it is addressed. The corporate auditor is charged with the task of observing this representational process with the objective of verifying and attesting the prescribed qualities of the reported accounting abstractions – that is, as stated above, in terms of their relevance and reliability. In order to complete this task, the corporate auditor evidences the accounting procedures which are followed in the construction and disclosure of these accounting abstractions. To do this expertly and with due professional care, sufficient evidential material must be available. If this assumption is not made, the corporate auditor enters an audit situation not knowing the probability of satisfactorily completing the audit task. The validity of this assumption has been recognized both in the USA (AICPA, 1991, p.121) and in the UK (APC, 1980b, para.4).

The postulate, however, is not narrowly phrased in terms of just the sufficiency and availability of audit evidence. It specifically requires sufficient competent and reliable evidence to be gathered and used within reasonable time and cost constraints. No corporate auditor should expect an abundance of evidential material to be immediately available for examination and judgment. Nor can the reporting corporate organization be expected to retain indefinitely all the material which evidences the processes of financial accounting. Yet, despite these constraints, it must be assumed that not only will the corporate auditor be able to gather evidence of sufficient quality to support his or her audit opinion, but that this can be done within a reasonable time and at a reasonable cost.

The corporate audit is required to be complete as soon as possible after the financial period-end in order to provide shareholders and other report users with timely information. It would be irrational to assume that any corporate audit of informational quality would delay its publication to a point at which its utility was significantly impaired. And it would be equally senseless to assume that the cost of corporate auditing outweighs its benefits to shareholders and others. Each of these points is consistent with the information economics approach to audit theory – that is, a demand for an external audit service will exist when its perceived benefits exceed its costs (Wallace, 1985, p.34).

The importance of this postulate was first stressed in 1972 (Lee, 1972, p.61), and is emphasized by Sherer and Kent (1983, p.21). It is also written in an alternative form by Schandl (1978, p.23) when he presumes that past, present and future evidence is required in an audit situation. And Flint (1988, p.22) puts it in a further alternative form by stating that the subject-matter of auditing is susceptible to verification by evidence. But Mautz and Sharaf (1961) are silent on the issue, despite a clear indication of the fundamental conceptional importance of evidence to informed decisions (p.68).

Wolnizer (1987, pp.11–27), on the other hand, extends the postulate of available audit evidence by prescribing such material as both independent and independently testable – that is, he believes audit evidence should be public knowledge and independent of the auditor and reporting management. To be credible, therefore, the verification and attestation of reported financial statements of corporate organizations is assumed to be based on sufficient and available evidence which is within the public domain, and therefore independently testable.

This latter view of evidence is supported in this text, particularly in Chapter 10. In terms of interpreting the term 'competent and reliable' audit evidence, it is taken to mean that it is independently testable. Unless the sufficiency and availability of audit evidence is viewed in this way, the independent authentication of the quality of reported financial statements is an unattainable audit objective. In particular, the ability of corporate auditors to attest the reliability or representational faithfulness of accounting information appears to require independent evidence being independently evaluated by (Wolnizer, 1987, p.159).

The accounting information contained in the reported financial statements to shareholders and other report users is free of major fraud and error.

The main objective of the corporate audit function is specified in this text in terms of the attestation of the relevance and reliability of reported financial statements. Thus, although the corporate auditor cannot and must not ignore such matters if they materially affect the informational content and prescribed qualities of these statements, and despite any public expectation to the contrary, the corporate audit is not assumed to be primarily focused on the detection of fraud and error. It is therefore further presumed that corporate auditors approach their work without pre-supposing the existence of either major fraud or error. To do otherwise would result in a fraud investigation of a type wholly incompatible with the corporate audit task specified by present regulation.

The absence of major fraud or error is largely determined by the existence and reliability of systems of control instituted by corporate management. However, even with such systems in place, fraud particularly can exist if it is of the type involving misinformation caused by very senior management. Under such circumstances, however, corporate auditors are typically held responsible by their professional body for detecting fraud and error when proper assessments of audit risk, and normal audit routines, should give them a reasonable expectation of revealing it (AICPA, 1991, p.56; and APC, 1990, para.7). It should not be assumed therefore that corporate auditors have no responsibility for the detection of significant fraud and error – merely that they are not required to make a prior presumption that it exists. It must be stated, however, that such an assumption is inconsistent with the current climate of opinion resulting from major fraud-related corporate failures (see, for example, Briloff, 1990; and Mitchell et al., 1991).

Mautz and Sharaf (1961, p.42) originally specified this postulate in two parts – verifiable financial statements are free of irregularities; and internal controls eliminate the probability of such irregularities. It was combined into one postulate in 1972 (Lee,

1972, p.62), and is used by Sherer and Kent (1983, p.21). It does not appear in the postulates outlined by Flint (1988) or Schandl (1978).

The relevance and reliability of reported financial statements to shareholders and other report users can be reported meaningfully to them by the corporate auditor.

This final postulate of corporate auditing makes the relatively common-sense point that the corporate audit report is the means of communicating the results of the corporate auditor's work to the shareholders and other report users as part of corporate governance and managerial accountability. Consequently, rational argument suggests that the effectiveness of such a communication is related to whether its readers can determine from it the meaning and significance of the auditor's comments on the quality of the verified accounting information. Unless it is assumed that financial statement users are capable of understanding and interpreting the auditor's attestation, the impact of the corporate audit is questionable.

The evidence to date on this point is not reassuring. Lee and Tweedie (1977, p.55; and 1981, p.79) reveal the corporate audit report as one of the most neglected areas of corporate financial reports. And Hatherly and Skuse (1991) review the long-standing debate concerning the frailties of the short-form report and the need for a more coherent long-form communication. The postulate, however, is recognized by Schandl (1978) in terms of assumptions that the audit requires a judgment in the form of a communicated opinion, and that such a communication is meaningful (p.23); and by Flint (1988, p.23) in terms approximate to this text.

An overview of the corporate auditor as a professional

Before proceeding to an explanation and discussion of the basic concepts of corporate auditing which relate to these postulates, it is useful to reflect briefly on certain aspects of what this chapter attempts to say about the corporate audit function generally, and about the corporate auditor particularly. The specified postulates portray an auditor who is in a functional position to be free to act as a professional, and who will functionally act with freedom when put in that position. More generally, the corporate auditor is assumed to behave in all audit acts in a professional way. He or she is expected to safeguard the public interest by unbiasedly providing a competent service of the highest quality to corporate financial report users, thereby also injecting stability to the process of managerial accountability in corporate economic affairs (Willmott, 1990, p.322). But this begs questions concerning the meaning and interpretation of the terms used such as 'profession', 'professional', and 'public interest'.

A profession can be interpreted as a specialist occupation which emerges from a temporally extended process of division of labour in an economic community (Johnson, 1972, p.10). As such, it becomes a profession by socially transcending other occupations which involve and depend on mechanistic or rule-based processes rather than expert judgments (Bledstein, 1976, p.88); and by establishing itself as an elite group in society due to its unique specialization (in terms of services provided), social separation (created by specialist education and training, and related to status and rewards) (Krause, 1971, p.14; and Larson, 1977, pp.2–3), and a unique linguistic discourse (Goodrich, 1987, p.81). In particular, this position is achieved by establishing a monopolistic control over a defined and systematized body of knowledge (Johnson, 1972, pp.16 and 32; and Larson, 1977, p.212) – or at least by making explicit claims to such knowledge (Hines, 1989b, p.74). Much of this claim is founded on terms (such as 'present fairly' and 'a true and fair view') which have their origins in an authoritarian legal discourse of infinite meaning, and which are therefore impenetrable to those outside the law (Goodrich, 1987, p.176) (or accounting and auditing for that matter).

Such a body of knowledge is to be seen in the form of both financial accounting (the subject of the corporate audit), and corporate auditing (the expert technology brought to bear on the verification of financial accounting data). It is also evidenced more specifically in the published financial reporting standards of accounting regulatory bodies, and the published auditing standards prescribed by similar entities. Indeed, Montagna (1974, pp.9–12) comments on the power and authority given to the accounting profession by stated and generally acceptable accounting principles. And Hines (1989b) argues that conceptual framework projects for financial reporting practice are examples of professional accountants attempting to demonstrate deliberately and explicitly the existence of a defined body of knowledge in order to legitimate themselves as professionals within society. Richardson (1988), on the other hand, evidences the financial rewards and social status achieved by professional accountants when adopting formal education requirements, and ensuring audit practice autonomy.

What these and other writers demonstrate, in the context of a professionalized activity such as corporate auditing, is the well-established relationship between power and knowledge – that is, where there is power, there exists knowledge; and where there is knowledge, there is the exercising of disciplining power. As suggested by social philosophers and historians such as Foucault (1977, pp.170–94), this leads to a conclusion that the possession of knowledge provides a means of disciplining human behaviour in society – not in the sense of physical punishment, but more from the point of view of an intangible, involuntary and, none the less, tyrannical restriction of behaviour.

This suggests an alternative view of corporate auditing – that is, a technical function whereby the profession of accountants can exercise power over individuals and organizations by verifying and attesting the quality of corporate management's accounting representations to shareholders and other report users. The presence and legitimized need for the corporate auditor implies a significant uncertainty about the possible existence of accounting abnormalities in audited financial statements – at least sufficient to create serious doubts about whether or not they are safe for use without audit. The corporate audit also implies that the auditor is competent and objective enough to clarify the uncertainties and remove the doubts.

The ability to provide stability and rationality in a previously unstable and irrational situation by the application of a significant body of knowledge is a powerful position. It is a typical situation with respect to designated professions. It creates calm, and also client dependency with respect to the professional service. By appearing to expertly and objectively remove uncertainty and doubt surrounding the accounting content of corporate financial statements in their unaudited state, the corporate auditor is helping to structure a credible representation of an implied corporate economic reality, and controlling for any inherent uncertainty associated with such an accounting representation. In so doing, the corporate auditor appears to be acting responsibly as the expert able to remove a significant sense of doubt in the mind of the report user so far as financial statement use is concerned. It is in this sense that the corporate audit can be perceived as ritualistic (Mills and Bettner, 1992).

These characteristics of corporate auditing are consistent with more general thinking about the nature and role of professions and professionals – that is, the existence of a profession implies crises needing to be resolved by the professionals concerned (Krause, 1971, p.79); professional knowledge providing rationality to a situation (Johnson, 1972, p.36); professionals dealing and coping with uncertainties (Johnson, 1972, pp.42–4); professionals exercising power through the resolution of such uncertainties (Montagna, 1974, pp.5–6); and professionals invoking potential disaster for their clients unless their services are provided, thereby creating client dependency (Bledstein, 1976, pp.89–90 and 99–100).

The corporate audit function can therefore be viewed as a professionalized activity conducted with the intention of occupational control and monopoly of service (Johnson, 1972, pp.45 and 52). Corporate auditors are seen as the custodians of a specialist body of knowledge called corporate auditing, and possession of that body of knowledge is interpretable as a form of social control (Larson, 1977, p.227). Auditors are perceived (by means of regulation particularly) as the only professionals who can practise the expertise which is embedded in the body of knowledge. This is further argued to breed public submission and passivity with respect to the exercising of such expertise (Bledstein, 1976, p.104). The corporate auditor's position as an expert in an area of uncertainty is not challenged. Indeed, the opposite is the case. There is both consent and compliance that he or she, as the professional, is the only person who can be entrusted with dealing with the uncertainty concerned (Larson, 1977, p.227). The success of the accounting profession in this regard is evidenced by the almost universal regulatory requirement for suitably qualified professional accountants to act as corporate auditors.

Altruism, the public interest and the corporate auditor

The corporate auditor is therefore observed as a skilled expert exercising competence in a designated body of knowledge acquired by means of a self-regulated education and training programme provided by a professional body. This competence gives corporate auditors social authority (Larson, 1977, p.231), in the sense that it sets them apart, and legitimates their technical actions on behalf of their client company and the public. In particular, corporate auditors in their role as competent professionals covenant to put their audit expertise to best use in the public domain on behalf of the immediate beneficiaries of their audit service, such as shareholders and other external financial report users. As mentioned earlier in this text, corporate financial statements are a form of public good, and the corporate auditor's report on their quality must be interpreted as also in the public domain. Thus, as professionals generally, and as corporate auditors particularly, they are expected to place their duty to serve the public interest above all other interests. The conflict for the auditor in this respect is balancing the public interest with self-interest (Montagna, 1974, pp.4–5), or at least not allowing the social and economic pressures of self-interest to dominate public duty.

More specifically, corporate auditors are in business to earn a living as competent professional attesters of the quality of published corporate financial statements. As such, they are concerned to act in the public interest, but they also have to consider their self-interest in the sense of maintaining their economic well-being. They would not be acting rationally in an economic sense unless this was so. Whenever corporate auditors accept an audit assignment, they assume a business risk – that is, they may lose their corporate client because of the latter's financial failure as a consequence of their audit actions (for example, an unfavourable audit opinion on the financial statements may lead to investment or debt activity which precipitates failure); or because of managerial disagreement or dissatisfaction with their audit service (for example, with regard to the disclosure of material information or explanations in the financial statements). In addition, corporate auditors always face the possibility of inadequate audit work leading to a successful lawsuit for damages against them. Thus, when corporate auditors are undertaking their audits, it is inevitable that matters relating to their business risk may influence their audit decisions and judgments – especially in situations when they are in disagreement with corporate management over particulars concerning the content of the audited financial statements. Whatever the business risk, however, the corporate auditor is presumed (rightly or wrongly) to put these behind public duty and expected altruism as a professional.

Whether the corporate auditor in practice is typically acting in a way consistent with the above professional specification is open to debate. Recent corporate failures in both the US and the UK have caused the role of the corporate auditor as a competent and caring individual in society to be brought into sharp focus. Indeed, there is a growing critical literature which suggests that the audit profession may not be acting in terms of its implicit covenant with society regarding the public interest. Instead, it is alleged, economic self-interest, and a natural alliance with corporate management, may be the driving force in audit situations – resulting in audit reports which are inconsistent with the underlying realities inherent in financial statements, specific audit failures to detect and report frauds which are so serious as to eventually lead to corporate failure, and an inevitable loss of auditor independence. Consider the following brief reviews.

Recent situations

Before discussing aspects of the corporate auditor's role in the context of the public interest, it is necessary to focus briefly on the context. In recent years, several major corporate failures have given rise to charges of mismanagement, fraud, poor accounting, and external audit failure. Some of these failures have resulted in court action, but most are pending that process. In any case, the full details of the situation concerned, particularly regarding audit failure, may never be known as settlements out of court appear to be a favoured strategy by the audit firms concerned. In the US, for example, there is a continuing legal process involving corporate auditors and the banking failures in the Savings and Loan industry; and large audit firms are settling for very large out-of-court damages in failed company situations (as with Coopers and

Lybrand and the MiniScribe Corporation). In the UK, the position is no different (for example, the settlement with Ferranti International), and potential litigation in cases such as Polly Peck, Bank of Commerce and Credit International, and Maxwell Communications suggest that the audit profession is under siege.

Desecrated covenant

Briloff (1990, p.7) accuses the audit profession particularly of failing to honour its implicit covenant with society regarding protection of the public interest. In the context of the US position, he castigates accounting practitioners, educators and standard-setters for this failure (pp.23–8). Willmott (1990, p.327) rationalizes this by suggesting that accountants have sustained this type of criticism in the past because of a lack of public accountability for their actions which focuses their attention on maintaining a status quo. Fogarty, Heian and Knutson (1991) discuss this lack of professional response within an institutional framework, in which there is no incentive to change because the benefits of a professional monopoly (such as corporate auditing) outweigh the costs of litigation (p.221). Instead, professional accountants can be seen to do 'nothing' whilst creating an image of compliance and potential crisis (p.222).

Doing 'nothing'

Paradoxically, the strategy of doing 'nothing' does involve doing 'something'. Sikka, Willmott and Lowe (1989) catalogue a number of UK corporate failures in recent years which have been investigated by government regulators who are members of the accountancy profession which is criticized for poor practice in their findings. This closed system, in which corporate auditors set their own audit standards, and then judge these standards on behalf of the state, gives rise to a suspicion that the audit profession may be content to do nothing about its so-called failures (p.65). In this respect, Gaa (1991, p.103) regards the relationship between auditors and the regulators of auditing as a strategic and political game to determine a mutually agreeable level of audit regulation. Willmott (1991, p.119) analyses the situation differently, believing that the institutionalized history of the principal–agent relationship has determined the present situation which is concerned with regulations being in place to maintain the privileged position in society of the principal–owners. Bynington and Sutton (1991), on the other hand, see the present audit situation as one in which the audit profession provides a public perception of meeting societal expectations regarding its role whilst, in reality, attempting to maintain its self-regulating monopolistic position (pp.327–8). Alternatively, Hooks (1992) argues that altruism and self-interest are not necessarily incompatible in explaining audit behaviour, both being capable of contributing to social welfare (p.129).

Whether these analyses of the role of the corporate auditor are correct is not the main issue in this text. What is of concern is the apparent position of a recognized and well-rewarded profession apparently in conflict with its public covenant. Such a covenant is implicit in the explanations of the role, objectives and postulates of corporate auditing in this and previous chapters. It is therefore important, in light of the above criticisms, to have an understanding of the main ideas which support corporate auditing in practice, and which are presently under such public scrutiny. Chapters 7, 8, 9 and 10 deal with these concepts in turn.

Further reading

R.K. Mautz and H.A. Sharaf (1961) *The Philosophy of Auditing*, American Accounting Association, pp.37–52 (the original formulation of audit postulates).

D. Flint (1988) *Philosophy and Principles of Auditing*, Macmillan, pp.19–41 (a combination of the postulates of Mautz and Sharaf (1961) and Lee (1972)).

H. Willmott (1990) Serving the public interest? A critical review of a professional claim, in D.J. Cooper and T.M. Hopper (eds), *Critical Accounts*, Macmillan, pp.315–31 (a critical examination of the auditor as a professional, with particular reference to the public interest versus self-interest issue).

Discussion and essay topics

1. Why study the postulates of corporate auditing? Explain what they are and the role they are used in by theorists.
2. Compare and contrast the audit postulates of Mautz and Sharaf with those of Flint and Lee.
3. Explain the justifying postulates of corporate auditing. What are they justifying?
4. Discuss the behavioural postulates of corporate auditing. Whose behaviour do they relate to?
5. To what aspects of the corporate audit function do the functional postulates relate?
6. Prepare a commentary on the corporate auditor as a professional person providing a needed service.

7

An independent corporate audit

Underlying the previous descriptions and explanations of the corporate audit is a general expectation that corporate auditors will act competently and honestly as professional people. In particular, they are expected to use their skills and knowledge relevantly and appropriately on behalf of the audit beneficiaries concerned and, in so doing, prevent their professional judgments and decisions being subjugated by corporate management. As indicated in various parts of this text, corporate managers may not wish their accounting representations to be stated in accordance with required specifications, or for the corporate auditor to state that that accord does not exist. It may consequently attempt to pressurize corporate auditors into compromises over the quality of the financial statements and their opinions on that quality.

Put more specifically, there is a conventional expectation held regarding the societal commitment of the corporate auditors – that is, they will act at all times independent of any interest, including their self-interest (Watts and Zimmerman, 1986, p.315; and Willmott, 1990, p.315). Whether this commitment is honoured or not in practice, it is its perception which underpins the usual prescription of an objective and honest audit assessment of the quality of reported corporate financial statements. These statements are received by shareholders and other corporate report users who are often intellectually and geographically distant from the reporting entity and its management. They depend on the corporate auditor acting not only expertly but also independently. This user dependence is a significant feature of the implied covenant which the corporate auditor enters into as a professional person providing a specialist service which impacts a variety of corporate constituents. This situation can be described in terms of agency and probabilities. The corporate auditor is acting as an independent agent for shareholder–principals by monitoring the accounting actions of managerial agents. In such a relationship, there exists a probability of the corporate auditor discovering accounting abnormalities created by management. The size of this probability varies according to the degree of competence and independence exercised by the corporate auditors – the more competent and independent they are with respect to discovering accounting abnormalities, the higher the probability of discovering and reporting them to shareholders and other interested corporate constituents.

A doubt, however, exists that, because of self-interest and despite their competence, corporate auditors will not act independently, and will not report on accounting abnormalities. An economic agency counter-argument to this is that corporate auditors have an incentive to be independent because there are economic consequences for them of not being independent when they are in disagreement with corporate management. In particular, the reputational effect of bending to managerial pressure could damage or reduce potential long-term economic rewards, even though such unprofessional action provides them with short-term financial benefits. In other words, not only is acting in the public interest beneficial to social welfare, it is also essential to the corporate auditor's personal welfare (Hooks, 1992, p.129).

Accountability, competence and honesty

As previously argued, the corporate audit has a major aim of enhancing the accountability of corporate management. In particular, as Flint (1988, p.57) concludes, it fulfils a societal function by bringing management to the point of accountability with ownership. It is a social mechanism by which corporate management is provided with an incentive to provide truthful accounting representations of the economic consequences of its actions on behalf of shareholders and other constituents. Indeed, it can be argued that corporate management will not report truthfully to shareholders and others (and thereby serve its short-term economic self-interest) if there appears to be no means by which the truthfulness of its financial reports can be determined and made public (Ng and Stoeckenius, 1979, pp.10–11). However, it can also be concluded that an expert and independent audit on behalf of shareholders and others is an authoritative attempt to compensate for any limitations in an otherwise unaudited corporate accountability process.

The requirement for and provision of a corporate audit signals a constitutional separation of the corporate auditor from the reporting company and its management (Flint, 1988, p.55). It also communicates the existence of a gap between shareholder–principals and their agent managers – a gap which, in the absence of the expertise and independence of the corporate auditor, leaves shareholders and other potential report users uncertain as to the quality of the reported financial statements; and provides management with at least an opportunity to report at a level of sub-standard quality. The size of this gap is not uniform. It varies from situation to situation, depending on such matters as the size of the reporting company and its shareholder community (the larger the latter is, the greater the gap is likely to be); and the degree to which the company is publicly owned (the more public it is, the greater the probability of a gap existing). Indeed, in practice, the need for corporate auditing appears to be positively associated with the size and public nature of the corporate organization (Page, 1991a, pp.212–13).

Audit theorists appear to be agreed that, so far as independence is concerned, much depends on the competence and honesty of the individual corporate auditor in a complex agency situation. For example, Flint (1988) writes of the fundamental importance of the technical and professional competence of the auditor (p.58), combined with professional probity or integrity (p.64). This linkage of professional virtues is emphasized by Schandl (1978, p.192) as objectivity and competence, and hypothesized by Watts and Zimmerman (1986, p.31) as competence and independence. Moizer (1991, p.35), on the other hand, concentrates on technical competence as a separable characteristic of the auditor.

However, despite this apparent consensus, little has been written on the reasons why it is expected that the corporate auditor will act competently and honestly. In this text it is argued to be insufficient to say that competence and independence are expected. These characteristics must also exist in practice if the corporate audit is to be meaningful in the sense of protecting shareholders and other legitimate report users from poor quality accounting information from corporate management. And, to exist, there have to be sufficient incentives for the corporate auditor to meet any prior expectations.

As suggested briefly above, incentives for the corporate auditor to act competently and independently can be examined in both economic and sociological terms. In particular, they are related to the economic consequences of auditor incompetence and dishonesty, and the connected effects on their social status as self-regulating professionals. The following paragraphs reveal reasons to explain why the corporate auditor attempts to act competently and independently in an agency situation involving a very clear potential moral hazard. In other words, they attempt to explain why, despite a situation in which the corporate auditor and management can collude to misrepresent the reported financial consequences of managerial actions, there appear to be incentives to prevent such collusion occurring (Antle, 1984, pp.17–18; and Watts and Zimmerman, 1986, p.315).

Incentives for auditor competence and independence

One argument regarding the competence and independence of corporate auditors focuses on the position that they are rational economic people who will act as auditors in such a way that they do nothing to impair their long-term economic well-being. In this sense, the argument is a simple one based on economics rather than morality. It suggests that, if economic sanctions from lack of independence are sufficient, the auditor will tend to resist the pressures of management (DeAngelo, 1981).[1]

As explained previously, corporate auditors are professional people charged with a social duty of protecting their clients and other corporate constituents from any malpractices of a designated managerial agent. They are therefore expected to be economically self-interested, but also to be committed to act independently of any sectional interest (including self-interest). This bilateral functioning provides a conflict for corporate auditors, requiring careful attention if their audit services are to be useful to their beneficiaries, and also economically and socially rewarding to them.

One fundamental problem for corporate auditors is that, if they are in conflict with corporate management concerning the quality of its accounting representations to shareholders, and attention is drawn to this conflict in their audit report, they run the considerable risk of damaging their economic well-being by losing the client company (and, possibly, other potential clients) at some future date (Watts and Zimmerman,

1986, p.316). By insisting on an accounting change, or by modifying their audit opinions to reflect the disagreement, they may satisfy their social duty as professionals but damage themselves economically. News of this situation may also cause other actual and potential corporate audit clients to move elsewhere to avoid an apparently difficult auditor. This compounds the initial economic loss of the original corporate client. Corporate auditors could therefore be tempted under such circumstances to serve their self-interest to the detriment of their social duty.

One counter to such temptation is that, although the corporate auditor may benefit economically in the short term by compromising independence and retaining a corporate client, in the longer term (due to reputational effects) the economic loss may well exceed the earlier short-term gain (Antle, 1984, p.18; and Watts and Zimmerman, 1986, p.315–16). The reputation of the corporate auditor for not exercising independence in matters of disagreement with management may become public knowledge, and this may have the effect of reducing individual and total demand for his or her audit services (Antle, 1984, p.18), or cause the state to interfere with or substitute the self-regulating audit profession (Moizer, 1991, p.38) (resulting in a significant loss of fee income as the price of audit services diminishes).

It can also be argued that corporate auditors will carry out whatever audit work is necessary to get them to the point at which they feel they have reduced the probability of a successful law suit for negligent work to an acceptable level – this point varying according to the auditors' perception of their risk and return in each situation (Moizer, 1991, pp.36–7). Indeed, they may also wish to perform at an above-average level of professional competence and honesty in order to secure a public knowledge of these attributes and, consequently, a public reputation justifying higher-than-average audit fees in the longer term (Moizer, 1991, p.37).

There therefore appear to be arguments suggesting that the position of potential moral hazard in which corporate auditors find themselves is not necessarily one in which loss of independence and short-term economic gain will prevail. Indeed, these arguments suggest that economically rational corporate auditors should take the longer-term view and preserve their independence in order to maximize, first, their reputation as competent and honest professionals and, second, their fee income. Indeed, as Moizer (1991, p.39) points out, there is a more general argument which states that the corporate auditor will always act independently in a state of enlightened self-interest involving a necessary balancing of public and self-interests (p.40; see also Hooks, 1992).

Watts and Zimmerman (1986, pp.316–18) support this view when they suggest that corporate auditors attempt to obtain enhancing reputational effects by means of a variety of mechanisms – for example, membership of recognized professional societies which regulate their professional behaviour (thereby presenting a public image that, if they act unprofessionally as auditors, they will be punished by exclusion from membership, and therefore lose the right to practise as corporate auditors); offering their audit services as partners in firms with unlimited liability (suggesting that, if sued successfully for not acting competently or independently, they will not only lose their right to practise as corporate auditors, but will also lose all or part of their personal as well as professional capital); and merging audit firms to achieve an economic size and public presence such that the firm name becomes a brand name (thus assisting to create a greater market share of available corporate audit services with a public position of independence).

A difficulty with the above thoughts and statements is that they are theoretical arguments rather than empirically tested and proven hypotheses. In particular, they do not say whether corporate auditors behave in this way in practice in order to meet the stated expectation of independence. For example, corporate auditors have to consider a risk factor other than the audit risk they assume when determining the quantity and quality of audit evidence they require in order to properly support their audit opinions on the quality of reported financial statements. Instead, and especially in situations in which they are in disagreement with corporate management over such reporting quality, they also have to consider their personal business risk – that is, the possible economic consequences of being sued successfully for incompetent or managerially-dependent work weighed against the chances of losing the audit engagement by publicly disagreeing with management.

This situation for corporate auditors can be expressed in terms of a simple relationship – the higher auditors perceive their business risk, the greater the probability of modifying their audit report with respect to the subject of disagreement or conflict. Contemporary evidence to support it is presently circumstantial. As mentioned previously in this text, there have recently been a number of very large corporate failures in the US, the UK and elsewhere which, pending court decisions, have caused commentators to question the independence of the auditors concerned. It would be inappropriate at this stage to second-guess the precise details of these situations – that is, until such time as the legal process publicly records the actions of the corporate auditors concerned. However, publicly stated disquiet about the independence of corporate auditors is a matter of literature record, and the reader is invited to investigate these concerns in the context of the broad independence principles enunciated in this chapter.

In particular, the US position can be examined in writings such as Briloff (1990), and the UK situation in the Mitchell *et al.* (1991) study. In doing so, however, the reader is reminded that, in many of these significant corporate failures in recent times, the corporate audit firm elects to settle for damages out of court – thus preventing its role in the affair becoming public knowledge. In this respect, such action can be construed as consistent with the general economic agency argument. The corporate auditor's long-term economic well-being could be damaged by the reputational effect of a known lack of independence. Thus, given a corporate failure and the short-term loss of a client, the cost of preventing such knowledge becoming public, by settling out of court, may be perceived by the corporate auditor to outweigh the long-term economic consequences of loss of reputation.

The possible consequences of these conclusions are considerable but complex. They could mean that, contrary to their implied societal covenant as professional experts, corporate auditors will consider their personal circumstances before any other. For example, if the financial health of the client company is weak, the auditor may act independently, and modify a report because of a fear that his or her lack of independence will be discovered at a corporate liquidation. On the other hand, the auditor may take the risk of loss of independence, knowing that the cost of an out-of-court settlement justifies the short- and long-term gains from not being publicly found out. Alternatively, and with respect to the size and public visibility of the client company, it can be argued that the smaller and less visible it is, the less independent and truthful in reporting the corporate auditor will be because the probability of being found out is small.

If these arguments are sound *vis-à-vis* corporate auditor competence and independence, they cause the corporate audit function, report and auditor to be viewed very differently from the conventional expectation of professionalism generally and independence specifically. Instead, the corporate auditor's report could not be trusted to be formulated either competently or independently, unless the company concerned is either very large, with considerable public visibility, or is financially unhealthy. Even then, settling out of court to avoid reputational effects prevents the corporate auditor's independence from being determined (as distinct from being questioned). And, for situations involving less than large and/or healthy companies, there would always exist a doubt concerning the independence of the corporate auditor.

The nature of corporate auditor independence

The above discussion of corporate auditor independence is relatively silent on the nature of the concept – except to suggest it concerns a human characteristic of the auditor and, specifically, the objectivity and honesty of judgments in corporate audit situations involving agency relationships between the auditor, management and shareholders. This restriction is relaxed in this section in order to provide a more complete understanding of the concept.

Corporate auditor independence is usually thought of and described as practitioner independence – that is, it is articulated in terms of the objectivity with which the corporate auditor approaches an audit situation as a professional practitioner, and how he or she copes with the gathering, evaluation and reporting on audit evidence in an unbiased way (Mautz and Sharaf, 1961, p.205). It is also traditionally perceived as a state of mind, in the sense of the corporate auditor's attitude to relationships with corporate management, shareholders, and other legitimate users of corporate financial statements (Mautz and Sharaf, 1961, p.206). Thus, in every corporate audit situation, there is a persistent question as to whether or not the auditor has been mentally independent of management, and of the pressures the latter can exercise when the auditor is making audit decisions. Flint (1988, pp.59–61) concurs with this view of the typical audit situation, describing auditor independence as a mental attitude, and further aligning it to the personal qualities of probity and strength of character (p.64).

But ascribing to the concept of auditor independence an intangible mental quality makes it also a relatively ambiguous term which is difficult to interpret in relation to the work of the corporate auditor. In particular, it is exceedingly difficult to give operational meaning to what is essentially a state of mind, and in a situation where the auditor is intellectually and geographically distant from the audit beneficiaries who are relying on his or her independence. However, at least there is a general agreement that independence is an attitude of mind which does not allow the viewpoints or conclusions of the corporate auditor to become reliant on or subordinate to the influences and pressures of conflicting interests. Corporate auditors must remain vigilant to counteract or avoid any influences and pressures which could impair or damage their impartiality, and thereby reduce the objectivity expected and relied on in their audit actions. They must remain true to their professional code of ethics and, particularly, they must at all times be honest.

In this sense, the expected independence of the corporate auditor can be perceived as not only a predicated state of mind, but also a public statement of assurance relating to the behaviour of a professional person, and of various possible pressures and influences on that person's integrity and honesty (Schandl, 1978, p.193). Consequently, it is essential to presume that corporate auditors are free from the influence of these pressures; that there are means of assisting them to withstand them; and that the expected position of independence can be sustained (Flint, 1988, p.60).

The appearance of corporate auditor independence

As indicated above, expectations of a state of mind are not ideal bases on which to place the trust and confidence of shareholders and other interested report users with respect to the corporate auditor's honesty in formulating an audit opinion. Indeed, it can be argued that it is far too intangible a quality to be the only aspect of corporate auditor independence which should be emphasized. The corporate auditor may be independent in thought and action, but it is only in rare circumstances that this can be seen to occur. In most situations not involving audit disputations which are reported to shareholders and other external constituents, there is little or no evidence to signal whether or not corporate auditors have avoided pressures on their independence and professional neutrality. Thus, as well as being mentally independent, it is also necessary that they are seen to be independent by means of explicit and public signals that this is so. At the very least, they ought to be in a position which effectively demonstrates they are capable of withstanding pressures against their independent state of mind. The confidence of shareholders and others in the honesty of corporate auditors and their reports is likely to be focused on these visible signals of their independence, rather than their relatively hidden state of mind.

The appearance of corporate auditor independence is usually taken to mean a physical positioning with the client company and its management. The ideal position is one in which the corporate auditor is completely isolated from every situation likely to be perceived as possibly jeopardizing the mental state of objectivity and impartiality. Unfortunately, the reality of a typical corporate audit is such that this state cannot be achieved without some compromise. For example, in order to conduct their audits, corporate auditors communicate and work closely with corporate management; and they receive their remuneration and reappointment on the recommendation of management, even though it may be shareholders who vote on such issues (as in the UK). Thus, specific mechanisms have to be put into place in an attempt to create a reasonable public image of independence for the corporate auditor. These mechanisms are explained and discussed in the sections which follow a broad review of the various dimensions of independence.

Alternative dimensions of corporate auditor independence

Mautz and Sharaf (1961, p.205) mention three dimensions to the concept of auditor independence. In particular, the auditor should be independent in thought and deed when, first, planning the audit; second, gathering and evaluating suitable evidence; and third, reporting the results of such activities in the form of an audit opinion. Mautz and Sharaf (1961, pp.230–1) also argue that auditors have to approach the audit with independence, conduct it independently, and provide explicit messages that they have been independent.

The thinking behind these prescriptions is that auditor independence should not be perceived either by the auditor, auditees or audit beneficiaries as a condition which relates only to the dimension of audit verification. Instead, it must be conceived as a condition which pervades every aspect of audit preparation, action and report. Auditor independence is all-embracing. It has to exist at all times, and on every occasion, if the credibility of the corporate audit process is to be maintained, and if the required qualities of the audited financial statements are to be confidently relied on by their potential users. In other words, *vis-à-vis* the audit function, auditor independence is a multi-dimensional concept.

Regulating for corporate auditor independence

The appearance of corporate auditor independence is achieved by a number of different regulatory mechanisms in practice. These regulations, which attempt to provide an image of independence for corporate auditors, and thus give confidence to those individuals who are the beneficiaries of their audit opinions, can be divided into two main categories – each dependent on the specific environment of corporate and professional regulation which is prevalent.

The first category relates to individual provisions which operationalize the corporate auditor's verification function. They are usually found in corporate legislation (or similar formal state regulations), or in the voluntary internal regulations of the corporate audit client. The second category deals specifically with corporate auditors and their expected behaviour as professional people. These provisions are typically contained in formal codes of ethics issued to members of bodies of professional accountants who are employed as auditors of corporate organizations. It is not the purpose of this text to spell out in detail the particular provisions on corporate auditor independence which are currently contained in various laws and codes, and which can change from time to time. Instead, it is useful to describe them in very general terms in this and the next section of the text, leaving the reader to investigate particular details which pertain to the individual corporate environment of which he or she is a part (see, for example, AICPA, 1991, pp.17, 4321, and 4411–20; and Securities and Exchange Commission, 1984 for the current US position; and ICAS, 1992 and Companies Act, 1985, Chapter V for the equivalent UK position).

The first broad group of possible auditor independence provisions deals with the extent to which the corporate auditor is free of corporate management in the context of administrative situations such as initial appointment, re-appointment, removal and replacement, resignation and remuneration. Typically in these situations, as for example in the UK, regulatory provisions are in place to control these matters. In particular, it is usual to require that shareholders approve any prior management decision or recommendation to them. If corporate regulation does not require this, then, as in the US, the corporate audit client's internal regulations may require any managerial recommendations on the appointment, etc. of its auditor to be approved by its non-executive board of directors or its shareholders.

If such mandatory or voluntary regulations are in place, they can be argued to permit corporate auditors to make known to the shareholders any views or statements they have concerning their appointment, dismissal or remuneration. They can do so without reference to corporate management, and before any vote on the matter. Such views can be given in writing or in person at an appropriate shareholder meeting. However, in practice, the reality is that the company's senior executive managers make the decisions regarding the auditor's appointment, remuneration and dismissal. Shareholders either are also the managers concerned (in smaller entities) or they are too distant from the company to object seriously to managerial recommendations on these matters (as in public entities). Thus, it should not be supposed that internal or external regulations, of themselves, create a situation in which the corporate auditor is protected from the direct or more subtle pressures of management to lose expected objectivity and impartiality.

Regulations can also exist with respect to giving corporate auditors effective independence by means of right of access to evidence they regard as necessary to their audit opinions. Such provisions, as in current UK corporate legislation, are designed to prevent corporate management from restricting the scope of the audit and, therefore, the opinions of corporate auditors. They attempt to free corporate auditors from the more obvious pressures which can compromise their independence. They constitute the regulatory licence which allows corporate auditors to undertake their duties and achieve their objectives without unjustified interference by management. However, as stated previously, such regulations can only create an environment for corporate auditor independence. They cannot guarantee it. Once given access to evidential material, complete independence can only exist if the corporate auditor is committed personally as a professional expert to act independently in all phases of his or her work.

A further and recent indicator of regulated corporate auditor independence is the professional requirement, as in the US, that the auditor provide an explicit expression of independence. Such a message appears as a heading in auditors' reports to shareholders, in which they describe themselves as independent. Of itself, this does not signal that independence has existed at all times and in all situations during the audit. Instead, its intention is purely one of providing an explicit reminder that the audit report has been prepared independently by a professional expert in accounting matters.

Regulations of professional accountancy bodies also usually require their members acting as corporate auditors to communicate with their successors on the occasion of a change in audit appointment. The idea is to provide an appearance of independence in which both the old and the new auditor is in a position to know as much about the situation as possible without interference by corporate management. For example, the outgoing corporate auditor may be in dispute with management. Despite pressures on independence because of the potential economic consequences of losing the audit, the auditor has not conformed to management's position. The details of the dispute, however, can be made explicit in a communication of events to the incoming auditor. And knowing these details, that person can then decide whether or not to take up the new appointment. Thus, the corporate auditor can communicate and have heard his or her version of events independently of corporate management. This reinforces the usual legal expectation of the corporate auditor being directly responsible to shareholders, irrespective of the proximity with which he or she has to work with corporate management in order to complete the audit function meaningfully.

Regulatory prohibitions and auditor independence

In addition to the aforementioned regulations and provisions with the capacity to allow the corporate auditor freedom to exercise independence, there may be others which are also intended to enhance the portrayal of this position. These relate to specific prohibitions concerning the relationships which corporate auditors can or cannot have with their client companies. As with all such regulations, they do not guarantee that they will be independent, for that is a matter of how they think and act in a particular situation. Instead, they are directed at providing explicit assurance that they are not in a position where their integrity can be questioned. If put in place, the prohibitions are consistent with the prescription of several theorists that there must be no unnecessary relationships which might detract from the corporate auditor's objectivity and impartiality (Lee, 1986, pp.91–5; Flint, 1988, pp.63–72; and Moizer, 1991, pp.41–5).

One of the most important of these prohibiting provisions states that corporate auditors cannot also be managerial officers of the companies they are auditing. The underlying principle at work here is that corporate auditors must not be in a position where they are verifying and attesting the quality of accounting representations of managerial activity in which they have an interest or for which they have a responsibility. If the corporate auditor is permitted to be a manager–producer of financial statements, as well as their verifier and attester, there can be no certainty for shareholders and other report users as to the reliability of either the accounting representations in the statements or the processes related to their verification. This prohibition can also extend to situations in which a former auditor is employed as an executive of a client company. In this case, the former firm should not act as auditor, particularly when the executive continues to have a financial interest in it.

A second example of provisions with the capacity to protect the appearance of auditor independence concerns professional provisions regarding the corporate auditor's fee income, and any undue dependence on an audit client. An individual fee may well be a significant proportion of the auditor's total income. Under such circumstances, there is an obvious danger of the auditor being perceived as too dependent on particular fees from individual clients – that is, of not being independent of a client company because of the economic consequences of losing the fee when in dispute with its management. Professional provisions (as in the UK) usually prescribe that no corporate audit fee may constitute more than a stated percentage of the auditor's total income.

A third professional prohibition relates to delimiting the potential effects on auditor independence of personal relationships they may have within the organizational structures of client companies. Such personal relationships endanger the appearance of auditor independence. For example, corporate auditors, or members of their staff, may be related to individual members of their client companies' management and workforce. Thus, unless specifically prohibited, and despite the corporate auditor being prevented by specific regulation from being employed other than as the auditor of the company, his or her spouse, children and other relations could be employed by it. For this reason, it is important to avoid any relationship which has the potential to harm the appearance of independence because of misperceptions of it by audit beneficiaries. If specific professional provisions do not exist in this area, it is common to find that individual audit partners and their firms adopt an appropriate voluntary code of practice.

The next area of potential concern regarding the image of independence relates to the existence of financial interests held by the corporate auditor. If the corporate auditor, or members of his or her staff, have financial interests in a client company, there is a significant loss of apparent independence. Indeed, there is the possibility of the corporate auditor being perceived as mentally influenced by such interests during the audit. For example, the nature of the audit opinion on the quality of the reported financial statements could influence the market valuation of shares he or she held in the company. Other examples of such conflicting financial interests include loans to and from such entities; and trading activities where the corporate auditor is a customer or supplier of the company. Professional provisions on these matters are generally universal in terms of the nature and direction of the prohibition. That is, partners and staff (and close relations of any of these individuals) are either prohibited or discouraged from holding shares in a client company, should not usually lend to or borrow from a client company, and should also avoid trading with it where at all possible.

Management services and auditor independence

There is a further situation involving the corporate auditor and the client company which can be construed as having a potential effect on the appearance and reality of independence. This concerns management services offered and given to a corporate client by its auditor. If the auditor provides, or could provide, such non-audit services to an audit client, the question is whether he or she is capable of being independent in the audit for fear of losing or not gaining the additional services and the related fee income.

There are solutions which have been prescribed to cope with this situation. For example, one extreme would be to ensure, by means of regulation, that such a conflict could not arise. Corporate auditors would be allowed to provide only audit services, and would therefore decline audit appointments in any company for which they are working in some other capacity. Alternatively, corporate auditors could be prohibited or recommended to limit their non-attest managerial services to those of a non-executive or non-accounting nature.

Generally, however, existing professional guidance on this matter is either very weak or non-existent. The reality is that such conflicts of interest exist for almost all corporate auditors in practice. The typical situation is therefore one of dependence on them to act prudently as professional accountants. It leaves them to judge how best they can avoid the potential conflict. This is despite the almost universal impression given by professional accountancy bodies world-wide that they would prefer the corporate auditor not to provide multiple services to audit clients (for example, AICPA, 1991, p.17; and ICAS, 1992, p.6).

The provision of management services by the corporate auditor, and the economic consequences of banning their provision, can be substantial. Arguments can be made that the integrity of corporate auditors, and their verification and attest functions, are not impaired because they can remain mentally independent as professional people. However, from the perspective of the appearance of auditor independence, an opposite argument exists. If the corporate auditor is involved in activities which impinge on the subject-matter of the audit, and/or there is a possibility of losing additional non-attest services if the auditor is in disagreement with the client management, there is a clear impression that objectivity in the audit situation could be impaired.

It is reasonably clear that a universal concern exists over this issue. But, as stated previously, professional bodies have been either reluctant or unable to prescribe on the matter, and the result is that individual corporate auditors are left to judge each situation on its merits and according to their personal preferences. Meantime, there is an unease, which occasionally is made public, that corporate auditors can only be truly independent if all matters of conflict are removed from their portfolio of activity. In this regard, it has to be remembered that the public, generally, and audit beneficiaries, particularly, do not necessarily have the detailed knowledge and understanding necessary to perceive the organizational separations which are possible in audit firms to allow for the co-existence of audit and non-attest services. In this context, it does not matter to what extent individual corporate auditors are assumed to be independent when they conduct their audits. External interests have no means of looking into either their minds or their organizational structure. Thus, the need to continue to review and discuss this issue is paramount if an existing expectations gap is not to be perpetuated, and if the value of the corporate audit is to be maximized by those who depend on it *vis-à-vis* the use of reported financial statements.

Auditor independence and the shareholders

One further issue ought to be discussed about the concept of corporate auditor independence, and that is the relationship of the corporate auditor to shareholders. The legal position is quite clear and universal in nature. The primary responsibility of the corporate auditor is to shareholders in the context of an agency situation – the auditor as agent acting on behalf of the shareholders as principal. However, corporate financial statements are a matter of public record and, as previously mentioned, can be interpreted as a public good in the sense that many individuals other than shareholders can use their informational messages. Thus, the corporate auditor can be argued to have a duty of care, including independence of mind and deed, well beyond the shareholder group.

This particular issue has not been directly addressed in regulatory provisions affecting the conduct of the corporate audit. Indeed, the usual approach in audit regulations is to conform to the principal–agent relationship between the shareholders and the corporate auditor, and to frame provisions affecting auditor independence within the context of that approach. Each of the areas of concern discussed previously is predicated on this basis. Thus, the need for the corporate auditor to be independent in mind and action *vis-à-vis* all groups of potential audit beneficiaries is usually unstated, but must be recognized if the general accountability objective of the corporate audit is to be achieved.

The concept of corporate auditor independence can therefore be extended further to cover a multiplicity of corporate situations. This is done by simplistically studying the relationship of the corporate auditor to the client company in terms of relative sizes of the organizations involved. For example, in the first situation, both the client company and its auditor are small organizations. Every fee earned by the auditor is critical to his or her economic survival, and the potential loss through disputation with the client is a serious matter. In addition, the corporate auditor in this situation builds a relationship with the client akin to that of a family doctor or lawyer. He or she provides other non-attest services, and works closely and directly with the managers who are usually also the shareholders. Thus, there are obvious pressures acting against the auditor's independence. But it can be argued that this is unimportant because of the relative lack of other audit beneficiaries. However, despite the smallness of the situation, there are beneficiaries other than shareholders (for example, bankers providing finance to the company), and they are entitled to assume that the auditor has thought and acted independently at all times.

At the other end of the organizational size scale, there is a situation where the client company is a very large entity and its auditor is also very large. Here it might be safely assumed that the size relativity concerned is such that corporate auditor independence is guaranteed. However, even in this case, there are circumstances which exist and act against independence, and which require to be recognized and resolved. For example, the company's external interests are bound to be both multifarious and physically remote from its activities and day-to-day management. It is therefore crucial that the corporate auditor is not only independent in mind and deed, but also that the image of this is projected reasonably to all external constituents. In addition, the very largeness of the client company creates independence issues for the corporate auditor. The economic consequences of not retaining the audit engagement are very material, not just in the sense of the absolute and considerable amount of fees to be derived from audit and other non-attest services they may provide, but also because of the reputational effects which the loss of the audit can have. Other actual or potential corporate clients may be unwilling to employ an auditor who is seen to be in serious dispute with a client. Such a view, if operationalized, will have significant repercussions on the long-term economic well-being of the corporate auditor. The large corporate audit also becomes increasingly a continuous work activity for the corporate auditor, involving an almost permanent working relationship with corporate management to be effective. To do the audit work required to support the audit opinion in a very large client situation, audit staff become almost part of daily corporate operations, and thus lose their image of objectivity.

These selected examples of potential impairment to corporate auditor independence are positions of extremes regarding relative organizational size and relationship. However, for any of the intermediate situations (large company and small auditor; or small company and large auditor), there exist similar pressures on independence – although to a lesser or greater degree depending on the specifics of the situation. Whatever the case, however, it appears to be mainly the appearance of corporate auditor independence which is in initial doubt. This is all that most external audit beneficiaries can hope to be able to judge, as they cannot enter the auditor's mind, and they certainly are not in a position to monitor personally his or her audit actions. It is therefore vital that corporate auditors' appearance of independence is not in question, and that all audit beneficiaries are confident that they can act objectively. It is also important to have various regulations attempting to provide this atmosphere of universal report user confidence in the corporate auditor's objectivity. Such regulations, however, only help to create a situation which will allow corporate auditors to cope with pressures acting against their independence. They cannot be regarded as a substitute for the personal integrity and honesty which is such an essential part of professional behaviour.

Recent corporate situations and auditor independence

The corporate auditor's personal integrity and honesty is currently under intense public scrutiny. As the previous sections have attempted to emphasize, the expectation is that the corporate auditor will act independently at all times. This is expressed well in the following US auditing standard (AICPA, 1991, p.17):

> It is of the utmost importance to the profession that the general public maintain confidence in the independence of independent auditors. Public confidence would be impaired by evidence that independence was actually lacking, and it might also be impaired by the existence of circumstances which reasonable people might believe likely to influence independence.

Recent events relating to considerable corporate failures in the US, the UK and elsewhere have unfortunately conspired to at least suggest that evidence may exist to refute the corporate auditor's independence in these cases. What must be made clear in this respect is that such 'evidence' is currently no more than a reasonable suspicion. However, the fact that these doubts exist puts the entire credibility of an independent corporate audit at stake. What cannot be denied is that situations such as the Savings and Loans banking failures in the US, and UK crashes such as Polly Peck, Bank of Commerce and Credit International, and Maxwell Communications Corporation, cause a fundamental question to be asked – that is, in light of these failures and previous unqualified audit reports from the auditors concerned, were the latter indeed independent or had they compromised their independence in some way? (see, for example, Briloff, 1990).

A further problem with contemporary corporate auditing is that, for auditor independence to exist, there should be choice for both the auditor and the client company (Murphy, 1991, p.23). The corporate auditor must be free to make an independent audit judgment, and the client must be free to choose an independent auditor. But the persistent concentration of audit firms, and their increasing provision of non-attest services, has reduced these choices to the point at which, when there is corporate failure, there is almost an automatic questioning of auditor independence. And reductions in such choices create arguments to strengthen the corporate auditors' position – that is, to give them teeth in situations in which a lack of financial control and bad accounting are prevalent (Holmes, 1991, pp.30–1; and Hatherley, 1992, p.33).

There is also a clear suspicion that the audit profession organizationally does not respond credibly to the issue of the independence of its members. For example, Sikka, Willmott and Lowe (1989) provide a detailed account of the UK Auditing Standards Board's unwillingness to reveal its standard-setting process, and charge that it was regulating auditing in such a way as to provide audit clients with the accounting flexibility they desire (p.65) – a charge which, if sustainable, brings the practical reality of lack of auditor independence into sharp focus.

Although at this stage the charge may be described as not proven, it is consistent with other critical auditing research. For example, Byington and Sutton (1991, p.327) provide evidence of the accounting profession acting as a professional monopoly by responding to public criticisms and pressures increasingly only when its self-regulating status is at risk. And Fogarty, Heian and Knutson (1991) demonstrate the profession's capacity to mount a public relations exercise in the face of criticism which, in effect does 'nothing', and is consistent with economic rationality. In other words, because of the financial rewards from attest and non-attest services, it makes long-term economic sense for the profession to bear the short-term costs of audit failures.

Proposed solutions for auditor independence

The previous sections suggest that specific regulations and professional provisions are designed to assist in improving the appearance of corporate auditor independence, and thus maintain the credibility of the corporate audit function as a process of organizational accountability. Despite these regulatory aids, however, corporate auditors remain in a practical situation in which pressures exist to impair their judgment and damage or remove their independence. In these circumstances, it is sensible to articulate further suggestions for improving not only the appearance of independence, but also the probability that the corporate auditor will act as an independent professional expert in a given organizational context. It is essential that his or her independence in practice is such that all audit beneficiaries can rely on it without question. On the other hand, the reality of the difficulties of combating pressures which erode it in practice must also be recognized, and continuing efforts must be made to sensibly reduce or remove their potentially harmful effects. In other words, public expectations regarding corporate auditor independence require a response. But any answer must be workable – organizationally, politically, socially and economically.

Basically, what each of the undernoted suggestions attempt to achieve is a multi-dimensional improvement in the environment of the corporate audit, such that the pressures on corporate auditor independence are significantly reduced or disappear. In each case, they relate mainly to appearances, and can do little to guarantee how each corporate auditor will behave in a given set of circumstances.

These proposals are made in addition to existing provisions, and have been described in very general terms earlier in this chapter. They should be read in the context of research findings by Lavin (1976). These suggest (p.49) that, so far as perceptions of expert users of corporate financial statements are concerned, state (for example, the US Securities and Exchange Commission) rulings on positions of auditor independence tend to be more conservative and stringent than those of the self-regulating audit profession (for example, the US AICPA). This conclusion from the mid-1970s is consistent with more recent arguments and evidence that the auditing profession acts as a self-regulating monopoly (Byington and Sutton, 1991).

Goldman and Barlev (1974, pp.716–18) categorize proposals to improve auditor independence in three ways. The first relates to attempts to decrease the potential power of management to pressurize auditors into compromising their objectivity and impartiality; the second is concerned with reducing the opportunity for auditors to lose or diminish their independence by imposing on them specific rules relating to both auditing and financial reporting standards; and the third seeks to adjust the structure of auditors' existing role by, for example, making them public employees with the state as the client, or expanding their explicit clients beyond shareholders to include other interested third parties. The suggestions which are explained below contain varying elements of each of these categories.

Suggestions for regulating corporate auditor independence

In corporate situations where it is possible for the corporate auditor to have financial interests or personal relationships in a client company, it can be argued that these interests and relationships should be banned by specific legislative or regulatory provisions, rather than relying on voluntary or discretionary action. Such interests include direct shareholdings, but could also involve indirect investment through subsidiary company holdings, loans and credit facilities, and even business and domestic transactions. Personal relationships for prohibition would involve connections between audit and client company personnel. Thus, even in situations where professional codes of ethics recommend that financial interests should be banned, and that personal relationships should be avoided or guarded against, this proposal adopts a more stringent policy that the state should proscribe these compromising situations (Sherer and Kent, 1983, p.31; Lee, 1986, p.100; and Moizer, 1991, p.43). The intention of this proposal is to ensure that no financial or personal conflict exists to influence the objectivity of the auditor. If put in place, such a regulation would require corporate auditors to be free of conflicting interests and relationships prior to and following appointment, in much the same way as they are required to be professionally qualified as accountants in order to continue to act as corporate auditors.

An apparently less drastic proposal suggests that the corporate auditor should be required to disclaim an audit opinion if financial interests and personal relationships exist vis-à-vis the client company (Lee, 1986, pp.99–100). That is, if auditors have such interests or relationships, they would not express an opinion because they would not be deemed to be independent. The idea behind this proposal is to permit corporate auditors to have financial interests in or personal relationships with client companies but, at the same time, to prevent them from describing themselves as independent, and from giving independent opinions, if they were unwilling or unable to divest themselves of the interests or relationships.

Other regulatory prohibitions which have been proposed to improve the appearance of corporate auditor independence include a regulatory ban on management services by auditors (Sherer and Kent, 1983, pp.31–2), or at least reporting that they are involved in the provision of such services to an audit client (Schandl, 1978, p.196). As previously stated, non-attest services by the auditor is one of the most vexed problems affecting independence, and these solutions are similar to those discussed above with respect to financial interests and personal relationships – that is, their objective is either to ban or publicly disclose them.

A further regulatory solution to auditor dependence is to limit the size of economic interest in the client company, such that no audit fee can exceed a given percentage of total income (Moizer, 1991, pp.41–2). The purpose of this idea is to formalize existing professional prescriptions to reduce the financial dependence of auditors, and thereby put them in an unambiguous position to resist the pressures of corporate management. However, given the business risks associated with corporate auditing, particularly in terms of potential litigation, such an audit fee restriction must take into account the need to provide professional accountants with sufficient economic incentive to assume the business risk of corporate auditing.

Suggestions which take a regulatory approach to the auditor independence problem have been made in a number of other forms. For example, it is argued that the relatively long-term nature of the corporate audit engagement tends to create an inevitable loss of independence due to a working familiarity with the client's management and staff (particularly in larger audits). For this reason, it is recommended that the audit appointment be rotated periodically in order to prevent these conditions from developing (Sherer and Kent, 1983, p.32; Lee, 1986, p.100; and Moizer, 1991, p.44). However, the advantages of this proposal must be weighed against the costs of investing in repeated audit start-ups.

In similar vein, it is suggested that the corporate auditor's position of independence can be improved if an audit committee is required to be formed – that is, comprising non-executive directors of the client company to whom the auditor could bring audit reports and any matters of conflict with executive management (Goldman and Barlev, 1974, pp.713–14; Sherer and Kent, 1983, pp.32–3; Lee, 1986, p.95; and Hatherley, 1992, p.33). These committees would act as a mandatory filter for any discussion with management over the audit, the audit opinion, and other matters likely to jeopardize auditor independence such as the audit fee (Sherer and Kent, 1983, p.33). Such an idea currently exists on a modest voluntary basis among very large companies, and appears to be reasonably successful (Marrian, 1988, p.32).

The regulatory approach to resolving the problems of auditor independence is extended further with two specific suggestions which take the existing audit function out of the free-market, private-enterprise sector and, instead, place it within the boundaries of the state. The specific proposals are, first, for an audit court (Spacek, 1958b; and Stamp, 1970, pp.119–28 and 168–87); and, second, the audit as a state appointment, including the existence of a state audit board (Lyall and Perks, 1976; Sherer and Kent, 1983, p.33; Lee, 1986, p.99; Moizer, 1991, pp.44–5; Fogarty, Heian and Knutson, 1991, pp.221–2; and Murphy, 1991, p.24).

The audit court proposal is premised on the observation that the auditor's independence has been eroded to such an extent that it is impossible to retain credibility in the situation – even with the various regulatory prohibitions mentioned above to improve the position. Thus, it is proposed that the independent audit judgment be removed from the auditor, and given to a judicial audit court where eminent professional accountants would be appointed as judges to attest the quality of the financial statements. The existing auditor would be relegated to an evidence gatherer, responsible only for presenting the accounting facts to the court for its judgment and opinion.

The other state-orientated proposal concerns the formation of a state audit board. The purpose of such a board would be to take over the existing functions of the professional accountancy bodies with respect to the corporate audit – particularly, the licensing of auditors and the promulgation of auditing standards. As with the idea of a required audit court, this proposal suggests that the debate over auditor independence is irretrievable, and that a fresh start has to be made in which the auditors are put in a position in which they cannot compromise their independence.

Non-regulatory approach to auditor independence

There are a number of other views on auditor independence which take a non-regulatory and, therefore, free-market approach to the problem. They are all concerned with the need for adequate independence on the part of the corporate auditor, but adopt a position that certain non-regulatory mechanisms can either take care of the matter or, at least, have the potential to do so. The first comment is a common-sense one of Goldman and Barlev (1974, p.714) that the discipline of potential legal liability has an important effect on auditor behaviour. They further argue that an extension of the legal relationship between the auditor and audit beneficiaries (specifically, third parties) improves auditor independence. If auditors know they can be sued for negligent work, not just by their primary clients, but also by others who depend on the competency and independence of opinion, they have a strong economic incentive to be both competent and independent. Such a wider audit responsibility is consistent with the self-interest argument of the auditor being able to justify the financial and social rewards associated with an independent professional audit (Gwilliam, 1991, p.71), but inconsistent with current court decisions regarding a strict limitation of the corporate auditor's duty of care (p.68). It is also inconsistent with the conclusion of Fogarty, Heian and Knutson (1991, p.222) that, to date, audit firms have been willing to settle lawsuits at great expense out of court in order to protect their reputation and avoid external scrutiny of the audit process.

Also pertinent to this discussion is the potential disciplining of corporate auditors as a result of their membership of recognized professional bodies (Watts and Zimmerman, 1986, p.316). They are usually required by regulation to be professionally qualified accountants and, in order to be so designated, they have to comply with standards laid down by their professional bodies. If they do not comply with these standards, and this is brought to the attention of these bodies, they risk exclusion from membership, consequential loss of the ability to conduct corporate audits, and serious loss of economic rewards from such activity. In other words, there is a powerful economic self-interest for the corporate auditor to behave professionally generally, and independently particularly.

In addition, as Goldman and Barlev (1974, p.714) point out, the auditor's professional body should be constantly issuing and reviewing auditing and accounting standards to reduce the reporting options available to a manipulatory corporate management, and thus diminish unnecessary pressures on the auditor's independence. The professional body should also be specifying rules of ethical behaviour for its auditor members, thereby ensuring that they are at least made aware of areas of potential conflict with their independence (Sherer and Kent, 1983, p.29). As previously mentioned, there are counter-arguments to at least part of this view of the role of professional accountancy bodies. These suggest that such bodies desire to maintain a status quo of a level of accounting and auditing flexibility compatible with the needs of audit clients (Sikka, Willmott and Lowe, 1989, p.65); act as a professional monopoly responding only to public threats to their self-regulatory position (Byington and Sutton, 1991, p.327); and, more generally, do 'nothing' of consequence to respond to accusations of malpractice because of their members' economic dependence on corporate clientele (Fogarty, Heian and Knutson, 1991, p.223).

Watts and Zimmerman (1986, pp.316–18) also argue that the structure of the auditing community is capable of maintaining reasonable levels of auditor independence. For example, they suggest (pp.316–17) audit firms are constituted as partnerships of unlimited liability, and that this acts as an incentive to be both competent and independent. If the auditor is found to be either incompetent or lacking in independence, to the detriment of a corporate client, the financial consequences in an unlimited liability situation are severe. This, however, is inconsistent with recent developments in the US and elsewhere to incorporate audit firms with limited liability – that is, the position taken by bodies such as the AICPA in the US that incorporation is permissible as a means of restricting the exposure of auditors to the considerable financial losses of litigation.

Watts and Zimmerman (1986, pp.317–18) also suggest that the contemporary trend of audit firm mergers which result in fewer but larger firms creates an organizational and economic structure less likely to cause firms to bend to the pressures of management in areas of audit conflict – thus helping to sustain a reasonable expectation of auditor independence. This point is also argued by Goldman and Barlev (1974, pp.715–16), but is disputed by Murphy (1991, p.23) on the grounds of fewer firms restricting choice for corporate organizations seeking independent auditors.

The need for a separate audit profession, mentioned above within the context of a regulated corporate environment, is also advocated in a private sector context by Mautz and Sharaf (1961, pp.228–30). In particular, they argue (p.228) that auditing and other non-attest services are incompatible and should be separated if independence is to be preserved; and, particularly, that audit work (being of a quasi-judicial nature) is something very different from these other services. Mautz and Sharaf also recognize (p.229) the potential economic hardship of making these separations in practice, and suggest that it should occur gradually by specialization and within the context of the audit firm. In effect, this recommendation has occurred in practice since it was made – at least to the extent of separate partnerships and divisions being created within audit firms. However, it has not allayed fears held about a potential loss of independence, and has resulted in the suggestions made previously for a separate and regulated audit profession.

A final suggestion to improve auditor independence within a free-market approach is that of peer review (Moizer, 1991, p.44). This involves one audit firm reviewing the work of another. However, such a review requires to be undertaken voluntarily if regulation is to be avoided, and it is difficult to conceive of who is going to pay the bill if such a system were put in place. Nevertheless, the idea has potential, if for no other reason than its capacity to restrain corporate auditors in situations where they might be tempted to compromise their independence. Self-interest arguments suggest they would not wish such compromising to be made explicit to their professional peers.

Audit independence versus auditor independence

One further aspect of the issue of corporate auditor independence requires to be considered in this text. This concerns the general argument of Wolnizer (1987) that the fault rests not with the auditor but with the audit subject-matter of reported financial information. More specifically, Wolnizer (1987, p.121) argues that the conventional notion of auditor independence is incomplete – that is, it is predominantly concerned with the auditor's behaviour in the audit context. It does not consider the independence of the accounting subject-matter of auditing. Thus, the conventional concept of independence is almost totally focused on an unobservable state of mind, and difficult-to-verify conditions surrounding that state of mind (pp.123–4). Not surprisingly, the issues surrounding the conventional view of independence concentrate on improving explicit signals of the appearance of auditor objectivity (p.129). Wolnizer argues that independence as an issue is stuck in an intellectual groove (p.146), in which it is perpetuated by indoctrination received in auditing education and practice (p.151).

What Wolnizer is suggesting is that there is no question that the need for auditor independence is paramount. But to focus on it as if it were simply a problem relating to the auditor's state of mind is oversimplistic – as is the approach of attempting to resolve it by means of improving the circumstances in which the auditor can appear to be independent. Improving images does not necessarily improve realities. Instead, Wolnizer (1987, pp.147–8) suggests that the basic problem is the nature of the content of conventional financial statements which are the subject of audit. Because they are not based on independently testable evidence, they are always going to be subject to the possibility of manipulation by reporting management. And, because such manipulation can take place, the auditor is always going to be potentially subject to the pressures of management to comply with the manipulation, thereby compromising independence.

The Wolnizer case for improved auditor independence is therefore to remove the opportunity for manipulation and compromise, and substitute a set of financial statements based on independently testable accounting evidence. It is a solution which challenges the need to be constantly concerned with appearances of auditor independence to provide comfort and reassurance to report users on such a matter. Instead, it attempts to get at the root of the problem – the nature of reported accounting information. This will be discussed later in Chapter 9.

A review and overall comment

Before proceeding to examine the issue of the corporate auditor's duty of care, it is useful to bring together some of the foregoing comments on corporate auditor independence. The first observation relates to the dichotomy between appearance and fact. The most important issue centres around the context of corporate auditors' behaviour and actions. Above all else, they must appear to be independent if financial report users are to trust the audit opinion and the quality of the audited information. In this sense, it does not matter how honest corporate auditors have been, or how much personal integrity they have. The fundamental issue is whether or not they can be seen to be in a position in which they can withstand the expected pressures by corporate management to compromise their position. Thus, all the efforts of legislators, regulators, and professional bodies is directed at constructing a clear image of potential independence.

The existing evidence from audit research supports this view of the pre-eminence of perceptions of auditor independence. For example, Pany and Reckers (1980, p.50) report on US shareholder perceptions of lack of auditor independence in situations where they are receiving gifts and purchase discounts from corporate clients, even if they are of minimal amount, and irrespective of the size of the client. Firth (1980, p.451) concludes from a study of preparers and users of financial statements that auditor dependence is perceived to impair investing and lending decisions, and that users are more sceptical than preparers of independence being possible. Shockley (1981, p.785), on the other hand, reports a general consensus between preparers, users and auditors concerning potential dangers to auditor independence – that is, the greatest risk is perceived to be related to auditors operating in a highly competitive market for their services, followed by their provision of management services, and then by the size of their firm. Knapp (1985, p.202) provides a further perceptual dimension – that report users perceive the auditor to be more likely to be independent when the corporate client is financially unhealthy rather than healthy. And Lacey (1986, p.23) reveals a reasonably consistent ranking of perceived auditor independence, with users more sensitive to independence issues than either auditors or preparers, but each group's perceptions being generally consistent with existing independence regulations (p.51).

A further crucial factor with respect to the concept of corporate auditor independence is that its achievement is related to basically economic incentives. The non-critical version of this position assumes economic rationality. It states that, irrespective of the morality of a professional person acting in the public interest, the corporate auditor has a long-term incentive to act independently because of the economic consequences of the reputational effects of being known to be dependent. The critical alternative, on the other hand, suggests that, in the absence of regulation, the corporate auditor has an economic incentive to act dependently because of the improbability of being found out. The existing provisions to regulate for independence, together with the available evidence on perceptions of independence, provide support for the critical view. This, of course, also brings into question the propriety of the theoretical argument and prescription of the corporate auditor as a professional acting in the public interest.

Note

1. There is also an argument to suggest that, when considering the concept of auditor independence, it is important to consider the independence of the individual auditor

(partner) as well as that of the audit firm (auditor) taken as a whole (Miller, 1992). Indeed, despite the potential economic consequences to the firm of inadequate auditing, the relationship between the individual audit engagement partner and the corporate client may be such that the economic benefits of loss of independence may outweigh the disbenefits of such behaviour to his or her firm (Miller, 1992, p.83).

Further reading

R.K. Mautz and H.A. Sharaf (1961) *The Philosophy of Auditing*, American Accounting Association, pp.204–31 (the first conceptual argument to support auditor independence in practice).

D. Flint (1988) *Philosophy and Principles of Auditing*, Macmillan, pp.54–86 (an updating and extension of the conventional Mautz and Sharaf (1961) argument for auditor independence, placed in the context of audit authority).

R. Antle (1984) Auditor independence, *Journal of Accounting Research*, Spring, pp.1–20 (an analytical argument for auditor independence in a principal–agent situation; concentrate on the qualitative argument, assuming Antle's mathematics are correct).

P.W. Wolnizer (1987) *Auditing as Independent Authentication*, Sydney University Press, pp.121–87 (an alternative view to auditor independence based on the notion of a need for independently testable accounting information).

P. Moizer (1991) Independence, in M. Sherer and S. Turley (eds), *Current Issues in Auditing*, Paul Chapman Publishing, pp.34–46 (a critical review of the auditor independence concept).

Discussion and essay topics

1. Think of the term 'independence'. What does it mean to you in terms of everyday usage, and how does it relate to the corporate audit situation?

2. Discuss the concept of corporate auditor independence in the context of economic agency.

3. How does corporate auditor independence relate to corporate accountability?

4. What incentives can be argued to exist to ensure corporate auditor independence?

5. Analyse and comment on the conventional concept of corporate auditor independence.

6. Why is the appearance of independence so vital to the credibility of the corporate audit?

7. Compare and contrast corporate auditor independence as a state of mind with the Wolnizer notion of independent testable audit evidence.

8. How have corporate regulators recognized the need for auditor independence?

9. Critique the dangers to and solutions advocated for corporate auditor independence in both regulated and non-regulated circumstances.

8

The corporate auditor's duty of care

Previous chapters specify the corporate audit function as a complex technical process to independently verify and attest the quality of externally reported corporate financial statements. The objectives of this process comprise a mixture of economic, psychological and social factors designed to reduce doubt about the quality of the accounting content of these statements, give assurance and protection to those individuals and organizations relying on them, and, more generally, assist in the task of effective corporate managerial accountability.

Underlying these prescriptions are three related postulates. The first is that those individuals and organizations who need protection from sub-standard reporting cannot personally verify and attest the quality of the financial statements. The second assumes corporate auditors are sufficiently skilled and experienced to complete their audits competently. And the third states that corporate auditors can be held accountable for the standards of their verification and attestation work. These assumptions collectively predicate corporate auditors as professional experts with generally accepted standards of professional competence by which their audit work and opinion can be judged in individual corporate circumstances. They make explicit a broad societal expectation that corporate auditors can and do conduct their function with the care appropriate to an expert and professionalized activity (Flint, 1988, p.144). And they are consistent with standards which are provided for the auditor in written statements of professional accountancy bodies (as, for example, in AICPA, 1991, pp.7–8; and APC, 1980b).

Corporate auditors are therefore expected not only to act competently and responsibly as professionals, but also to be able to justify their audit actions according to adequate standards of competence and care. Thus, they must be aware of relevant standards, and apply them appropriately in their work. They must also be sensitive to changing societal expectations which require their audit standards to vary over time. As needs, knowledge and expectations change in society, professional experts such as corporate auditors must respond accordingly when these changes impact their work. This is primarily what distinguishes professional from other organized activities.

A major problem, however, is determining from time to time what standards are appropriate in a constantly changing environment (Flint, 1988, p.148). What is acceptable corporate audit activity at one point of time is not necessarily acceptable at a later date. Indeed, it is not always clear what is acceptable. For example, in relation to the issue of the auditor and the detection of fraud and error, and despite written guidance concerning the need to assess the risk of the existence of material fraud or error (as, for example, in AICPA, 1991, pp.55–65; and APC, 1990), the corporate auditor has to consider the nature and magnitude of such risk on a case-by-case basis, using experience and knowledge to observe each individual set of circumstances on its merits.

Corporate auditors' duty of care does not change the primary responsibility of corporate management for the overall quality of verified financial statements (Mautz and Sharaf, 1961, p.114; AICPA, 1991, p.5; and APC, 1990, para.8). But it does require them to be aware of the precise boundaries of their responsibility with respect to those individuals and organizations relying and acting on their opinions, and the standards they are expected to meet in formulating those opinions (Mautz and Sharaf, 1961, p.111; and Flint, 1988, pp.151–2).

Given that corporate financial statements are a form of public good, the major issues for corporate auditors are, first, identifying from the broad spectrum of members of society who rely on their audit opinions those individuals and organizations to whom they have a reasonable professional duty of care; and, second, determining the level of professional standards which express the competence below which their audit actions and opinions must not fall if such a duty of care is to be satisfied. To be effective, therefore, parameters of professional responsibility in corporate auditing should be known, accepted as reasonable, and adopted in practice. This process involves all contributors to the corporate audit debate – that is, corporate management, audit beneficiaries, state regulators, and auditors.

A professionalized activity such as corporate auditing can only work effectively in the public interest if its practitioners are informed, willing to accept and capable of implementing prescribed standards of behaviour. Corporate auditors cannot be expected to have an unlimited duty of care because that would be unreasonable and unfair. But they cannot be allowed to practise their skills with no responsibilities. The essential issue is establishing a reasonable and fair balance between these extremes. Striking such a balance is a continuous process where individual events can alter the status quo. It is also a process in which society, rather than auditors and their professional bodies, specifies the ultimate standards they are expected to attain. This is usually achieved by means of state regulation, court decisions, and other forms of public expression (including media and literature comment and criticism).

The contemporary collective attitude of the auditing profession to matters of professional responsibility is one of treating them with extreme caution – that is, by either responding only when under extreme pressure or threat to do so (Byington and Sutton, 1991), or by basically doing little or 'nothing' irrespective of whether or not such pressure exists (Fogarty, Heian and Knutson, 1991). A typical response to explicit criticism is to issue a statement which seeks to limit the duty of care to what is acceptable to audit practitioners and their regulating bodies, rather than to meet the public expectations contained in the criticism. An example of this style is the current position held by individual auditing writers and professional bodies that, despite a public expectation to the contrary, the detection of fraud and error is an important but subsidiary audit activity to the primary focus of giving an opinion on the accounting quality of reported financial statements (AICPA, 1991, p.56; and APC, 1990, para.9; see also Tweedie, 1991, pp.28–9).

The propriety and sense of this approach to the duty of audit care is debatable – specifically with respect to the long-term economic and social consequences of appearing either to renounce or to decline an area of expertise which has been persistently and historically associated with audit activity, deny a service which could provide considerable economic and social benefits, and refuse to deal with difficult and risky issues of public interest (Mautz and Sharaf, 1961, p.130). Indeed, the need to maintain the credibility of corporate auditing as a professionalized activity attracting reasonable financial and social rewards appears to require a more positive approach by accountants to the duty of corporate audit care. On the other hand, rational economic argument suggests that corporate auditors will assume audit responsibilities only when they perceive the economic benefits to them to exceed the related economic costs (including the cost of litigation).

As Mautz and Sharaf (1961, p.116) argue, the growth and development of the audit profession is at stake with respect to audit responsibilities. In particular, until there is a societal consensus on the issue, there is a continuing need to monitor those audit responsibility standards which are currently operated by the corporate auditing profession. Such practical prescriptions exist in several different forms – that is, either as written auditing standards and guidelines, and rules of professional conduct issued by bodies regulating audit practitioner behaviour (for example, AICPA, 1991); or as court decisions in which the work and opinion of individual auditors has been questioned and judged (see Godsell, 1991). Thus, the responsibility of the corporate auditor is interpretable at any point of time in terms of a mix of legally and professionally prescribed standards of audit behaviour within a framework of changing public expectations (Flint, 1988, p.146).

The concept of the prudent auditor

Mautz and Sharaf (1961, p.131) propose that the concept of audit care is based on the prudent practitioner of auditing. This is an approach also favoured by Flint (1988, pp.149–50), and is adopted for purposes of discussion in this text. Adapting the Mautz and Sharaf argument to corporate auditors, the notion of the prudent practitioner proposes an expert who will exercise audit judgments with care and skill at least equal to the norms of professional peers and current expectations, and with respect to his or her previous audit experience (Mautz and Sharaf, 1961, pp.132–3).

Such a prescription of responsibility is arguably reasonable with respect to both the corporate auditor and audit beneficiaries. Auditors are expected to be competent in their actions, but no more expert than the average of the auditor community of which they are a part. In other words, they are not expected to perform to unattainable levels of competence and expertise. And, by achieving feasible levels of performance, the beneficiaries of their work can reasonably expect to be protected from sub-standard financial reporting (Mautz and Sharaf, 1961, p.134). It therefore appears to be in everyone's interest to require the corporate auditor to perform to a reasonable and effective level of competence and care. If this is not the case, the corporate audit function becomes an activity in which the expectations of its beneficiaries can never be met by the auditor. Such a situation has the potential to create frustrations, doubts, and loss of credibility in the corporate audit.

Mautz and Sharaf (1961, pp.135–40) extend their explanation of the prudent practitioner with a number of criteria which assist in understanding what is expected of responsible corporate auditors. For example, they should be aware of those audit beneficiaries who could be damaged if their work and opinions are sub-standard (for example, a specific potential investor in or lender to the client company). This awareness should be sufficient to avoid the danger of ignoring the known needs of a specific user not covered by relevant audit regulations.

Corporate auditors should also give special attention to circumstances in which there appears to be unusual audit risk – as, for example, when corporate internal controls are weak or non-existent. By means of appropriate audit actions, they should attempt to remove or minimize their doubts concerning the material uncertainty. If, following such appropriate actions, they are unable to resolve the issue, they should report accordingly.

Finally, corporate auditors should keep abreast of professional developments in their area of expertise with the objective of updating their audit skills. In particular, they should ensure that there are adequate reviews of all audit procedures completed in order to monitor their appropriateness in light of known best practice. If they fail to adapt their expertise to changing circumstances, they run the risk of not meeting currently prescribed work standards.

The specifics of what is deemed to be an adequate discharge of the duty of care owed by the corporate auditor to audit beneficiaries are ultimately determined within courts of law (Flint, 1988, p.148). Even though in practice the standards of the prudent audit practitioner are determined personally, with the assistance of guidance and prescription from relevant professional accountancy bodies and corporate regulators, what and to whom the corporate auditor is responsible can never be precisely mapped until the specifics of an individual case are tested and judged in a court of law (Flint, 1988, pp.145–8).

Prudent corporate audit practice is shaped in part by the cumulative application by generations of auditors of specific auditing standards in individual corporate circumstances. But, because societal expectations of corporate auditors change over time, and are not necessarily reflected in prescribed standards, they may find their work subject to challenge in courts of law when audit beneficiaries believe they have been damaged by them. In this respect, as discussed later in the chapter, a faithful implementation of existing audit standards may be insufficient to meet societal expectations. Consequently, as the ultimate authority in such matters, a judicial court may prescribe a standard higher than that which corporate auditors, their peers, and their regulating professional bodies believe to be adequate. In other words, such a court is not bound in its decision by existing standards of audit performance (Flint, 1988, p.147). Instead, it must interpret the auditors' performance in light of current needs and expectations of the corporate auditor.

Corporate auditors thus require to constantly monitor their duty of care in relation to statements of public expectation regarding their audit function (Flint, 1988, p.148). In these circumstances, explicit corporate auditing standards are no more than guidelines for individual audit practitioners who are concerned with adequately discharging their duty of care. Although standards have an authority and, if implemented, can be persuasive, they should not be regarded as conclusive evidence of competent corporate auditors at work (Flint, 1988, p.156). Corporate auditors must therefore always be aware that, as skilled professionals, they work in an expert area in which standards are dynamic and not static, minima rather than maxima, and ultimately determined by courts of law as custodians of the public interest.

Determining reasonable audit care and skill

What the previous section boils down to for the individual corporate auditor in practice is determining what is negligent audit work and then, essentially, avoiding this in decisions and actions. More specifically, the auditor must at all times act with reasonable care and skill in the circumstances (Gwilliam, 1987, p.137). In this respect, and as implied in the previous section, what is determined as reasonable care and skill must involve attention to judicial attitudes and verdicts (pp.137–8), specific contractual audit duties (pp.138–9), adherence to explicit standards laid down by professional and other regulatory bodies (pp.139–42), the degree to which corporate management can be relied on (p.142), the possibility of fraudulent activity (pp.142–3), the appropriateness of audit evidence and tests for and of evidential material (pp.143–5), and the strengths and weaknesses in internal controls (pp.145–8). Each of these matters will be discussed appropriately in this and later chapters (see also Godsell, 1991, pp.1–14, 58–82 and 106–15).

The corporate auditor's responsibility for specific tasks

Corporate auditors are responsible as prudent practitioners for ensuring that their stated audit tasks are completed by the competent application of those auditing standards which are known by them to be the most appropriate practice for the corporate situation being verified. Currently, they have an over-riding responsible for observing and judging the propriety of the accounting processes by which identifiable corporate activity is described in the form of a specific set of financial statements as part of corporate governance and managerial accountability. Their opinions are on the quality of these processes and statements as they relate to stated information criteria. They are formulated with due attention to available evidential material concerning the accounting construction of the financial statements. Corporate auditors are therefore directly responsible for the following audit-related tasks:

- **Familiarization** with their specific duties as contained in those contractual, regulatory and professional provisions which govern the nature and conduct of the required audit of corporate financial statements. In this way, they bound their audit work within prescribed and explicit limits.

- Maintaining an adequate position of **independence** *vis-à-vis* the corporate audit client and its management in order to maximize the confidence of its shareholders and other beneficiaries of audit work who may rely on the objectivity of the audit opinion.

- Effectively **planning** the conduct of their audits in such a way that they will meet the procedural standards expected of them in terms of obtaining sufficient competent evidence to support their opinions. In practice, given the stated qualities expected of financial statements, this means obtaining adequate evidence to support the presumption of relevant and reliable accounting information.

- Utilizing audit **practices** known to be generally accepted by their professional peers as suitable for purposes of obtaining and judging the evidential material necessary to support their audit opinions on informational relevance and reliability.

- Ensuring that their audit **opinions** are compatible with the findings of their review and analysis of the evidential material they have gathered for audit purposes. The credibility of the corporate audit is directly related to this factor. Just as the financial statements are expected to be relevant and reliable, so too is the auditor's report.

- Suitably reporting their audit opinions to shareholders and other interested individuals and organizations so that the quality of the verified financial statements is clearly expressed and capable of being **understood**. The utility of the audit is dependent on corporate auditors' ability to express their audit findings in such a way that the users of the verified financial statements are in no doubt about their relevance and reliability.

- Properly **supervising** their audit staff in such a way as to determine whether or not they are complying with each of the above requirements of the auditor's duty of responsibility to meet stated objectives. The value of the corporate audit is linked to the integrity and expertise of all audit staff, and not just to the auditor's behaviour. Failure to comply with accepted standards by any staff member can jeopardize the credibility of the entire audit effort.

In undertaking each of these related tasks, corporate auditors are actively pursuing their duty of audit care in terms of specific goals. However, comprehension of this position, particularly by individuals and organizations mentally and/or physically distant from the audit function, tend to be clouded by misperceptions of the corporate auditor's objectives and related responsibilities. This is usually described as the expectations gap, and relates to differences between what auditors and audit beneficiaries believe to be the reasons for and achievements of the corporate audit (Guy and Sullivan, 1988, p.36; and Sikka *et al.*, 1992, p.2).

In fact, there are many such misperceptions and the expectations gap is therefore a multiple phenomenon (see evidence of this in Lee, 1970b; and Humphrey, Moizer and Turley, 1992a). However, the most publicly discussed are those described in the following sections.

- **Detecting and preventing fraud and error** This topic is discussed in detail in the next chapter within the context of the qualities expected of reported accounting information. The undernoted is therefore only a brief introduction to the issue concerned.

There has been a continuing debate concerning the history of the corporate auditor's responsibility for detecting and preventing fraud and error (see Brown, 1962). As previously mentioned, it is usually assumed by the audit profession that the primary responsibility for these matters is with corporate management to provide adequate control systems (AICPA, 1991, p.5; and APC, 1990, para.4). This principle has also been recognized for some time in judicial decisions. For example, in *S.P. Catterson and Sons Ltd* (1937), the auditor was found not to have been responsible for detecting fraud when management had ignored a previous audit warning concerning weaknesses in the company's internal controls. The judge in the case stated:

> It is not the auditor's business to tell the directors how to carry on and conduct their accounting system; they make their recommendations, and if they are not acceded to, the responsibility is not the auditor's responsibility, but it is the responsibility of the directors.

This judgment clarified a number of earlier court decisions in which it was determined that the auditor had only a limited responsibility for fraud and error detection (even in times when that was regarded as the primary audit objective). For example, in *Kingston Cotton Mill Co.* (1896), the judge concluded that the auditor must not be made liable for detecting complex frauds, particularly by senior management, when his suspicions were not aroused. In other words, as in *Irish Woollen Co. Ltd* v. *Tyson & Others* (1900), the auditor was seen to have a major responsibility for fraud and error detection only when he failed to use reasonable care in what were suspicious circumstances. And such circumstances had to exist at the time of the audit (*Henry Squire (Cash Chemist) Ltd* v. *Ball, Baker & Co.* (1911)).

The crucial point, however, was and remains – what is reasonable care in suspicious circumstances? In a more recent case, *Thomas Gerrard and Son Ltd* (1968), this matter was clarified to some extent. The judge ruled that the auditor is guilty of negligence if he or she fails to detect fraud because the nature and quality of the audit procedures were below what is regarded as best practice, and were therefore insufficient to arouse the auditor's suspicions in circumstances in which they should have been activated (the fraud had been perpetrated over several years). This ruling put the onus on the corporate auditor to be aware of what are the most appropriate procedures to apply in any given audit situation, but it did little to meet the challenge of a persistent concern about the auditor's role *vis-à-vis* fraud and error detection. It also emphasized a point made by Gwilliam (1987, pp.163–6) that this issue needs to be judged on individual circumstances rather than by general rules.

Public expectations of corporate auditors with respect to fraud and error are typically stated in terms of a perception that they have a duty to verify that the audited financial statements are free of such matters (Connor, 1986, p.77; Gwilliam, 1987, pp.167–8; and Guy and Sullivan, 1988, p.37). The auditor community, on the other hand, believes that it is impossible to design an audit to detect all illegal acts, but that auditors should be sensitive in their audit decisions and actions to the possibility of material fraud and error existing (Carmichael, 1988, p.41).

The state of this issue is therefore one in which the public expectation exceeds the apparent capability of the corporate auditor to satisfy the perceived audit objective. Yet auditors know it does not make sense to completely deny such a responsibility (Gwilliam, 1987, pp.168–70). The present position therefore involves a muted affirmation of that responsibility by auditors in their published audit standards (AICPA, 1991, pp.55–65; and APC, 1990). Whether this is sufficient to appease the perceived public expectation, or give adequate guidance to individual auditors, is debatable. It certainly indicates an area of audit activity in which the duty of care is bounded in relatively ambiguous terms, and in need of greater clarification. Evidence is available from the research literature of a growing ambiguity in this area, and a consequent enlarging over recent years of the expectations gap between auditors and audit beneficiaries (see Lee 1970b; and Humphrey, Moizer and Turley, 1992a).

- **Warning of business failure** Typically, public disquiet about the role of the corporate auditor is made explicit when there is a major corporate failure (Connor, 1986, p.77; Briloff, 1990, p.10; Humphrey, Moizer and Turley, 1992a, p.3; and Mitchell *et al.*, 1991). The magnitude of such an organizational disaster is usually such that the relevance of the corporate audit is brought into question in terms of its potential as an early warning system to investors and other interested individuals and organizations. As Connor (1986, p.77) and Godsell (1991, p.6) argue, business failures are perceived as audit failures.

The reason for this position may be due to knowledge that the corporate auditor has a duty of care to verify the legitimacy of the going concern assumption which underlies conventional financial reporting (AICPA, 1991, p.197; and APC, 1985, para.6) – that is, to verify whether or not the reporting company has an indefinite financial future, and to take this factor into account in the attestation of the financial statements. Corporate auditors therefore assess the financial strength of companies as part of their audits and, in these circumstances, it is unsurprising to find they are also perceived as having a more specific responsibility regarding financial failure when that arises.

The response of the auditing profession to this issue has been similar in kind to that on fraud and error detection – that is, recognizing it has a limited duty of care, and describing this in relatively ambiguous circumstances. These concern a professional expectation that the corporate auditor will evaluate whether or not there is substantial doubt about the reporting organization's ability to stay in business over the next year following the relevant reporting date (AICPA, 1991, p.197; and APC, 1985, para.6). However, nowhere in existing audit standards is there clear instruction as to what is meant by substantial doubt with respect to an issue such as potential corporate failure. The corporate auditor is thus left in the serious dilemma of deciding whether or not the financial condition of the corporate client is sufficiently poor to warrant reporting on it in the context of giving an opinion on the reported financial statements. If the auditor does not report on such a matter, audit beneficiaries may be financially damaged when relying on statements which do not warn about financial ill-health. On the other hand, specifically reporting on the company's financial health may precipitate a financial crisis unnecessarily, thus damaging audit beneficiaries and, possibly, also the auditor because of subsequent litigation.

What these two examples of corporate auditors' duty of care indicate is that they are professional experts required to give an objective opinion on the quality of an informational product on which other individuals depend for decision purposes. More specifically, corporate auditors are in a situation in which they are privy to evidence concerning the propriety of company operations, and the financial viability of the company as a going concern.

These are matters which are obviously material to a variety of different decisions but, in many respects, go beyond the verification of the quality of accounting numbers in reported financial statements. The corporate auditor's claimed expertise is concerned with accounting rather than more general business matters. Inexpert warnings by the auditor of possible fraud, illegal acts, and potential financial failure could create financial problems for the company and audit beneficiaries.

Yet all these matters also in some way impact the quality of the financial statements being verified, and therefore affect the auditor's work and opinion. To deny any of these responsibilities could be interpreted as an act of a professional not prepared to protect clients' or the public interest (with potential reputational effects and long-term economic consequences). To accept them, on the other hand, could appear to be claiming non-accounting expertise which corporate auditors do not usually have (again with long-term reputational and economic repercussions).

The present position, therefore, is one of ambiguity, doubt and concern. Corporate auditors' objectives with respect to attesting the stated qualities of reported financial statements are clear. Equally clear is the impossible position they are in if they attempt to meet public expectations which are known to exist (Humphrey, Moizer and Turley, 1992a, p.23), but which demand skills, time and resources which they may well be unable to provide in adequate quantities, and involve immeasurable economic consequences.

The same conclusion can be made about a variety of other roles for which the corporate auditor may be felt to be responsible, but which do not appear to be functions which are regarded by auditors as part of the normal audit function (see Lee, 1970b, p.294; and Humphrey, Moizer and Turley, 1992a, p.29 for full listings). These have not been as prominent or as well-articulated as those relating to fraud, illegal acts, or business failure. None the less, they exist, and should be treated as seriously as these latter problems. They represent further facets of the overall expectations gap which exists concerning the corporate auditor's duty of care. They are described briefly below but in no particular order of importance.

- **Ensuring all regulatory requirements affecting corporate organizations have been complied with** The corporate auditor is normally (but not always) regulated by specific provisions concerning the verification of the accounting for and reporting of financial information to shareholders and others with a legitimate interest in the reporting company. Auditors are not typically charged with a wider regulatory responsibility, nor do they necessarily have the expertise necessary to detect and evaluate such matters – as, for example, activities by the reporting company which violate non-accounting laws or regulations. As discussed above, the corporate auditor does appear to have a responsibility for fraud or other irregularities when these affect the quality of the financial statements. Similarly, other illegal acts may impact these statements, and the auditor is advised to be watchful, and to take appropriate audit action to investigate when such acts are believed to materially affect the quality of the financial statements (AICPA, 1991, p.68). However, because of the non-accounting nature of many illegal acts, the auditing profession appears to regard its members' responsibility in this area as limited to a consideration of their financial effects – and only when and if they are detected during the normal course of the audit (AICPA, 1991, pp.68 and 70). Others disagree with this limited approach to corporate accountability, believing that the corporate auditor has a much broader and deeper social responsibility beyond the accounting quality of reported financial statements – particularly as it relates to the corporate organization's impact on the community and environment of which it is a part (Tinker, 1985, pp.203–7; and Gray, 1990, pp.106–10).

- **Guaranteeing the accuracy of the accounting content of verified financial statements** The nature of reported accounting information is such that it attempts to communicate the financial consequences of economic operating activity by the reporting company over a given period of trading. It is therefore a limited portrayal of such matters. It can never provide the pictorial correspondence of a photograph or film. But it should not have the uninterpretable quality of a totally abstract painting. Particularly to satisfy the criterion of reliability, it should faithfully represent what it purports to describe. As FASB (1980, para.76) states on this issue:

> The financial statements of a business enterprise can be thought of as a . . . model of the enterprise. Like all models, it must abstract from much that goes on in a real enterprise. No model, however sophisticated, can be expected to reflect all the functions and relationships that are found within a complex organisation. To do so, the model would have to be virtually a reproduction of the original. In real life, it is necessary to accept a much smaller degree of correspondence between the model and the original than that. One can be satisfied if none of the important functions and relationships are lost.

Thus, the accounting process in practice should identify these functions and relationships on the basis of their relevance to report user decisions, and compress them into a relatively few accounting messages which meaningfully conform with the criterion of reliability. In doing so, the reporting accountant is concerned with the subjective application of financial accounting standards. These involve measures of judgment which mean that no set of financial statements can be regarded as accurate or absolutely correct. And corporate auditors therefore cannot be expected to guarantee them. They are not guarantors, for that would be an economically and technically impossible task. Instead, they are professional experts required to give a caring opinion on the general quality of the informational content of corporate financial statements. This is contrary to an alternative view of the corporate auditor as an insurer, with the audit fee being regarded as the cheapest form of insurance against defaults in the principal–agent relationship in corporate activity (Gwilliam, 1987, pp.55–6).

- **Judging the efficiency and adequacy of corporate operations and management** As will be discussed in later chapters concerning the corporate auditor's use of evidential material, a major part of the duty of care as a prudent auditor is to review the client company's systems of internal controls (Mautz and Sharaf, 1961, p.142). In effect, the corporate auditor is expected to review the entire internal control structure (the control environment and procedures, and the accounting system) in order to understand it sufficiently to plan the audit; assess the control risk (the risk of material misstatement in the financial statements derived from the internal control structure); and test controls to assist in such understanding and assessments (Temkin and Winters, 1988; and, more specifically, AICPA, 1991, pp.73–4; and APC, 1980f, para.7).

Undertaking these audit tasks involves the corporate auditor in aspects of corporate activity much broader than accounting processing, and includes operational and managerial features of corporate systems. However, this may give the impression that the corporate auditor is, first, ensuring that the internal control structure is adequate; and, second, verifying and reporting on the quality of corporate operations and management. Except when these matters impact the quality of the financial statements being verified, such audit roles are not required by conventional audit regulations. This does not mean that such additional roles for corporate auditors are not desirable; or, indeed, that they do not conduct them in their capacity as providers of management services. Instead, it is a reminder that the contemporary corporate audit task is conceived by corporate regulators in terms of an accountability function which depends on a regular reporting of financial statements of a certain quality – which is a matter which is only partially determined by the strength or otherwise of internal controls. It should be noted, however, that the recent incidence of corporate failures has caused a serious question to be asked as to whether the corporate auditor ought to be required to report directly to shareholders on the quality of internal and, particularly, financial controls in the reporting company (Holmes, 1991, p.30).

In summary, therefore, corporate auditors are specifically responsible at the present time for reporting on the accounting quality of corporate financial statements. Their major activity is centred on the uncertainties which surround specified informational qualities – that is, finding sufficient competent evidence with which to come to an expert and informed opinion on whether or not these statements meet these criteria. Their duty of care is driven by such a focus, although this is not to say that other responsibilities (such as those discussed in this section) are not equally worthy alternative ways of discharging the overall audit role in corporate accountability. Indeed, given the current corporate climate, there are compelling reasons to investigate the appropriateness and feasibility of these alternative roles.

The corporate auditor's responsibility to report users

The previous sections in this chapter concentrate on explaining and discussing the nature of corporate auditors' duty of care in two different ways. The first relates to the idea of them as prudent professional experts whose actions are measured against accepted standards of behaviour. The second outlines in broad terms what they are responsible for with respect to the expected qualities of reported financial statements. Each of these discussions is important to an understanding of corporate auditors' responsibilities. But neither provides knowledge of the audit beneficiaries to whom they have the stated duty of care. Indeed, the text has been ambivalent on this matter to this point, preferring to describe corporate audit beneficiaries in the broad terms of shareholders and other individuals and organizations with reasonable rights of access to verified accounting information. This section attempts to redress this imbalance by more rigorously identifying corporate audit beneficiaries who could be damaged by substandard auditing, and who have the right to seek recompense if damaged. The crucial issue is therefore determining those audit beneficiaries to whom the prudent corporate auditor primarily owes a duty of care.

The primary beneficiaries of the corporate audit

The fundamental legal principle which has governed the corporate auditor's potential liability to an audit beneficiary is privity of contract – that is, a potential liability exists only within the context of a contractual relationship to provide an audit service to a specific beneficiary. If the latter individual can prove in court that he or she relied on the work of the auditor when this was substandard, and was quantifiably damaged by it, the auditor can be held liable for such damages (*Winterbottom* v. *Wright*, *(1842)*). Liability to any other potential beneficiary, on the other hand, is determined by the law of tort in terms of a civil wrong independent of a contract (Mannix, 1976, p.1).

These distinctions create problems with respect to determining those individuals and organizations to whom the corporate auditor has a duty of care and a potential liability for professional negligence (see Godsell, 1991, pp.15–57). Such problems are twofold.

Company or shareholders?

The primary report user group identified with the corporate audit is that of shareholders. However, the corporate auditor is legally contracted to the client company, usually by means of a written statement to its management of his or her intentions and objectives with respect to the conduct of the audit engagement. This communication conventionally describes their willingness to provide an expert opinion on the quality of the company's financial statements to its shareholders. In other words, although the audit contract defines the separate legal entity of the company as the primary beneficiary, it is its shareholders who receive and rely on the financial statements and audit opinion (Gower, 1979, p.523). The company (by means of its management) can therefore take action against the auditor in terms of the audit contract, thereby leaving individual shareholders who are damaged to seek redress by action in tort (Mannix, 1976, p.1). Thus, it is reasonably clear that the corporate auditor has a duty of care at law to both the company and its shareholders, despite the long-standing rule to the contrary in *Foss* v. *Harbottle* (1843).

This has been the legal position for many years, and several specific UK cases can be cited to support it as a general principle in the area of corporate auditing. For example, in *London and General Bank* (1895), the judge ruled that the auditor must fully report the facts to the shareholders when the company's balance sheet has been inadequately prepared. This general decision was also followed in *Rex* v. *Kylsant* (1931). In *London Oil Storage* v. *Seear, Hasluck & Co.* (1904), the auditor was defined as an officer of the company with a duty to protect both the company and its shareholders. The judgment in *Candler* v. *Crane, Christmas & Co.* (1951) was more specific – the duty of care was to the company and its shareholders, and not to any third party relying on the audit opinion. This UK position is compatible with the privity of contract decision in the US case of *Ultramares Corporation* v. *Touche* (1931). However, despite the apparent consistency of these rulings, the issue over third-party liability is far from clear, and court attitudes on the matter have changed over time.

The above situation has been complicated in recent times by the UK case of *Caparo Industries* v. *Dickman* (1990), in which the judgment indicated a need to make a further distinction between the collective body of shareholders and individual shareholders. In particular, the decision indicated that the corporate auditor is responsible to the body of shareholders, but not to any individual shareholder who may rely on his or her work or report (Godsell, 1991, pp.41–2).

Responsibility to third parties?

The subject-matter of the corporate auditor's work is the set of financial statements which are annually addressed directly to shareholders, but which are also available and accessed by a variety of other users – to the extent that they have become, albeit unintentionally, a form of public good. In this respect, the obvious problem for corporate auditors is whether they have a legal duty of care to any third-party user who has suffered a quantifiable loss as a result of relying on the audited statements when the audit work has been negligent. Over many years, courts have attempted to resolve this issue within these terms, the most important separable factor being the need to establish a non-contractual duty of care (Gwilliam, 1991, p.61). No universal agreement, however, has been reached on the issue.

This creates a problem for the corporate auditor, particularly, and the accountancy profession more generally. In fact, there is a considerable public interest issue at stake (Gwilliam, 1991, pp.71–2). The corporate auditor is legally required to protect the company and its shareholders from poor quality financial reporting. The time and effort involved in such monitoring is already committed from a social welfare point of view (p.72). And auditors and their profession have a self-interest to assume a wider responsibility in order to justify the financial and social rewards which can be received from auditing (p.71). But the problem is one of fairness to the auditor when opening the door to potential liability to any third party who may access and rely on the quality of audited financial statements. In this respect, the courts over several decades have established a number of key factors to assist in a consideration of the dilemma.

The first of these factors is a combination of concepts described as just and reasonable foreseeability and proximity – that is, the corporate auditor can reasonably identify a just and reasonable third-party liability in circumstances where there is sufficient proximity between the company and the third party to anticipate the latter's reliance on the former's audited financial statements. This multifaceted general principle has evolved from a series of decisions in the US. For example, *Rusch Factors Inc.* v. *Levin* (1968) and *Ryan* v. *Kanne* (1969) extended the auditor's liability to third parties who are members of a known but limited class of audit beneficiaries. And *Rosenblum Inc.* v. *Adler* (1983) extended the liability to beneficiaries whom the auditor could reasonably foresee.

The latter position was accepted in the New Zealand case of *Scott Group* v. *McFarlane & Anors* (1978), and in two cases – *Jeb Fasteners* v. *Marks Bloom & Co.* (1981) and *Twomax* v. *Dickson, McFarlane & Robinson* (1983). In other words, the combined effect of these cases over a number of years in several countries appears to confirm that the concept of reasonable foreseeability is firmly established, and that corporate auditors must accept that they have a duty of care to those persons who might rely on their work and would suffer loss if an action for professional negligence can be sustained – that is, assuming that such possible reliance is known to the auditor or should have been reasonably foreseen.

However, more recently in the UK, in *Caparo Industries* v. *Dickman* (1990), a second modifying general principle of third-party liability has been introduced. This centres around a legal test that the auditor knew the audited financial statements were to be given to a known third-party for a known specific purpose (Godsell, 1991, p.42; and Gwilliam, 1991, p.68). Factors which influenced this judgment were the court's belief that the key purpose of corporate financial statements is stewardship and not investment decision-making; the need to look at individual circumstances; and, more generally, the difficulty in each circumstance of establishing foreseeability, proximity, and a just reasonableness (Gwilliam, 1991, pp.67–8).

There therefore appear to be signs of a judicial move back to the legal position enunciated in the *Ultramares* case in the US in the 1930s, and the *Candler* case in the UK in the 1950s. This is a situation which is confusing and troublesome for corporate auditors. In particular, it takes a narrow view of the auditor's role in corporate accountability, and specifically ignores the realities of financial statements being accessible by report users making decisions in a variety of markets. It is also contrary to the prescriptions of accounting policy-makers such as FASB (1978 and 1980) and ASB (1991b) concerning the requirement of audited financial statements of corporate organizations to be decision-useful generally, and relevant and reliable particularly. It is sensible to ensure that corporate auditors are not being asked to assume legal responsibilities for potentially negligent work which are unfair and unjust to them. But it is equally important to recognize the societal utility of corporate financial statements, and the variety of social and economic roles which the corporate auditor has in establishing the quality of such statements (as discussed in Chapter 3 of this text). Somehow, defining the corporate auditor's duty of care in this broad environment has to be a matter of priority – such that the self-interest of auditors can be reasonably met, and the public interest in their function can be properly satisfied. Neither of these matters should exclude the other if the corporate audit is to serve a meaningful purpose. In this respect, Godsell (1991, pp.9–10) argues a need for innovative legislation which involves a feasible rather than ideal solution to this dilemma, recognizing the need to accommodate the respective positions and needs of the producers, users and auditors of corporate financial information.

Holding the corporate auditor accountable

The previous sections attempt to outline the legal position of responsibility with respect to the office of corporate auditor. However, this is not the only way in which auditors' duty of care can be observed. They also have an ethical responsibility as members of a designated profession. Particularly as members of recognized professional bodies, they are subject to the regulations of these bodies which exist to ensure they act in ways which comply with stated and accepted professional standards of behaviour. Thus, corporate auditors must be conscious of their responsibilities to their corporate clients (and, possibly, other interested individuals and organizations with legitimate interests in these clients), and to their profession.

Corporate auditors can be held accountable for the quality of their work in a number of different ways. First, there is the mechanism of a formal complaint to the auditor's professional body leading to disciplinary procedures and, if he or she is found guilty, punishment including expulsion from membership. In this way, the professional body is fulfilling its implied covenant with society to protect it from sub-standard work by its individual members. The second mechanism is the one alluded to throughout most of this chapter, and that is the law suit seeking damages for alleged negligent work by the corporate auditor. As mentioned above, this can be done either by the company in terms of the audit contract (thus effectively acting on behalf of the body of shareholders) or, less frequently, by individual shareholders or other third parties under tort. Such a legal action is formulated on the basis of the nature of the specific complaint against the corporate auditor. It may be criminal if the work of the auditor is felt to have been deliberately dishonest or fraudulent. Or it may be in the form of a civil action when the complaint concerns negligence when audit behaviour does not meet accepted work standards.

A third form of accountability which is rarely discussed is the internal mechanisms within audit firms which are designed to control the actions of individual audit engagement partners. Individual corporate auditors cannot be regarded as stand-alone professionals when they are members of a firm involving other professional colleagues with joint and several liability for negligent work. Thus, individual auditors are subject to internal standards and procedures which effectively evaluate the quality of their audit activities. These may be explicit mechanisms involving internal peer review, or they may be more subtle and indirect pressures to perform to a specific standard of behaviour and competence. In this respect, individual audit partners and their colleagues must guard against pressures which compromise audit quality for short-term economic benefit (see, for example, Miller, 1992).

Responsibility and changing corporate audit standards

What the previous sections in this chapter attempt to describe are the difficulties which the corporate auditor faces when charged by legislators or other regulators with the specific task of giving an expert and objective opinion on the quality of reported financial statements. Such a function tends to be dynamic rather than static in nature, particularly because the financial statements concerned can be accessed and used by a variety of individuals and organizations who are not specifically contracted to the corporate auditor. In addition, the expected qualities of the financial statements can be interpreted and perceived in different ways, at different times, and by different individuals and organizations. Thus, it is difficult for corporate auditors to know at any particular point of time, and in relation to any individual set of corporate circumstances, what is legally expected of them in terms of a duty of care involving best practice and potential audit beneficiaries. The situation is fluid, and it should not be surprising to find the corporate audit profession as a social grouping tending to consistently prescribe limitations to its members' audit responsibilities.

A justification for this cautious approach can be made by reference to a number of court decisions made at various times which have caused concern to individual corporate auditors and the accountancy profession generally, some examples of which now follow.

- **Rex v. Kylsant** (1932) The corporate auditor in this case was accused of aiding and abetting the publication of misleading financial statements which had damaged the company's shareholders. The statements were deemed to be misleading because they overstated the profitability and financial position of the company as a result of undisclosed transfers from reserves and provisions. At the time of the case, this practice was not only used by companies but was also generally accepted by the accountancy profession. However, the judge held that, because such undisclosed transfers were intended to deceive report users by not revealing the truth about the company's profitability and financial position, the auditor had a duty to reveal the truth of the situation.

What is important about the decision in this case is the fact that the court set an accounting standard beyond what was then determined by the accountancy profession as best practice. In other words, use of what is regarded as best practice as a defence in a negligence suit is inadequate in circumstances where the court determines that such practice does not adequately protect the company and its shareholders. Thus, despite the existence of prescribed accounting and auditing standards, corporate auditors must look to the circumstances of the individual audit to judge whether, in the interests of the audit beneficiaries, they need to go beyond these standards.

- *Escott* et al. v. *Bar Chris Construction Corporation* (1968) In this US case, the corporate auditor was found guilty of not re-visiting a previous audit to determine the continuing validity of his original opinion on the financial statements concerned. This was a prospectus situation in which evidence available after the audit affected the quality of the information reported in the prospectus statement. Corporate auditors' duty of care was judged to be one which, contrary to then existing best practice, does not stop when they complete their audits and write their opinions. Instead, if such opinions are relied on in the future in circumstances in which they no longer remain valid because of new evidence, they should verify and report this appropriately.

- *United States* v. *Simon* (1969) This was a case in which the corporate auditor had verified certain loan transactions between the company and an affiliate, but had failed to investigate the use to which the funds had been put, and thus had not determined their recoverability. The auditor followed what was then best practice, but the court set a higher standard which had not been anticipated by him. From the decision in this case, it would appear that corporate auditors are expected to go well beyond the companies they are auditing to verify the quality of the information they attest. How far they have to go in order to satisfy this requirement is problematic. What is clear is that they must treat each audit situation on its merits – irrespective of what existing standards suggest, and always with an enquiring mind.

- *Pacific Acceptance Corporation Ltd* v. *Forsyth and Others* (1970) *Pacific Acceptance* was an Australian case dealing with a situation similar to the findings of a Canadian Royal Commission Report on *Atlantic Acceptance Corporation Ltd*. In both instances, the judgments indicated that the corporate auditors concerned had followed existing best practice by relying on the truthfulness of external certificates and opinions concerning the existence of securities, and by not investigating qualified audit opinions on subsidiary company financial statements. The effect of these judgments was to cause US and UK auditors to clarify their approach to reliance on the work of other specialists and other auditors (this is now contained, respectively, in AICPA, 1991, pp.157–9 and 299–305; and in APC, 1986a and 1986b).

- **United States v. Weiner (1978)** The implications of this US case for the auditing profession were such that a special committee was formed in 1975 to consider the main issues. The case (*Equity Funding*) centred on a major fraud which was not discovered by the auditor. The corporate audit issues identified by the AICPA committee (AICPA, 1975) involved the consequences of loss of independence when the auditor becomes too close to client management; the need to clarify the duty to report on fraudulent activity to shareholders and regulators when management is defrauding; and the need to be competent with respect to computerized information systems.

Each of these issues remains a problem to the present community of corporate auditors. The effectiveness of the corporate audit depends to a significant degree on co-operation and good relations between the auditor and management. But to what extent these relations can be taken depends on each set of circumstances. The need for the corporate auditor to report on the consequences of fraudulent acts other than to senior management is unclear – particularly when senior managers are part of the fraud (the auditor's duty of confidentiality is usually assumed to be paramount – AICPA, 1991, pp.62–3; and APC, 1990, para.31). And computer technology appears to change continuously, requiring a level of expertise beyond that with which the typical auditor is currently equipped.

Responsibility for evidential material in corporate auditing

The recurrent theme of this text is the role of the corporate auditor in the process of corporate governance and managerial accountability. More precisely, this is expressed as the expert and independent verification of the expected quality of reported financial information. The duty of care of corporate auditors is therefore incompletely stated unless there is an indication of what is required of them with respect to completing such an audit. In particular, attention should be paid to the corporate auditor's responsibility to obtain and evaluate sufficient evidential material with which to formulate an opinion, and the corresponding duty to report that opinion meaningfully. These duties are explicitly expressed by standard-setting bodies – for example, with respect to sufficient competent evidence on which to base an opinion (AICPA, 1991, p.7; and APC, 1980b, para.4); and a meaningful opinion (AICPA, 1991, p.7; and APC, 1989, para.6).

A number of court cases have reinforced these principles of corporate auditing. The need to seek adequate evidence beyond the verification of the arithmetical accuracy of the financial statements has been emphasized in early cases such as

Leeds Estate, Building and Investment Co. v. *Shepherd* (1887), *The London Oil Storage Co. Ltd* v. *Seear, Hasluck & Co.* (1904), and *Arthur E. Green & Co.* v. *The Central Advance and Discount Corporation Ltd* (1920). The need to get away from a recomputation type of audit was highlighted in the case of *City Equitable Fire Insurance Co. Ltd* (1924) (with respect to independent external confirmations of asset and liability characteristics); and *Westminster Road Construction and Engineering Co. Ltd* (1932) (in relation to exploring evidence beyond the accounting records and explanations of company officials).

The need for adequate audit evidence was particularly brought to the attention of reporting accountants and corporate auditors in the 1941 Securities and Exchange Commission investigation of *McKesson and Robbins Inc.* This audit situation made explicit the corporate auditor's duty of care with respect to going outside the client company's accounting system for independent evidence to confirm or deny the validity of the accounting numbers reported in the financial statements (by, for example, physical inspections of inventory and external confirmations of receivables). This situation, arguably more than any other in the history of corporate auditing, had the effect of changing generally accepted audit practice almost instantly – especially with respect to evaluating evidence from a reliable source. Other cases already mentioned in this chapter merely emphasize this last point (for example, *BarChris*, *Continental Vending*, *Pacific Acceptance*, and *Equity Funding*). In other words, the corporate auditor's duty of care with respect to audit evidence is not determined solely on the basis of the quantity of evidence obtained. It has much to do with its quality and, particularly, the quality of the evidential source. The major issue today is determining evidence and evidential sources which are capable of supporting an opinion on the expected quality of the reported financial information. This will be the subject of the remaining two chapters of the text.

A review and overall comment

This chapter outlines and discusses the accountability complexities associated with the corporate auditor's function of agency. In particular, it is clear that, as part of the principal–agent relationship between corporate management and shareholders, the auditor is also acting as an agent accountable to the latter group. What is less clear is his or her position with respect to a society in which a broader corporate accountability is expected.

The focus of this problem is the public availability of audited financial statements, and the potential multiplicity of uses associated with them. The corporate auditor's task is usually defined by regulation as the reporting of an expert opinion on a stated quality of these statements. The auditor is expected at law to conduct such a function according to appropriate standards of care and skill as a prudent practitioner. A major problem in this respect, however, is that such standards tend to be dictated by societal expectations of the audit function at a particular point in time. And expectations can change over time as societal attitudes and tolerances to behaviour change. Corporate auditors therefore have to be sensitive to attitudes, tolerances and expectations concerning their function. Their difficulty is that such matters may only become apparent *ex post* to a significant and public corporate failure. Thus, corporate auditors, and their regulating professional bodies, are always in the difficult position of attempting to predict changes in societal expectations *vis-à-vis* the corporate audit function.

Attempts by the corporate auditor to match public expectations should be made in the context of what is regarded as fair and reasonable. There are limits to what any professional practitioner can be expected to achieve in his or her function. It can be constrained by factors such as available time, appropriate skill, and economic cost. It is therefore unfair and unreasonable to ask the corporate auditor to be accountable for audit tasks which are significantly constrained by factors which have not previously been recognized and addressed. A case in point is the present situation with respect to criticism of the corporate auditor for failure to detect fraud or to warn of impending business failure. These tasks can be undertaken, but not within the strict limits of a function designed to report on the accounting quality of disclosed financial information.

The current situation with respect to articulating a clear statement of corporate auditor responsibility is confused not just by public criticism reflecting expectations incompatible with possible achievement, but also by ambiguous signals from courts of law, professional bodies, and audit firms. Public expectations can be articulated by guardians of the public interest such as academics and politicians. Their main task is signalling the critical rationale for auditor responsibilities, rather than searching for meaningful solutions (see, for example, Mitchell *et al.*, 1991; and Gray, 1992). Courts, on the other hand, have tended over many years to provide both variety and, more recently, conservatism in their decisions with respect to the auditor's duty of care (Gwilliam, 1987, p.151). This, coupled with a current tendency to set standards beyond those expected by the accountancy profession (Gwilliam, 1987, p.157), has created considerable uncertainty as to what the corporate auditor is and should be doing, and for whom he or she is acting.

Professional accountancy bodies have reacted to this uncertainty typically by denials of responsibility beyond what is conventionally regarded by the accounting community as a reasonable duty of care and skill. This response is understandable as a counter to an uncertain and ambiguous situation, but it also provides a signal of a conservative profession unwilling to change to meet the needs and expectations of relevant groups in society. The situation has been further complicated by individual corporate auditors in situations of corporate failure being sued for negligence but settling out of court. What this procedure does is prevent the details of the situation becoming public knowledge. Thus, the concept of corporate auditor responsibility is not being discussed in an appropriate public forum, and the difficulty of matching expectations and achievements is perpetuated.

Further reading

D. Godsell (1991) *Auditors' Legal Duties and Responsibilities*, Longman (a recent review and discussion of the many facets of the auditor's duty of care).

D. Flint (1988) *Philosophy and Principles of Auditing*, Macmillan, pp.144–50 (a warning that auditor responsibility is a concept governed by changing societal expectations).

D. Gwilliam (1991) The auditor's liability to third parties, in M. Sherer and S. Turley (eds), *Current Issues in Auditing*, Paul Chapman Publishing, pp.60–75 (a discussion of the changing concept of auditor responsibility to third parties, with specific regard to recent court decisions).

D.P. Tweedie (1991) Fraud – managements' and auditors' responsibilities for its prevention and detection, in M. Sherer and S. Turley (eds), *Current Issues in Auditing*, Paul Chapman Publishing, pp.22–33 (an up-to-date review of the problem of assuming a responsibility for detecting fraud).

S.R. Byington and S.G. Sutton (1991) The self-regulating profession: an analysis of the political monopoly tendencies of the audit profession, *Critical Perspectives on Accounting*, 2(4), pp.315–30 (critical research to reveal the slowness of the audit profession to respond to criticisms of its standards).

Discussion and essay topics

1. How can the corporate auditor be held accountable for the quality of his or her audit work?
2. Comment on how the corporate auditor copes with changing circumstances and expectations regarding the duty of audit care.
3. To what extent should corporate auditors be held accountable for the quality of their audit work? Should this be to shareholders or to a wider group of potential audit beneficiaries?
4. Relate the concept of corporate auditor responsibility to that of economic agency.
5. Compare and contrast the notion of audit risk to that of the corporate auditor's business risk.
6. Prepare a critique of the conventional concept of the prudent corporate auditor.
7. Prepare a commentary outlining the matters for which corporate auditors are believed to be responsible, and those for which they deny responsibility.
8. Discuss the problems associated with holding the corporate auditor responsible for the detection of fraud and error.
9. Review existing case law regarding the corporate auditor's duties to audit beneficiaries.

9

Attesting corporate financial statement quality

The purpose of this and the following chapter is to examine critically the 'what' and the 'how' of corporate auditing. Previous chapters are primarily concerned with the function's 'why' and its 'who'. There is therefore a need to redress this imbalance by introducing the reader to the subject of auditing as distinct from that of the auditor. Before doing this, however, and as a preparation for the detail of this chapter, it is useful to review what is stated in earlier parts of the text with respect to the corporate audit generally, and the quality of audited financial statements particularly.

The corporate audit is fundamentally an agency situation, in which the separation of the agent–manager from the principal–shareholder creates doubts for the latter about the actions of the former. Such doubts are the stimuli for an accountability exercise in which corporate management reports directly to shareholders (and indirectly to others) by means of formal financial statements containing accounting-based messages about its performance. The recipients of these statements may take decisions based at least partly on them. But, because of the potential moral hazard of management manipulating the information, and adversely affecting the nature and quality of the decisions, the corporate auditor is employed as an agent of the principal–shareholders to verify independently the financial statements' accounting quality.

This quality is typically expressed by regulators of corporate activity in terms of over-riding and undefined characteristics such as 'present fairly' and 'a true and fair view'. Recently, however, accounting policy-makers have prescribed and defined the primary reporting qualities as relevance and reliability. The significance of this emphasis for corporate auditors is that they appear to have a regulated responsibility to give an opinion which effectively states whether or not the audited financial statements from corporate management are capable of impacting specific user decisions, and that they correspond with stated economic phenomena. This perception of the corporate audit presumes, *inter alia*, that the auditor has knowledge of user decisions, and can observe reportable and verifiable economic phenomena. It also assumes that such a function is needed and is feasible. The purpose of this chapter is to examine and discuss the reasonableness of these assumptions.

Corporate business activity and auditing

Corporate financial reporting is essentially an information system designed to construct and represent abstractions of the state and effects of specific empirical events which comprise the business activity of a corporate organization. A company is legally created in order to facilitate and control the use of scarce economic resources by means of contractual exchanges which are funded from a variety of external sources. The rationale for such a legal structure is that it is more efficient and economical to transact in this form than by individual market exchanges (Williamson, 1975, p.8). More specifically, Williamson (1981, p.1537) views the corporate body as a natural consequence of transaction cost economics:

> . . . the modern corporation is mainly to be understood as the product of a series of organisational innovations that have had the purpose and effect of economising on transaction costs.

Corporate financial reporting is therefore an informational technology which observes business activity as it occurs in transactional arrangements within and between corporate structures, and re-presents it in a calculational form at a later time to shareholders and other external corporate constituents. Such representational abstraction of corporate business activity is intended as a substitute for direct experience of it for those who could not be there when the events concerned took place.

In these circumstances, the task of the corporate accountant is to create and present abstract accounting messages of former economic exchanges on behalf of management. He or she therefore brings the corporate past into the present by representing it in a set of financial statements. In doing so, shareholders and other external constituents of the reporting company are given a limited access to and vision of past events and related empirical phenomena. The main objective of this representation of the company's past is to facilitate future economic action by those individuals and organizations interested in but separated from the corporate structure.

Hopwood (1990) argues generally for this perception of the role of accounting in organizational activity and, for purposes of this chapter, it has been extended to the corporate audit function. In particular, the ability of corporate management and its reporting accountants to recreate and make visible aspects of a company's economic past by means of accounting calculation, and to influence future economic action as a result, is a very powerful reason for requiring an audit function.

For example, making visible parts of the economic past of a company implies the presence of a selection process used by its reporting management and accountants, in which other parts remain invisible (Hopwood, 1990, p.9); quantified but subjectively-based accounting calculations provide an apparent precise realism to economic phenomena which would otherwise be imprecise and unreal (pp.9–10); and economic actions, which otherwise might not be, are enabled to take place by the visibility created by the calculations (p.10).

In other words, the corporate accounting process is both selective and judgmental, and can have organizational consequences which justify a verification function to establish the quality of the accounting selections and judgments, and their potential effects on economic actions. More specifically, this text argues that the corporate auditor's main task *vis-à-vis* accounting representations of corporate business activity is to provide an expert opinion on whether they are adequate representations of a past for those individuals and organizations who were not then present.

The corporate audit is therefore an expert function to verify whether those aspects of past corporate activity made visible by accounting for stewardship purposes are relevant to shareholders and other external interests, and have been reliably calculated and presented in a way which will not lead to inappropriate economic action. Conversely, the corporate auditor has a responsibility to determine whether aspects of past corporate business activity which are potentially relevant, and can be reliably represented, have not been left invisible by the corporate management process of accounting selection and judgment.

The above arguments appear to support the existence of a two-tier duty for the corporate auditor with respect to attesting reporting quality in terms of defined prescriptions and undefined over-rides. In particular, it is possible to conceive of an audit situation in which the auditor attests the relevance and reliability of the reported information (in the sense of what is reported reasonably complying with these criteria), but where the over-riding quality objective of 'present fairly' or 'a true and fair view' is not met for purposes of corporate accountability (because of what is not reported).

The corporate accounting process and the auditor

As indicated in the previous section, the main focus of the contemporary audit of the corporate accounting process is the past business activity of the reporting company. Such activity usually takes the form of a physical reality of empirically-testable economic exchanges of goods and services which form part of conventional trading. Operationalizing this reality is typically achieved by a management of contracted transactions, although non-transacted events external to the company (such as price or foreign exchange movements) may also be part of it. Corporate auditors therefore have a considerable interest in those transactions and non-transacted events which are (or are not) captured by the corporate accounting process. Their primary task is to determine the adequacy of the consistency between the observable corporate physical reality, the reported accounting reality, and the decision needs of report users (that is, the reported information's relevance and reliability).

Corporate economic exchange involves managers and employees interacting continuously over time with individuals and organizations comprising the company's customers, suppliers, bankers, government agencies, debtholders and shareholders. These individuals and organizations constitute the potential audience for the verified informational output from its accounting process. The two major components of the company's business activity which form the basis for conventional accounting processing are the stocks and flows which result from selected economic exchanges. These are conventionally described in terms of accounting calculations of assets, liabilities and equities (which, when combined, form the company's financial (accounting) position at a designated point of time); matched sales revenues and related operating expenditures (which describe its financial (accounting) profit-ability); and related inflows and outflows (which constitute its financial (accounting) cash flow).

These financial accounting calculations are typically articulated into a set of financial statements which form the regulatory object of the corporate auditor's attention and opinion. They represent the company's past business activity to its shareholders and other external constituents, and the auditor is expected to comment on the quality of the representations as a set. He or she does so in terms of observing the physical reality, verifying the accounting process of abstracting that reality, and judging the presentation of the resultant abstractions.

Reality and the corporate accounting process

The function of a company's accounting system in relation to external financial reporting is to observe empirically its economic exchanges, identify and select those internal transactions and related external events for which there requires to be an accounting, process the selected transactions and events in an appropriate way to construct an accessible accounting data bank (usually by means of the well-established rules of double-entry bookkeeping), further select from this data bank those recorded accounting data which are judged to be reportable to shareholders and other external constituents, manipulate[1] the selected data in an acceptable way to provide reportable accounting calculations (usually by reference to a prescribed and authoritative set of accounting standards) and present these calculations in the form of accounting messages about the company's selected economic exchanges (usually by reference to mandated corporate regulations for external disclosure as part of corporate governance and managerial accountability).

The accounting process which the corporate auditor is required to verify and attest is therefore a complex judgmental sequence involving selection, processing, manipulation, compliance and presentation by corporate management and its reporting accountants. It empirically observes a largely physical reality of corporate economic exchange, and describes this in an abstract accounting form according to certain accepted rules and procedures which are judged to be appropriate for the specific circumstances. Corporate auditors are expected to attest the adequacy of financial accounting observations, judgments and procedures prior to the entry of the financial statements into the physical world of economic exchange which they partially represent. Their work is therefore a crucial element of that world.

What the previous paragraphs suggest is that, once audited and disclosed, the company's accounting abstractions of its business activity constitute a further physical reality in the form of a set of corporate financial statements which are available for use in decisions affecting future activity. These public representations of the corporate past therefore become part of a complex mix of present and future economic, political and social realities. The information they contain is used in a variety of decision and action settings and, consequently, has the potential to impact numerous economic, political and social discourses. As Hines (1988) argues, when accountants attempt to communicate aspects of reality to financial statement users, they also create the further reality of the statements themselves which, in turn, and when used in decision-making, reshape reality. Morgan (1988, p.484) describes this sequence in terms of accountants being enmeshed in the process of reality construction when attempting to help financial statement users to perceive that reality by means of accounting messages. Tinker (1991, p.305) also identifies the often conflicting and entwining political and social roles which the corporate accountant plays when attempting to reflect so-called economic reality.

In other words, the corporate audit is part of a complex process of reality construction. Audited financial statements form an important component of economic, political and social relationships. In these circumstances, attesting the quality of the reported output of the corporate accounting process should not be regarded as an independent and neutral function. As explained in Chapter 7, corporate auditors need and are expected to be independent in thought and deed in order to give credibility to their opinions. However, their reports are attached to the disclosed financial statements, effectively giving considerable authority to their use in a variety of contexts.

In particular, corporate auditors' independent opinions can be interpreted as explicit permissions to use the verified statements with confidence, and their audit work can be regarded as a major determinant of what is or what is not disclosed to shareholders and other external constituents. On each reporting occasion, a combination of regulators, corporate management, and the independent auditor effectively establish which aspects of the output of the accounting process are to be made visible, and which are to remain invisible. And, as stated above, this determination inevitably impacts individual decisions and, equally inevitably, results in economic, political and social consequences which reshape reality.

Economic reality and the corporate auditor

These thoughts are presented in the context of a corporate financial reporting function which increasingly appears to be expected to contain audited accounting messages reflecting so-called economic reality. Accounting theorists from the early 1960s onwards have invoked images of the potential of the accounting process to represent and correspond with an underlying economic reality (for example, Chambers, 1962, p.17; AAA, 1966, p.10; Sterling, 1970b, p.41; Staubus, 1977, p.44; Stamp, 1980, p.78; Ruland, 1984, p.224; and McMonnies, 1988, p.18). It is also to be found in the accounting policy-making prescriptions of standard-setters – particularly with respect to their mandate for reliable information which faithfully represents or corresponds to the economic phenomena or reality it purports to describe (for example, FASB, 1980, para.63 in the USA; and ASB, 1991b, para.30 in the UK). Indeed, one of the most significant advocates of this perception of accounting's potential describes the function's failures in terms of its conventional inability to report accounting numbers with an association of an economic nature (Sterling, 1979, p.213):

> The primary problem of accounting is that our figures do not have empirical referents. The fault lies neither in the abstract nor in the concrete but in ourselves – we do not know

how to adjust our accounts. If figures do not represent empirical phenomena, then it is the preparers and purveyors of the figures who are at fault, not the phenomena.

The solution to the problem is to adopt the objective of reporting figures that represent empirical phenomena. The first, and most important, generally accepted accounting principle should be that we account for empirical phenomena. The kind of phenomena that we decide to account for is important, but secondary. We must first decide to account for some kind of phenomena. A corollary of this principle is the establishment of the generally accepted auditing standard that reported figures be empirically tested. The first, and most important, objective of auditing should be the assurance that the figures accurately represent the empirical phenomena that they are intended to represent.

The role of the corporate auditor in this respect is not an easy one. As this text attempts to describe, the production (and quality) of financial statements by corporate management is not (and cannot be) a neutral process (as has been recently suggested by writers such as Solomons (1991, p.294) or accounting standard-setting bodies such as FASB (1980, para.101) and ASB (1991b, para.31)). As stated previously, reporting management makes choices as to which phenomena to report (and, therefore, which not to report), as well as on how to report those phenomena which have been chosen (Hines, 1989a, p.68; and Tinker, 1991, p.305).

These reporting decisions are typically determined only in part by regulation. In practice, the accounting choice of corporate management is influenced by a variety of economic, political and social pressures and conflicts affecting its self-interest. For example, it may regard the socially-desirable but not required disclosure of a contingent cost for environmental pollution by the company as neither economically or politically astute with respect to its short-term contracts of employment. And yet, because of potential litigation because of its environmentally-damaging behaviour, the long-term financial health of the company may be at considerable risk. Given the reporting over-ride of 'present fairly' or 'a true and fair view,' and assuming corporate compliance with detailed reporting requirements, the question must be asked as to whether so-called reality is being fully and properly revealed in such circumstances.

A major difficulty for corporate auditors in this respect is that they are paid by management and yet are expected to be independent of the latter (Sterling, 1979, p.15). They can independently attest the quality of what is reported in terms of what is specifically required to be reported. But they are on much less firm ground regarding disclosures which are not required but which, because of an undefined reporting quality over-ride, could be and are not.

Thus, despite their independence, corporate auditors can only minimize rather than eliminate inherent biases in corporate financial reporting. A positive audit opinion on the quality of corporate financial statements does not free these documents of the effects of economic, political and social pressures and conflicts with the potential to induce (or not) a particular user decision or action. In particular, adopting the general argument of Tinker (1991), it is impossible to assume that the accounting process is or can be independent of the corporate economic reality it purports to describe. It can only partially reveal corporate business activity because of, first, the subjective accounting selections by management and, second, the typical compression (using subjective accounting rules) by reporting accountants of reported data into a relatively few numbers and messages. Even the classical economic self-interest argument of agency theory recognizes this point when it includes in its description of a rational economic world a normative prescription for audit – that is, a need to verify the consistency of the accounting with the terms of the contracts concerned (Watts and Zimmerman, 1986, p.312; and Ball, 1989, p.39).

The role of the corporate auditor *vis-à-vis* the accounting process should therefore be perceived as verifying and attesting the quality of the partial access to information which corporate management has allowed shareholders and other external constituents by means of its financial statements. In particular, the auditor is reporting on the adequacy of the visibility provided in terms of the accountability contracted between the company and its stakeholders by means of internal and external regulations. The main audit problems in this respect concern what is meant by quality in terms of a partial access, and by adequacy in terms of the visibility provided by such access. Each of these issues focuses both on what the accounting process recognizes for reporting purposes (the recognition problem), and how it is reported (the measurement problem). The following sections deal with each of these matters in turn.

The recognition problem and the corporate auditor

As explained in Chapter 1 onwards, the principal reporting quality criteria on which this text is based are relevance and reliability. For example, ASB (1991b, paras. 23 and 26) defines these terms, respectively, as follows:

> To be useful, information must be relevant to the decision-making needs of users. Information has the quality of relevance when it influences the economic decisions of users by helping them evaluate past, present or future events or by confirming, or correcting, their past evaluations.

> To be useful, information must also be reliable. Information has the quality of reliability when it is free of material error and bias and can be depended on by users to represent faithfully in terms of valid description that which it purports to represent or could reasonably be expected to represent.

FASB (1980, paras. 47 and 59) prescribes similar criteria – except that relevance is described in terms of potential to influence decisions.

These prescribed informational characteristics are based on common-sense notions which are difficult to put into effect – that is, report users need information about the reporting corporate organization which they can trust and use in order to make sensible decisions relating to it. However, as mentioned previously in this chapter, in order to establish the consistency of reported financial statements with these criteria, the corporate auditor needs to examine what aspects of corporate business activity have been selected for accounting purposes (informational relevance), and how the relevant aspects have been processed through the accounting system (informational reliability). In doing so, the corporate auditor will also be answering the questions of what has not been recognized, and how different the accounting could have been using different processing methodologies. This section is concerned with recognition, and therefore predominantly with informational relevance. As such, it also relates to the prime objective of corporate auditing which is to assist in the process of managerial accountability – a matter recognized both by FASB (1980, para.50) and

ASB (1991b, para.14) in their specification of relevant information for stewardship purposes.

With respect to accounting recognition, this text takes a position consistent with Johnson and Storey (1982, p. 123) – that is, the corporate auditor's general attention is focused on specific events affecting the financial condition of the audited company and, more particularly, on economic events in which it has been involved over a past period of time. This approach is adopted for two reasons. First, events embrace external matters other than specific internally-managed transactions affecting the corporate condition. And, second, whilst recognizing the importance of arguments such as those of Tinker and Neimark (1990, p.45) that a focus on economic exchanges limits the reported portrayal of corporate activity (because it ignores the political and social dimensions of transactions) this text prefers to concentrate the reader's attention primarily but not exclusively on the conventional audit task (as argued in Chapter 1).

A primary function of the corporate auditor is to verify and attest whether the reporting company's accounting system has recognized all internal and external economic events affecting its financial condition which have the potential to influence the decisions of its shareholders and other external constituents, and thereby to affect the stewardship reporting of management. More specifically, the corporate auditor observes and tests for the effects of economic transactions and other events on the corporate organization's designated assets, liabilities and equities (see Johnson and Storey, 1982, pp.123–43).

Implied in this prescription of the corporate audit is an assumption of explicit practical criteria to assist the auditor in the recognition of such accountable phenomena. In fact, accounting standard-setters have attempted to produce criteria, although they exist in relatively naive form (as, for example, in FASB, 1984 and FASB, 1985 in the US; and ASC, 1990 in the UK). Indeed, there is recognition in these pronouncements of the difficulty of prescribing recognition criteria for every reportable situation (ASC, 1990, para.3.3).

Of particular concern to corporate auditors is that, when they examine an economic transaction, or observe an external event affecting the reporting company's financial condition, they have adequate means of determining whether it has been properly classified for accounting purposes (according to its nature), and accurately recorded (according to its exchange value) – in both cases relating these judgments to user decisions and managerial accountability. For example, they are concerned to verify that, within the company's accounting process, capital transactions are properly distinguished from revenue transactions. Inadequacies in this distinction can result in serious distortions of accounting relationships used to assess corporate economic and managerial performance (such as profit returns and financial position indicators) and, thus, managerial stewardship.

The difficulties facing corporate auditors in this area are considerable. In particular, they have very little means of operationalizing the relevance criteria *vis-à-vis* their audits. If properly adhered to, it requires them to assess recognition in accounting in relation to the influence of information on user decisions. As they have no formal guidance or knowledge of these decisions in particular circumstances, they can only presume such influence. This makes relevance an exceedingly difficult prescription to presently build into the corporate audit.

In addition, the corporate auditor has to determine whether the reporting company has adhered to what has become a major but ill-defined principle of financial accounting – that the observed transaction or event is accounted for according to its economic substance rather than its legal form. Alternatively, that the economic intention of the transaction or event, rather than its legal camouflage, is recognized in the accounting process (see, for example, AICPA, 1972, p.127 and AICPA, 1973, p.57 in the US; and ASC, 1990, para.2 and ASB, 1991b, para.30 in the UK – it should be noted that FASB (1980, para.160) prefers to use the alternative faithful representation criterion). The main intention of this audit task is to counter a growing tendency of corporate management to enhance its accountable performance by reclassifying transactions to comply with the legal propriety rather than with their economic intention (see Briloff, 1972 and 1976 for a general US review of this problem; and Griffiths, 1986; Rutherford, 1988; and Tweedie and Whittington, 1990 for equivalent UK commentaries).

A major problem for the corporate auditor in this area is determining what is the economic substance of a specific transaction in a given set of circumstances. Corporate organizations' creativity in this area appears to be in advance of auditors' ability to respond effectively. The current issue for the accountancy community is therefore to provide corporate auditors with accounting standards which are sufficiently detailed, consistent and unambiguous to challenge effectively the propriety of their corporate clients' accounting recognition judgments (Rutherford, 1988, p.33; and Tweedie and Whittington, 1990, p.97). The problem is not just one of corporate managers deliberately constructing transactions to distort their financial statements. It is also concerned with developments in business activity which create new forms of transaction which require classification for the first time in accounting systems (ASC, 1990, para.2).

A useful summary of these recognition issues is given by Tweedie and Whittington (1990, pp.88–91). They describe the problems faced by corporate auditors in such matters as:

- **Off-balance sheet financing** – in which significant corporate resources, income and cash flow are never brought into the audited financial statements because of the terms in which the relevant contracted transactions are written (for example, leases, quasi-subsidiary companies, joint ventures, and contingent contracts). This is a good example of the visibility issue mentioned earlier – things that should be made visible by accounting are, instead, made invisible yet consistent with legal contracts. The possibility of relevant reporting being achieved with off-balance sheet financing is questionable.
- **Accounting for groups of companies** – in which the acquisition transactions are engineered in such a way as to make visible or invisible significant corporate resources (such as goodwill) and, in each case, depending on what management wishes to reveal. Again, the potential for relevant information under such circumstances is questionable.
- **Brands** – in which, in the absence of observable transactions, corporate management makes visible significant intangible resources (such as brand names) in order to effect specific corporate strategies (for example, to counter potential takeover bids). The reality of these 'resources' is a major matter of concern for a corporate auditor attesting informational relevance.

- **Capital issues and financial instruments** – in which corporate management can legally engineer debt and equity situations for financial reporting purposes different from the substantive position. These situations, too, bring the question of relevant information sharply into focus.

Each of these broad categories of accounting issue presents the corporate auditor with a substantial challenge *vis-à-vis* attesting the relevance (and reliability) of audited financial statements. The common thread running through them is the difficulty, in the absence of agreed standards, of recognizing unambiguously what is an asset, liability, revenue, operating expense, debt, or equity for reporting purposes – all accounting fundamentals, yet all relatively unresolved by accounting and auditing standard-setters at the present time. Corporate governance and managerial accountability is not enhanced by this situation.

Literature prescriptions for recognition in accounting

Writers on audit theory and practice have tended to follow an implicit principle that accounting and auditing are essentially two parts of the same subject. Thus, when auditing is discussed, its subject-matter is assumed as the financial statement output of an accounting system. As Flint (1988, p.49) argues, organizational accountability is usually exercised by means of periodic financial statements which require to be attested by an auditor who is a professionally qualified accountant. This is particularly the case with respect to conventional corporate accountability.[2] Thus, much of what is written about corporate audits, and the audit of financial statement quality, is concerned with how the accounting takes place rather than with what is accounted for.

For example, within the context of a discussion of the audit concept of fair presentation, Mautz and Sharaf (1961) briefly recognize, but do not discuss, an expectation that financial accounting should reflect an underlying economic reality of events, transactions and their effects (pp.158, 165 and 168). They concentrate instead on the acceptability of accounting practices to reflect that assumed reality, dealing particularly with the nature, incompleteness, authority, effect and essence of generally accepted accounting principles (pp.160–9). In other words, they recognize the problem of how to account but take what to account as a given. For example (p.169):

> Although the auditor borrows generally accepted accounting principles from the field of accounting, he does so with full recognition that he may have to reject their application in some cases. To the extent they are satisfactory in bringing about a realistic portrayal of the facts of business activity and conditions he is grateful for them; to the extent that they fail, he must draw upon his knowledge of their goals and develop solutions which his experience and judgment tell him are constructively useful.

This approach is mirrored by Lee (1972). While prescribing a primary corporate audit objective in terms of verifying accounting's ability to correspond with a reality of economic activities and transactions (p.30), and explaining briefly the nature of the business activity cycle (pp.113–16), his main emphasis is on the principles of producing accounting information describing this activity (including data processing, internal controls, financial statements, generally accepted accounting principles, and disclosure) (pp.116–37).[3]

Schandl (1978) represents the first serious attempt by an audit theorist to grapple with the accounting recognition problem. He discusses the process of accounting abstraction (pp.107–13), prior to describing the audit process as one of verifying the 'truth' (defined in terms of reality (p.117)) of accounting statements using available evidence (pp.114–27). In particular, he describes (pp.124–5) the ultimate audit focus of audit evidence, and the main audit task as one of determining the truthfulness of such evidence in relation to a norm of reality (p.122):

> The auditor has to arrive at an opinion (judgment) on the truth of the purported evidence. In this phase of the audit he is using the norm system of 'reality' for his judgment.

The idea of auditing being concerned to verify an underlying economic reality by empirically testing reported accounting figures is advocated by Sterling (1970b, pp.323–6; and 1979, p.213). In adopting this perception of the auditor's task, he has influenced audit theorists such as Wolnizer (1987) and Ruud (1989), both of whom endorse the prescription of financial accounting providing descriptions of empirical phenomena, and of auditing verifying the truth of such correspondence (Wolnizer, 1987, p.2; and Ruud, 1989, p.20). Indeed, Ruud (1989, pp.153–4) provides a particularly clear advocation:

> Financial reporting should adopt an objective for describing economic reality. Auditing would be defined as a verification process to ensure the information's correspondence to economic reality. Financial accounting and verification should be seen as an integrated process, with the same subject matter.

Wolnizer (1987) goes even further than Ruud when looking at the audit evidence process. In particular, he suggests that an audit function should seek to demonstrate the correspondence of abstract accounting representations with an underlying economic reality, and with the auditor using and testing evidence from sources independent of the reporting entity – that is, evidence which satisfies the description of being independently testable (pp.186–7). In other words, for financial statements to be fit for use, they require to be based on data from independent sources, and such data need to be independently verified (p.187).

The problem with these advocations is that they are long on general principle but short on practical guidance. As the previous paragraphs attempt to demonstrate, there is a growing literature concern for an audit function which is directed at attesting accounting's ability to represent a past (mainly) physical reality relating to the reporting entity. However, little authoritative guidance is available about what aspects of that reality should be reported. And, consistent with the earlier writings of audit theorists such as Mautz and Sharaf (1961), the main attention appears to be on how to report – for example, Wolnizer (1987, p.70) recommends the use of market prices for accounting purposes; and Ruud (1989, p.133) implies a similar approach.

There is therefore much to be thought through with the idea of a corporate audit with a corporate accountability objective of assessing the reporting quality of user relevance in terms of an accounting recognition of economic reality. In particular, the problem has to be addressed of what should be recognized as relevant economic reality for purposes of financial accounting and reporting. This appears to have much to do with the nature of the decision models of shareholders and other interested users.

User decisions and the corporate auditor

Decision utility has become an almost generally accepted primary objective of corporate financial reporting. For example, in the USA (FASB, 1978, para.31):

> The role of financial reporting in the economy is to provide information that is useful in making business and economic decisions, not to determine what these decisions should be.

And in the UK (ASB, 1991b, para.12):

> The objective of financial statements is to provide information about the financial position, performance and financial adaptability of an enterprise that is useful to a wide range of users in making economic decisions.

Each of these conceptual prescriptions additionally provides a brief and broad description of user decision groups such as investors and creditors (FASB, 1978, paras. 34–6; and ASB, 1991b, para.9). But neither provides sufficient detailed analysis and insight of decision categories to give the corporate reporting accountant or the corporate auditor a template with which to judge the relevance of particular reported information to specific types of decision model. Lack of knowledge about individual report user decision models is one reason why accounting theorists such as Sterling (1967, p.107; and 1972, p.200) advocate a general-purpose approach to decision utility in financial reporting – generalization being a convenient means of coping with the variety of specific types of decision. This approach is, of course, consistent with the practical history of financial reporting, and the current approach of bodies such as FASB (1978, para.30) and ASB (1991b, para.6).

But broad arguments relating to the convenience of a general purpose approach lead to legitimate concerns about the utility of particular accounting information to a vague generality of report users (Fraser and Nobes, 1985, p.146); the assumed rationality of these users with respect to their use of reported information (Williams, 1987, p.169; and Page, 1991b, p.31); and, particularly, the economic 'goodness' of such decision use (Williams, 1987, p.172). These doubts also affect any consideration of the role of corporate auditors *vis-à-vis* reporting quality and corporate accountability. They appear to be expected to provide opinions on the general relevance of reported information to the vaguely specified decision models of shareholders and others. But they have no detailed guidance available to them to make appropriate audit decisions about this indeterminate aspect of reporting quality.

More particularly, the corporate auditor has no means of authoritatively judging the reported information's decision utility in terms of whether relevant aspects of the corporate organization's past business activity are recognized for accounting purposes. In other words, until the recognition issue is adequately addressed in financial accounting, the corporate auditor will require to pay lip-service to the reporting and auditing matters of informational relevance and decision utility – despite the assumptions of user rationality and expertise implied by writers associated with accounting policy (such as Solomons, 1989, p.11; and Whittington, 1991, p.33). Ensuring that reported accounting information corresponds with economic reality thus remains a relatively hollow aspect of corporate auditing because the audit objective of relevance verification is so hard to achieve knowingly.

The corporate auditor and informational reliability

The previous sections in this chapter concentrate their reader's attention on the corporate auditor's task related to what is or what is not reported. Such an analysis centres on the reporting quality of relevance in relation to the reporting objective of decision-usefulness. The commentary has touched on the related quality criteria of reliability, but has not explored the topic in depth. This and subsequent sections repair such an omission.

Before proceeding to examine the notion of reporting reliability, it is useful to recap and expand the general prescription given in Chapter 2 that the corporate auditor's function is, in part, intended to give an opinion on the reliability of the accounting content of reported financial statements. For this purpose, such a prescription is derived from the statements of concepts of accounting standard-setters in the USA and the UK. For example, FASB (1980, para.59) defines reliability as follows:

> The reliability of a measure rests on the faithfulness with which it represents what it purports to represent, coupled with assurance for the user, which comes through verification, that it has that representational quality.

Thus, there is a publicly expressed expectation that, to be reliable, corporate financial statements should contain accounting information which has been verified and found representationally faithful. In this respect, FASB (1980, para.63) defines the latter quality as:

> . . . correspondence or agreement between a measure or description and the phenomenon it purports to represent. In accounting, the phenomena to be represented are economic resources and obligations and the transactions and events that change those resources and obligations.

Verifiability is described by FASB (1980, para.81) in terms of:

> . . . a significant degree of assurance that accounting measures represent what they purport to represent.

What these definitions and descriptions do is put the criteria of reliability firmly within the purview of corporate auditors.[4] That is, they are expected to verify how well reported accounting information describes the underlying economic activity recognized as relevant for accounting and reporting purposes. The problem for them is that, as with relevance, they have little guidance other than their experience to determine to what extent there has been faithful representation. ASB (1991b, para.30) in the UK attempts in very general terms to provide such assistance by relating the issue to a prescription for reporting economic substance:

> If information is to represent faithfully the transactions and other events that it purports to represent, it is necessary that they are accounted for and presented in accordance with

their substance and economic reality and not merely their legal form. The substance of transactions and events is not always consistent with that which is apparent from their legal form, especially if that form is contrived.

But this puts the onus on the corporate auditor to determine what is the economic substance of each transaction or event, and to distinguish this from its legal form. No significant and generally accepted guidance is available in this respect at the present time, and attention must be paid therefore to specific prescribed accounting standards for given situations. With this in mind, it is useful to discuss the reliability issue for the corporate auditor in the context of the accounting process which attempts to provide reliable information – that is, with respect to data processing and internal controls, and the application of accounting standards forming so-called generally accepted accounting principles (GAAP).

Data processing, internal controls and corporate auditing

As Mautz and Sharaf (1961, pp.158–9) point out, the auditor is essentially concerned with establishing and reporting on the propriety of disclosed accounting information. In the context of this text, propriety is interpreted as relevance and reliability. In particular, reliability is dependent on the effectiveness of the accounting process which observes corporate business activity, and translates selected aspects of it into an accounting form. Part of this sequence involves a system of processing data (including the presence of sound internal control procedures to maintain its integrity); and another part concerns the application of accounting standards to express the processed data in reportable form (involving standards in place which not only are applicable but have sufficient authority to be applied). This section of the text looks at the first part of the sequence, and the following section discusses the second part.

The verification of corporate data processing by the auditor is not just about determining whether or not the rules of double-entry bookkeeping have been correctly applied as in audits of old (see Moyer, 1951, p.4). Instead, the issue begins with the recognition problem discussed earlier in this chapter – that is, whether user-relevant transactions and events have been observed and captured by the data processing system. This requires the presence of controls to monitor these procedures, and to signal deficiencies. Recognition is then followed by a sequence of appropriate documenting, recording and collating procedures. In this respect, corporate auditors are concerned to verify the accuracy of the application of data processing rules. They are also concerned with the existence and efficiency of controls at each of these stages in data processing.

The entire system of producing accounting data will vary from corporate organization to corporate organization, such variation depending on factors such as entity size, and the volume and complexity of the transactions and other events to be processed. Consequently, the data-processing system examined and tested by the corporate auditor may involve manually-produced, machine-based or computer-driven data (or some relevant mix of these media). Each information technology involves different skills and competencies on the part of corporate auditors, but each suggests that they should expertly evaluate the strengths of the internal controls in operation.

This last point is fully recognized by current audit standard-setters. For example, the AICPA in the US prescribes it as a specific field work standard (AICPA, 1991, p.7):

> A sufficient understanding of the internal control structure is to be obtained to plan the audit and to determine the nature, timing, and extent of tests to be performed.

Further guidance on this standard is provided in a more detailed statement (AICPA, 1991, pp.73–96), and will be discussed more fully in Chapter 10. Meantime, within the context of discussing informational reliability, it is pertinent to explain the substance of the guidance – that is, corporate auditors should be fully aware of the strengths of the corporate organization's accounting controls within the broader context of the overall entity control structure, and should assess their audit risk of not detecting material accounting misstatements (AICPA, 1991, p.73; see also Temkin and Winters, 1988). Similar audit guidance and prescription exists to assist UK corporate auditors (APC, 1980b, para.5; and 1980f).

Generally accepted accounting principles and auditing

The previous section states that the informational quality of reliability is partly dependent on the existence and effectiveness of the system of data processing and its related controls. It is also contingent on the application of an accounting body of knowledge with the capacity to translate individual accounting data into reportable representations of corporate business activity. This body of knowledge largely comprises financial accounting standards, and has been given the generic label of GAAP. Corporate auditors have a significant interest in these principles as their current function is regarded in practice as one which reports on the compliance of the corporate client's financial statements with GAAP. For example, in the US (AICPA, 1991, p.7):

> The report shall state whether the financial statements are presented in accordance with generally accepted accounting principles.

And in the UK (APC, 1980c, para.8):

> When expressing an opinion on the financial statements . . ., the auditor should be satisfied, *inter alia*, that the accounting policies adopted: (a) are appropriate to the circumstances of the enterprise; (b) have been consistently applied; and (c) have been adequately disclosed. In determining whether the accounting policies are appropriate the auditor should have regard to Statements of Standard Accounting Practice . . . or any other relevant accounting requirements.[5]

These UK audit standards provide a useful introduction to considering the relevance of GAAP to the corporate audit task of attesting the quality of corporate financial statements in terms of reliability. In particular, consistent with Mautz and Sharaf (1961, p.159), and in order to attest reporting quality, the corporate auditor needs access to accounting principles which are generally accepted, have authoritative support, and are capable of improving and raising the quality of the audited financial statements to a satisfactory level.

In the context of this text, such a level refers to whether the financial statements are a faithful representation of selected relevant aspects of the company's business activity. Whether the existing body of accounting standards which constitute GAAP succeed in this mission is, at best, uncertain and, at worst, unknown. What is certain and known, however, is that there is such a body of practices, at least partially contained in formal accounting standards issued prescriptively by bodies such as FASB in the US (Statements of Financial Accounting Standards (SFAS)) and ASB in the UK (Financial Reporting Standards (FRS)). Indeed, these bodies are explicit in relating existing standards to the notion of GAAP. For example, the AICPA (1992, para.5) stipulates pronouncements of FASB and similar bodies as constituent parts of the latter, and ASB (1991b, para. 43) designates its accounting standards as a basis for the over-riding 'true and fair view'.

The problem for the corporate auditor is that few FASB, ASB or other accounting standards relate the prescribed practices they contain to the reporting quality criterion of reliability. Indeed, within the US context, FASB conceptual statements are not referred to in statements of standards, and are not to be regarded as standards (see, for example, FASB, 1978, para.3). In the UK, the ASB (1991b, para.2) is very clear in its proposed 'Statement of Principles' dealing with quality reporting criteria:

> This Statement of Principles is not an accounting standard and hence does not define standards for any particular measurement or disclosure issue. Nothing in this Statement of Principles over-rides any specific accounting standard.

Thus, corporate auditors are in a considerable dilemma. They are charged with an implied responsibility to verify and attest the quality of reported financial statements in terms of their reliability or faithful representativeness. They are also charged explicitly with a responsibility to verify and attest the financial statements' compliance with GAAP (defined typically in terms of prescribed accounting standards). But, because there is no deliberate or even loose linkage between these standards and reliability, they have no way of easily determining whether the standards applied in a particular corporate situation mean that reliability has or has not been achieved.

GAAP and corporate audit practice

The previous section outlines the conceptual relationship between GAAP and corporate auditors. It indicates in general terms the problems they face when attempting to relate GAAP to their audit objectives. The situation gets no easier when the matter is examined in more detail. The following paragraphs explain this in the context of what a corporate auditor is required to do in practice with respect to GAAP implementation.

Accounting principles are generally accepted and appropriate

Corporate auditors are typically expected to verify that the accounting standards used by the reporting company are generally accepted or acceptable (for example, AICPA,

1992, para.4; and APC, 1980g, para.2). For this purpose, they are directed to sources from which such authority can be found (AICPA, 1992, para.5; and APC, 1980g, para.6). And these sources can describe their standards as having authority (ASB, 1991b, para.15). However, as Mautz and Sharaf (1961, pp.162–3) argue, such authority is relative rather than absolute. Accounting standards issued by bodies such as FASB in the US and ASB in the UK have no real claim to general acceptance because it is so difficult to determine such a position. Any authority they have comes from the mandatory status given to them in terms of expected reporting compliance (for example, AICPA, 1992, para.3; and ASB, 1991b, paras. 7 and 15), rather than from the definitive and unambiguous nature of their accounting prescriptions. Thus, all that corporate auditors effectively attest, despite the required wording of their reports, is that their client companies have or have not adopted certain standards issued by the main accounting standard-setting authority.

In this sense, corporate auditors presume rather than know that the GAAP applied by the corporate organization is appropriate to its circumstances (Mautz and Sharaf, 1961, pp.165–6). They are typically expected by regulators to attest the appropriateness of GAAP to the individual corporate circumstances they are verifying (for example, AICPA, 1992, para.4; and APC, 1980g, para.2). However, because individual accounting standards are not typically demonstrated by their sponsoring bodies to be reliable (in the sense used in this text), it is virtually impossible for the corporate auditor to be definitive in his or her opinion. As ASB (1991a, para.16) states, the application (and, presumably, audit) of accounting standards should be guided by the spirit and reasoning behind them. Corporate auditors are therefore still very much on their own in terms of making audit judgments about the spirit and reasoning of GAAP – having to treat each corporate circumstance on its merits, and consequently being under the potential pressure of management to conform with its interpretation of GAAP.

GAAP is incomplete

One of the most obvious comments to make about the accounting body of knowledge which is generically described as GAAP is that it is incomplete. It is impossible to conceive of a situation in which accounting standard-setters prescribe for every imaginable situation. This is recognized in the professional literature – for example, the AICPA (1992, para.7) mandates what an auditor should do if the accounting applied is not covered by authoritative standards prescribed by recognized bodies; and ASB (1991c, para.2) describes its role of developing new standards in changing circumstances.

In other words, corporate auditors may require to go beyond the existing framework of prescribed standards to judge the quality of GAAP applications by client companies. And here they may run into problems of judgment in a situation of pressure. Incompleteness of prescribed GAAP causes the reporting corporate organization to either fall back on custom and habit or innovate (Mautz and Sharaf, 1961, pp.161–2). And such incompleteness is to be expected because of accounting standard-setters' predilection for responding to GAAP issues only when pressurized to do so (see Mautz and Sharaf, 1961, p.165 for the argument; and Byington and

Sutton, 1991 for evidence to support it). Custom and habit are difficult to change, and the corporate auditor may agree to continuity of accounting standard use on the grounds of being expected to attest accounting consistency (for example, AICPA, 1991, pp.7 and 239–44 in the US; and Companies Act, 1985, Sch. 4 Part II, s.A, para. 11; and APC, 1980g, paras. 2 and 6 in the UK). But this may not be appropriate because of changed corporate circumstances.

Nor will corporate auditors necessarily find the incompleteness of GAAP easy to cope with when their corporate clients respond by innovating. In these circumstances, it is difficult to challenge the new accounting by reference to an authoritative source, and they may acquiesce to avoid any conflict with corporate management. Professional guidance on this matter is vague (for example, AICPA, 1992, para.9).

Observations of contemporary corporate reporting situations indicate that accounting innovation in the absence of authoritative GAAP exists, and that the auditor is in the front line of criticism of that innovation when it appears to breach the general reporting principle of adhering to economic substance rather than legal form (see, for example, Griffiths, 1986 in the UK; Briloff, 1990 in the US; and Tweedie and Whittington, 1990 for a general review).

Meaning of GAAP in practice

As stated previously, the corporate auditor is charged with the duty of attesting the compatibility of the accounting practices used by a client company with the general framework of GAAP (AICPA, 1991, p.7; and APC, 1980g, para.6). What this means in practice, given the existing accounting emphasis, is adherence to accounting standards which support the historic cost accounting system (see Companies Act, 1985, Sch. 4 Part II, s.A, paras. 10–12 for an explicit regulatory recognition of this point in the UK). In other words, the corporate auditor is expected to attest the reliability of financial representations of corporate business activity derived from accounting calculations which are based on the conservative allocation of historic costs.

Such a system has persistently and consistently been subject to criticism regarding both its relevance and reliability. It would be inappropriate in this text to discuss the nature of this criticism in depth, but a few relatively recent examples will support the point. Tilley (1975, p.197) concludes that the current system of reporting is irrelevant for decision-making, lacks realistic assumptions, and is internally inconsistent. Sterling (1981, p.112) challenges supporters of historic cost accounting to prove its decision relevance. And McMonnies (1988, p.34) complains of it being inconsistent, illogical, and incapable of reflecting economic reality.

In other words, the present system (and its related GAAP) is capable of being severely criticized for its lack of relevance and reliability. Given the nature of historic cost accounting, it is difficult to think of the corporate auditor doing anything other than recalculate the reported accounting numbers in accordance with the calculative rules contained within GAAP. It is therefore unsurprising to find this role being criticized on the grounds that it supports a reporting system in which compliance with legal form predominates over that concerned with economic substance, and in which the corporate auditor's task is to search for suitable loopholes in GAAP to assist management in its reporting (Zeff, 1987, p.67). Gerboth (1987, p.98) describes this as accounting opportunism:

> Even worse has been the erosion of that sense of personal responsibility which is the essence of professionalism. Strict conformity to accounting rules transfers responsibility for the results from the accountant to the rules . . . We have all seen it: the otherwise responsible accountant who points to the ever-growing, multi-coloured volume of authoritative accounting pronouncements and demands, 'Show me where it says I can't!'

Adequate disclosure and the corporate auditor

As well as verifying the compliance of corporate financial statements with GAAP, the corporate auditor is required to ensure that the accounting results of such compliance are adequately disclosed to shareholders and other interested external constituents (see, for example, AICPA, 1991, pp.7 and 245 in the US; and Companies Act, 1985, s.235, and APC, 1980g, para.2 in the UK). This requirement can be expressed as follows (AICPA, 1991, p.7):

> Informative disclosures in the financial statements are to be regarded as reasonably adequate unless otherwise stated in the report.

Adhering to this audit standard creates considerable difficulties for the corporate auditor, despite the typical specification of minimum levels of disclosure by formal regulation (as in Schedule 4, Companies Act, 1985 in the UK). As Mautz and Sharaf (1961, p.170) point out, adequate disclosure concerns two matters – the detail and scope of disclosed accounting messages.

Message detail relates to the effect of taking numerous relevant transactions and events and, by means of the accounting process (including GAAP), compressing them into a relatively few accounting numbers in the income, cash flow and financial position statements which are reported. The corporate auditor must therefore carefully review these statements to ensure that their content has been disclosed sufficiently to meet the over-riding quality standard of 'present fairly' or 'a true and fair view'. For example, in the UK, guidance on this matter is expressed in the following terms (APC, 1980g, paras. 8 and 10):

> The auditor should consider whether the results of operations and the state of affairs of the enterprise as reported in the financial statements are consistent with his knowledge of the underlying circumstances of the business.

> The auditor should consider the information in the financial statements in order to ensure that the conclusions which a reader might draw from it would be justified and consistent with the circumstances of the enterprise's business. In particular, he should bear in mind the need for the financial statements to reflect the substance of the underlying transactions and balances and not merely their form. He should consider also whether the presentation adopted in the financial statements may have been unduly influenced by management's desire to present facts in a favourable or unfavourable light.

Such statements relate to the general theme of this text that the corporate auditor appears to have a major responsibility to verify and attest the relevance and reliability of corporate financial statements. But as stated earlier in this chapter, knowing when such an objective has been met satisfactorily is exceedingly difficult to judge – that is, in the absence of detailed knowledge of user decisions, resolution of the recognition issue, and given the nature of current accounting practice and GAAP. Thus, judging the adequacy of the detail of corporate accounting disclosures is problematic.

So too is an audit judgment on the scope of corporate disclosure. Typically, corporate regulation specifies the form and content of audited financial statements (for example, Companies Act, 1985, Schedule 4 in the UK). However, individual circumstances may dictate that, in order to comply with the over-riding reporting quality, there needs to be additional disclosure. Corporate auditors must therefore consider the company's need to report beyond the minimum prescribed by regulation, and also the sensitivity and confidentiality of additional information if released to shareholders and others.[6] In particular, they should consider any possible economic disbenefits to the corporate organization of additional, unrequired disclosures.

In making audit judgments about the adequacy of disclosure, the corporate auditor has to consider the report user. As Mautz and Sharaf (1961, pp.172–88) argue, the financial report user community is increasingly more expert and knowledgeable about accounting matters (a situation continuing to the present day). This has caused audited financial statements to be considered by accounting policy-makers in terms mainly of those users who are able to understand them (or make the effort to understand them) (FASB, 1978, para.34; and ASB, 1991b, para.38). In other words, the corporate auditor judges the quality of reported information in terms of assumed user understanding.

Whether this assumption is reasonable is a matter of debate. The existing evidence is to the contrary. For example, Lee and Tweedie (1977, p.131; and 1981, p.141) indicate that annual corporate financial statements are potentially only understandable by expert users and, even then, expertise is no guarantee of understanding accounting information. And apparent reliance on the auditor's opinion by expert and inexpert shareholders is not high (Lee, 1977, p.92; Lee and Tweedie, 1977, p.54; Lee and Tweedie, 1981, p.78; and Hines, 1982, pp.298–301).

A fundamental corporate audit problem

The above discussion indicates considerable problems for the corporate auditor in verifying the reliability of reported accounting information. Part of the problem is undoubtedly related to the current accounting model and the state of GAAP which operationalizes it. What is suggested above is that the conventional system of reporting utilizes an accounting technology in the form of historic cost allocations which is inherently incompatible with the notion of a faithful representation of selected aspects of corporate business activity. In other words, no matter how good GAAP is in covering individual reporting situations, and no matter how good the disclosure is in presenting a comprehensive and comprehensible reporting of the accounting calculations, the fundamentals of historic cost accounting will act as a barrier to effective communication and accountability between corporate management and shareholders and other interested constituents.

The nature of reportable and auditable phenomena

Part of the problem is the nature of the phenomena which are reported and audited. Earlier in this chapter, it is stated that the fundamental subject-matter for corporate accounting and reporting is events and their effects on the financial condition of the reporting corporate entity. Much of these events and effects form an empirically observable and testable reality – that is, the corporate auditor is relating and evidencing a physical reality. For example, sale and purchase events result in contracted transactions which reflect the physical exchange of goods and services between the company and its customers. The economic effect of these events on the company can be demonstrated in accounting terms – that is, by measurable changes in its physical resources such as cash and inventory.

However, these specific transactions also result in changes to a less physical corporate reality which is, at times, less easy to account for and to attest (for example, liabilities, equity and income). In other words, what the company's reporting accountant and auditor are conventionally concerned with are accounting representations of economic phenomena of differing types. As mentioned above, some are of a tangible and physical nature (usually, but not always, the designated assets of the reporting company); some are intangible and constructed from social relationships (typically, legally contracted, and representing debt and credit); and others are social constructs derived from a prior recognition of the above physical and social realities (such as periodic income and temporal equity).

These distinctions are argued in detail by Mattessich (1991) in a general challenge to the notion that accounting does not reflect empirical phenomena (as argued, for example, by Sterling, 1979, p.213). In effect, Mattessich (1991, pp.3–4) argues that accounting is concerned with a practical (rather than a scientific) representation of a mix of physical and social realities. These involve human relationships in economic exchange as well as physical things (p.5), and form the so-called economic reality for accounting purposes which is embedded in the reliability criterion with which corporate auditors are concerned. Thus, they have to verify and attest the representational faithfulness of some 'things' which can be empirically tested, and other 'things' which are less easy to observe because of their social construction.

This creates substantial problems for corporate auditors. For example, a crucial part of their function is attesting the reliability of periodic income. Although derived from empirically observable events and transactions, the accounting calculation of income is largely dependent on the application of arbitrary accounting rules (or conventions) which form part of GAAP. As Sterling (1979, p.22) points out, the selection of conventional rules by practitioners (such as corporate auditors) puts them in an untenable situation of arbitrarily attempting to fit the conventions to the circumstances.[7]

Put differently, it does not appear possible that corporate auditors can determine the representational faithfulness of the conventionally-reported accounting numbers on the basis of an arbitrary GAAP. Instead, their main task appears to be one of recalculating the numbers to ensure their calculational compliance with the rules of GAAP and the specific corporate circumstances. However, it is equally hard to accept normative prescriptions for a more scientifically-based accounting when the reportable phenomena are a mix of physical and social realities.

For example, Ruland (1984, p.224) uses the cartology analogy in his prescription for faithful representation – the financial statement being a map of economic reality. Ingram and Rayburn (1989, p.62) challenge this view of accounting in a manner consistent with Mattessich (1991) that accounting cannot map reality because of a lack of empirical referents. Heath (1987, pp.3–4) goes further by suggesting that accountants and non-accountants confuse the map for reality – particularly assuming a physical status for a socially-constructed reality (for example, by inferring that income is cash flow (p.7)).

The problem for corporate auditors in this respect is that they are assisting the report user to gain access to an unseen economic activity by means of attested but arbitrary accounting representations of it. By giving a positive audit opinion on these representations, they are signalling their accessibility for various decision purposes, and attempting to complete a crucial stage in corporate managerial accountability. In this sense, the attested accounting is no more than a surface metaphor of words and numbers with the capacity to allow access to a deeper economic meaning (Thornton, 1988, p.8). The danger is, as suggested by Heath (1987), that the report user goes no further than the surface – that is, the reported numbers and words in audited financial statements become the corporate reality rather than a gateway to the unseen economic events, transactions and consequences. They take on an independent existence (or reality) which, if not related to what it attempts to represent, causes its user to be unaware of what it is or is not making visible about corporate activity and management (see Hines, 1989a, pp.56–62).

The duality inherent in formal communications about aspects of so-called reality is recognized by other writers and in other ways – particularly in science. It is therefore not unique to either accounting or audit theory. For example, the philosopher John Locke (Popkin, 1981, p.199) distinguishes two levels of reality in terms of objects and the effects of objects. Sterling (1970b, pp.41–2) reminds his reader that reality in science is more than just phenomena – it is also about the messages about the phenomena. This distinction is more clearly seen in the philosophy of science literature. Davies and Brown (1986, p.24), for example, write of scientists demoting real-world things to abstract status, with familiarity providing their reality (p.86). Gregory (1988, pp.182–4) describes scientists observing the world that cannot be seen, and creating reality by talking about it. He further sees physics as being a subject fashioned as a tool to see the world (p.3), but with the need for a shared language to give meaning to the world which is talked about by physicists (p.192). These ideas seem very similar to the general problem faced by corporate accountants and auditors. Accounting (and auditing) is the means of talking about a corporate economic world unseen by shareholders and other external constituents. But there needs to be an agreed language to do the talking. Accounting is that language, and auditing is a means of attesting the quality of its message and meaning.

The meaning of corporate reporting quality over-rides

The meaning of reported corporate accounting messages is explained and interpreted in this text in the context of the reporting quality over-rides which exist – that is, the ultimate qualities which are expected for purposes of corporate accountability, and which subordinate prescriptions such as relevance and reliability to a secondary position. These over-rides are described in Chapter 1, and throughout this text, as 'present fairly' (in the US) and 'a true and fair view' (in the UK (and Europe and the Commonwealth)). The purpose of this section is to complete the review of corporate financial reporting quality by examining the nature and role of these terms in the context of the corporate audit. Much of the analysis is derived from a more extensive study (Lee, 1992b).

Terms such as 'present fairly' and 'a true and fair view' can be regarded as explicit labels which the corporate auditor uses to describe the quality of reported financial statements in a situation of corporate managerial accountability. The use of such labels has a long history – they existed in pre-corporate business situations of the eighteenth and nineteenth centuries (including court cases), and became a continuous part of UK and British Commonwealth corporate legislation from the mid 1800s onwards. They were transferred to the US in the late 1800s by immigrating accountants, and eventually incorporated into SEC corporate regulations in the 1930s. What is reasonably clear from this situation is that reporting quality over-rides originated in legal sources, and that McGee (1991, p.876) has cause to conclude that a label such as 'a true and fair view' is a matter of law rather than of accounting, and that its meaning can only be determined ultimately by a court of law according to specific circumstances (p.877).

What is also clear about the existence of over-rides is that they have always been reporting quality labels directed specifically at the corporate audit function. But they have never been defined by legislation or regulation. Perhaps surprisingly, given their crucial importance to corporate accountability, this undefined position has caused explicit concern only to a relatively few accountants over the years. For example, Chastney (1975, p.4) complains of the dangers of a proliferation of individual meanings by accountants and others with respect to the UK notion of 'a true and fair view;' and Storey (1964, p.62) concludes that, in the absence of definition in the US, it is doubtful if even accountants understand one another on the issue of fair presentation.

The UK situation with the requirement for 'a true and fair view' is the most vague. It is completely undefined, as if it were not necessary to define it because each corporate auditor would intuitively know what it meant on each audit occasion (Shaw, 1980, p.7). But, as Flint (1988, p.34) states, such a label must be susceptible to sufficient universal understanding to be operationally viable. On the other hand, he argues (Flint, 1982, p.30) that lack of definition is a strength as it allows re-interpretation of the notion of corporate accountability over time. Such a view is compatible with the actions of UK legislators for many decades, but it has not prevented individuals attempting to interpret the term. In most cases, this has been done with reference to GAAP generally, and compliance with prescribed accounting rules particularly (for example, Skerratt, 1982, p.70) – an approach also recently adopted by UK auditing standard-setters (APC, 1980c, para.7). Others, however, have suggested an interpretation consistent with the reliability criterion that the reported accounting numbers infer a correspondence with an underlying reality (Wolnizer, 1987, p.94). Whatever the perception, the notion of 'a true and fair view' appears to be an article of belief, a credo and a symbol (Parker and Nobes, 1991, p.357).

The US position is very similar to that of the UK with the exception that fair presentation is explicitly associated with compliance with GAAP (AICPA, 1992).

Over a period of many years, and with a small but persistent criticism about lack of definition, 'present fairly' has been linked to GAAP, and GAAP has been interpreted as accounting standards with substantial authoritative support (Zeff, 1972, p.266).

This situation has persisted in both the US and the UK in the increasing presence of regulatory prescriptions for a reliability criterion, and the principle of economic substance over legal form. In other words, the consistent lack of definition of over-rides is a curious feature of an otherwise reasonably defined activity such as corporate auditing. A possible explanation is available in the context of a perception of accounting professionals seeking to maintain their place and rewards in society by laying claim to a formal body of knowledge (Hines, 1989b). And it also appears to relate to the use of reporting quality labels with an origin in a legal profession which uses language to exercise professional power in society (Goodrich, 1987).

Corporate reporting labels and professional power

The previous section reveals corporate financial reporting's ultimate quality criteria as part of a legally-based discourse contained in statute and regulation. As such, it is relevant to examine briefly the concept of statutory legal language to determine whether reporting's quality over-rides can be explained in that context. The first thing to be said is that there appear to be two views of such a concept. The first can be loosely attributed to realist arguments which suggest that the law can operate as a rational function with an objective ('scientific') reasoning of the facts (Moore, 1991, pp.767–9). The second is more recent in origin and appears more concerned with critically examining the law in order to provide alternative explanations of its non-rational functioning (p.769).[8] Each of these views is examined in order to relate them to the question of corporate financial reporting over-rides and the auditor.

The rational justification for the presence in statute of undefined legal terms is that their meaning is context- and use-dependent (Bowers, 1989, p.132), and subject to change over time (p.149). Definition is perceived to create a false temporal stability of meaning, in which specific terms are divorced from their current real-world context (p.163). Under these circumstances (p.162):

> It is probably more effective not to attempt a close definition of an indeterminate term but to allow the court to interpret it by a *libre recherche scientifique*, to work on analogy with the legislature, to apply the principle underlying the legislation to the new situation before it.

Thus, Bowers (1989, p.130) believes statutory legal terms are constructed with a capacity to allow courts to accommodate future events in their meaning – necessarily leaving them open-ended with qualities of ambiguity and vagueness (p.131), and trusting to the good sense of courts to identify their purpose in relation to case specifics (p.150). Such terms are therefore viewed as instruments of meaning rather than meaning itself (p.155), and should not have meaning forced on them (p.152). Statutory definitions are denied on three grounds – they, rather than the court, ultimately and substantially judge each situation (pp.167–8), they confuse because of alternative meanings (p.169), and they create a circularity in reasoning (p.169).

In other words, this view of statutory legal terms suggests that their lack of definition creates a greater flexibility for lawyers in changing times, and that their interpretation should be left entirely in the hands of these professionals. It further assumes that the latter persons will act rationally and expertly in relation to the lack of definition. In particular, that their body of expert knowledge will be sufficiently competent to reflect objectively current conditions and expectations in relation to the matter to which the undefined statutory term relates. This is a view consistent with the arguments of Flint (1982, p.30) that a lack of statutory definition of the term 'a true and fair view' assists the auditor to interpret corporate accountability according to changing societal expectations. On the other hand, McGee (1991, p.887) argues for an explanation of the term (with regard to report user expectations) so long as it is provided by lawyers rather than accountants.

What the above discussion and the previous section suggest is a situation in which undefined corporate financial reporting quality over-rides have been constructed by lawyers for purposes of corporate accountability; adopted and maintained in undefined form by accountants (by general reference to a body of accounting rules), interpreted on a case-by-case basis by auditors (by reference to the same body of rules), and ultimately judged when necessary by lawyers in court (according to individual circumstances and the body of rules). This is a situation involving a closed loop of thinking and action. It concerns two professions which have come together in the area of corporate accountability to determine the quality of financial statements in terms of internally-constructed bodies of knowledge (which are assumed to reflect current societal needs and expectations).

This conception of financial reporting quality, and the role of the expert practitioners involved, suggests an example of a professional monopoly at work (Goodrich, 1987). Goodrich regards the existence of specialist legal text, which can only be interpreted by lawyers, as evidence of an economic elite exercising its position of power in society (p.81). In particular, such language is impenetrable from outside the legal profession (p.176). Legal terms are given meaning, not by definition but, instead, by the role they play in a game with rules devised by lawyers (p.51). Such terms have no empirical referents but are intended to impose a normative order (p.54). They command, permit, authorize and communicate an expected behavioural conformity (p.71). They are self-referential in the sense of one term or rule being dependent on another (p.55). And they are separate but generic linguistic entities supporting a range of meanings which allow for contradiction, exception, limitation, extension and manipulation (pp.177–9). In other words, they provide lawyers with the greatest scope or power of judgment (p.180). The image of such language is of authority and persuasion (p.183).

These thoughts can be applied in the context of the legally-based terms used by corporate auditors. 'Present fairly' and 'a true and fair view' are undefined terms which legally describe the overall quality expected in corporate financial statements. Their role is one of generally prescribing quality by mandate, and persuading and authorizing reporters and auditors to provide it. They are also self-referential in the sense of usually being interpreted in terms of a body of accounting rules (and vice versa). For example, in the US, 'present fairly' is explicitly related for auditing purposes to a conformity with GAAP (AICPA, 1992, para.3), and GAAP is conceived largely in relation to rules devised by the accounting community of which the auditor is part (para.5). A similar logic is applied in the UK to 'a true and fair view' (APC, 1980a, para.3 and 1980g, para.6; and ASC, 1986, para.2). Both terms are undefined (except in so far as they are related by accountants to an apparent accounting body of knowledge), thus providing maximum scope for varied meaning by their accounting and auditing users. Indeed, corporate auditors are reminded of a duty to allow for different circumstances when referring to their body of knowledge (AICPA, 1992, para.4(b); and APC, 1980a, para.2(a)).

The use of 'present fairly' or 'a true and fair view' therefore seems to be a reasonable example of the use of undefined language to create an image of professional power and authority – what Goodrich (1987, p.183) describes as the image of language. In this sense, the reader is asked not to think of interpreting these terms according to some technical accounting meaning but, instead, to observe them as tools used by accountants and auditors when laying claim to a body of knowledge which they control and use, and which is the basis for their wider claim to being professionals. In this way, these terms can be regarded as resource elements in the provision of audit services for financial reward and social status (Larson, 1977, p.208). Terms such as 'present fairly', 'a true and fair view', and 'GAAP' explicitly signal the potential existence of a body of knowledge controlled and used by accountants and auditors. And, by not defining these terms, exploration of its existence is prevented. In other words, and adapting Goodrich's (1987, p.176) argument to auditing (by insertion):

> . . . the specialisation of legal [auditing] discourse, in all but its most general forms of prohibition and specification, is impenetrable to those outside the incestuous verbalism of the legal [auditing] code.

Images and the corporate auditor

These conclusions are compatible with those of Hines (1989a and 1989b) regarding the perceptions created by accountants regarding their claim to be professionals. Such perceptions can be interpreted as deliberately constructed and maintained images of professionalism – that is, of corporate auditors not only being professionals but also appearing to be professionals; and of retaining control over their key resource which is their body of knowledge. What better way to do so than by retaining its explicit existence in undefined or ambiguously-defined forms which cannot be easily interpreted from outside their profession?[9]

The production of images by individuals and organizations to create a social reality is a reasonable, well-known phenomenon, and its use as a device by corporate auditors ought to be put in that context. For example, religious sources such as the Bible are full of written imagery of the power, authority and, thus, separation of God and man (for example, Guthrie, 1968, pp.188–93)). Similar imagery is evident in the construction of palaces by royalty to establish its hierarchical relationship with its populace (Thurley, 1991, p.14). Indeed, Burke (1992, pp.25–8) writes of the archeology of royal image with respect to Louis XIV. Ewen (1988, p.215) develops these ideas in the context of corporate organizations constructing images of technological possibility and rational business judgment. He describes this as a technology of representation, and as an aesthetic of power (p.213). Harvey (1989, p.287) goes further by suggesting that these images in business are a resource or commodity, symbolizing order (p.355) and portraying power and authority (p.288).

Thus, the corporate auditor's involvement with undefined but over-riding prescriptions of reporting quality can be interpreted in terms of a powerful and authoritative professional grouping in society. Members of such a grouping seek to exercise power and gain authority as judges of that quality in relation to publicly-available information which will be accessed for a variety of decision purposes. In these circumstances, it does not appear to be in the interest of the audit profession to define these terms. Definition would restrict corporate auditors' ability to judge each situation differently, and would make their body of knowledge more visible than hitherto.

What is remarkable in this situation is that defined quality criteria have been prescribed for the corporate financial reporting function and its audit in the form of relevance and reliability. However, it should be noted, as explained earlier in this chapter, that these definitions assume a knowledge which is hard to determine. Audited information's influence over decisions and its faithful representativeness are not matters which the accounting profession has prescribed in detail as yet. Indeed, accounting standard-setters explicitly deny the status of standards to such quality criteria (FASB, 1978, para.3; and ASB, 1991b, para.2).

A review and overall comment

What this chapter has attempted to provide is a detailed discussion of the audit of quality expected of corporate financial statements within the context of corporate accountability. Such quality is typically governed by prescribed regulations which are never defined. In recent times, however, these terms have been supported by less mandatory prescriptions by accounting standard-setters which contain defined quality labels for reported accounting information. Despite their definition, these labels leave much in the hands of the individual corporate auditor to determine their meaning in specific audit engagements.

Normally, the meaning of reporting quality over-rides and related criteria is interpreted in terms of an accounting body of knowledge. Increasingly, this connection is made by accounting regulators in their definitions, explanations and instructions regarding the audit of reporting quality. In other words, the existence of GAAP, and its relationship to reporting quality, is what drives conventional corporate audit. It essentially signals that the latter function is an accounting-based exercise as part of a broader activity of corporate accountability. This, of course, ignores the potential for the corporate audit to be used for other corporate accountability tasks. That is, the reporting of audited accounting numbers is not the only means by which corporate management can be held accountable for its actions and performance.

The existence and use in corporate auditing of undefined reporting quality over-rides which are part of legislative prescriptions is an interesting example of professional monopoly at work. By relating such over-rides to a body of knowledge described as GAAP, as well as to criteria which reflect decision relevance and repre-sentational faithfulness, corporate auditors create images of their power and authority in the accessing of corporate financial statements by shareholders and others. They signal their capacity to provide information which reflects notions such as truth and fairness, and relevance and reliability.

Keeping these terms vague and ambiguous appears consistent with the idea of professional monopoly. Corporate auditors are essentially saying they can determine these reporting qualities by use of their specific body of knowledge. By keeping that body of knowledge hidden from the consumers of their services, they maintain their monopoly (and, thus, their financial rewards and social status). The major problem in this respect is that the accounting body of knowledge which they draw on is incompatible with achieving the stated qualities – especially if the focus is on decisions (which are not well known), and economic substance (rather than legal form). In other words, the corporate auditor may be laying claim to a body of knowledge which does not presently exist.

Notes

1. The use of the term 'manipulation' in this context should not be taken to imply a meaning which suggests fraudulent distortion in order to hide the truth of the situation. Instead, it should be interpreted in terms of accounting as a technical process which involves a skilled control of accounting procedures to ensure conformity with explicitly stated practice.

2. It would not be the case if accountability were interpreted in a much wider social context. The type of information so reported need not be accounting-based, and the auditor need not be an accountant. In this respect, an interesting introduction to the issue of constructing new accountabilities and creating new audit pressures is contained in a discussion of environmental auditing by Power (1991).

3. A similar approach is adopted by Lee in subsequent editions of his text (for example, 1986), with extensions to cover more recent developments in accounting practice such as the introduction of supplementary current cost accounting statements. Flint (1988), on the other hand, is even more sparse in his consideration of what accounting recognizes as auditable subject-matter, virtually ignoring the matter, and paying little attention to the related audit issue of the role of generally accepted accounting principles (p.34).

4. The equivalent to FASB in the UK utilizes similar prescriptions and definitions (ASB, 1991b) – that is, for reliability (para.26) and representational faithfulness (para.28). However, it does not mention verifiability. Both FASB and ASB support their main criteria with secondary qualities – such as precision and uncertainty, bias, and completeness in the case of FASB (1980, paras.72, 78 and 79 respectively); and substance, neutrality, and prudence in the case of ASB (1991b, paras.30, 31 and 32 respectively).

5. In the UK, these accounting requirements are contained in corporate legislation – specifically, the Companies Act, 1985, Schedule 4, Part II, s.A, paras.10–15 which deal with prescribed accounting principles.

6. Existing evidence of voluntary disclosure is sparse. What seems clear and reasonably consistent is that companies typically disclose less than is desired by report users (see, for example, McNally, Eng and Hasseldine, 1982, p.17).

7. Sterling's (1979, p.24–5) solution to this problem is a scientific basis for accounting. This is concerned with scientific principles involving empirical observation and testing of decision-relevant economic phenomena (pp.65–6). For example, in relation to periodic income, he argues that, if the accounting for assets satisfies these principles, then so too will their income derivative (pp.191–4).

8. Such a distinction is very similar to that in accounting and auditing – that is, the rationality of the economic agency arguments for financial reporting and auditing, versus the socio-political critical approach which explores alternative explanations denying accounting's

neutrality and representational accuracy. This text makes this distinction at various stages in its explanations of corporate auditing. For a discussion of critical legal studies as compared with its accounting counterpart, see Moore (1991).

9. This may also partly explain why accountants respond to but do not resolve issues on which they are criticized (Brief, 1975, p.285; Sterling, 1979, pp.3–4; and Richardson, 1988, p.393). It may also support the findings of Fogarty, Heian and Knutson (1991, p.222) of an accounting profession that practises doing 'nothing' whilst creating images to rationalize this approach. In other words, to prevent penetration to the body of knowledge, definitions of the over-riding quality criteria are not made.

Further reading

R.K. Mautz and H.A. Sharaf (1961) *The Philosophy of Auditing*, American Accounting Association, pp.158–203 (financial reporting quality expressed in the conventional terms of GAAP and other regulations).

D. Solomons (1991) Accounting and social change: a neutralist view, *Accounting, Organisations and Society*, **16**(3), pp.287–96 (a conventional view of the objectivity of reported accounting information *vis-à-vis* users and the reporting organization).

T.A. Lee (1992) Financial reporting quality labels, image-making, and the social construction of the audit profession, *Working Paper*, University of Alabama (a critical argument for the role of reporting quality labels as claims to a body of knowledge necessary to the social construction of the audit profession).

A.J. Briloff (1990) Accountancy and society: a covenant desecrated, *Critical Perspectives on Accounting*, **1**(1), pp.5–30 (an attack on the failures of the audit profession with respect to the quality of reported accounting information).

T.J. Fogarty, J.B. Heian and D.L. Knutson (1991) The rationality of doing 'nothing': responses to legal liability in an institutionalised environment, *Critical Perspectives on Accounting*, **2**(3), pp.201–26 (research to reveal the audit profession's tactic for survival when under attack for the quality of reported accounting information).

Discussion essays and topics

1. Discuss the role of the corporate auditor in terms of making visible aspects of corporate activity, and of reality construction.
2. Describe the relationship between the corporate audit process and the accounting process.
3. Prepare a commentary on the corporate auditor and the accounting recognition problem. What accounting characteristic is fundamental to this comment?
4. Prepare a commentary on the corporate auditor and the accounting measurement problem. What accounting characteristic is fundamental to this comment?
5. To what extent is the corporate auditor concerned with report user decisions?
6. Discuss the role of GAAP in the corporate audit function.

7. A major problem for corporate auditors is the nature of the phenomena they are asked to audit. Discuss.
8. The corporate auditor is asked to report in terms of undefined reporting quality labels. Discuss the difficulties and advantages of this.
9. Discuss the problems facing the corporate auditor with respect to the existence of defined reporting quality labels prescribed recently by accounting policy-makers.

10

Corporate audit evidence and evidential material

This final chapter of the text brings together many of the subjects and issues dealt with in earlier chapters. In particular, it attempts to describe and explain the procedures by which corporate auditors evidence their opinions on the quality of corporate financial statements reported to shareholders and other corporate constituents. By giving these opinions, corporate auditors are fulfilling the various economic and social roles outlined in Chapters 1, 2 and 3, and attempting to achieve the objectives specified in Chapter 4. They do so in the context of the historical traditions and habits described in Chapter 5, and the expectations inherent in the postulates of Chapter 6. Their audit behaviour is outlined in Chapters 7 and 8 as independent and caring professionals who are expected to attest the financial statement qualities prescribed by legislators and regulators, and discussed in Chapter 9. This chapter has the objective of identifying how corporate auditors proceed to give such attestations, and debate the various problems they face in doing so.

As mentioned in Chapter 1, this text is concerned with theoretical matters relating to the function of corporate auditing. As such, it is primarily devoted to conceptual rather than practical issues. However, in this chapter, because of the nature of the subject-matter, there is more attention paid to audit practices than hitherto. Nevertheless, the main emphasis continues to be conceptual. The subject is corporate audit evidence and the role it plays in the audit task of presenting an expert opinion on the specified qualities of corporate financial statements. The text examines the processes of gathering and evaluating evidential matter, and the use of such evaluations to judge reporting quality. The central feature of the analysis is audit risk.

The assumption of verifiability and corporate auditing

If the corporate auditor is charged with the responsibility of providing an expert opinion on the quality of corporate financial statements, it is logical to assume that they can be verified in this way, and that he or she is capable of doing so. The competence of the corporate auditor is usually presumed and provided for in legislative and regulatory provisions which require a professionally-qualified account-ant as auditor (s.11, Securities Act, 1933 in the US; and s.389, Companies Act, 1985 in the UK). 'Verifiability', on the other hand, is less explicitly assumed in corporate governance provisions, but has been well supported by individual accounting theorists and policy-makers over several decades.

These contributors prescribe reported accounting information as capable of verification and (presumably) attestation. Paton and Littleton (1940, p.18–21), for example, explain the need for accounting information to be based on and verified by objective evidence. But, in most recent writings, the informational quality of verifiability is associated with the primary qualities specified for reported financial statements. For example, the AAA (1966, pp.10–11) stipulates verifiability in conjunction with relevance to user actions (pp.9–10). In particular, it describes the concept as an attribute of reported information which allows individuals working independently of one another to come to a similar conclusion about it (p.10).

This notion of independence in relation to the verification of informational quality is inherent in other accounting theories of the last 25 years. For example, Chambers (1966, pp.84 and 148–9) advocates relevant information with the attribute of objectivity or its capacity to be independently corroborated. More recently, Sterling (1985, p.22) prescribes verifiability in addition to relevance and specifically in relation to reliability. His concern is that reported information should be verifiable in the sense of independent observers having the capability of achieving consensus regarding its faithful representation of economic objects and events, and of providing assurance of this (p.22). These ideas are incorporated into the conceptual framework of FASB (1980, paras. 59, 81, 82 and 84) in the US, and Solomons (1989, p.34) outlines a similar prescription in the UK context. Curiously, despite Solomons' earlier work, verifiability is not part of the UK proposed framework (ASB, 1991b), and it is not advocated in the US with the same conceptual linkages as prescribed by the earlier theorists. Indeed, FASB (1980, para.81) specifically disconnects the primary reporting quality from verification, leaving the latter prescribed solely in relation to reliability:

> Verification contributes little or nothing toward insuring that measures used are relevant to the decisions for which the information is intended to be useful.

This is a problem which is addressed later in this chapter. But, meantime, it should be noted that the verifiability prescription of accounting theorists and policy-makers has been incorporated into the audit literature. In general terms, it appears as an explicit postulate of auditing in a number of texts – for example, Mautz and Sharaf (1961, p.42); Lee (1972, p.55); Sherer and Kent (1983, pp.19–20); and Flint (1988, p.22). And it is extended by Wolnizer (1987) in a model of auditing based on a duality of independence concerning the auditor and audit evidence. Wolnizer's general thesis is that not only must auditors be independent but so too must their audit materials. If the latter are not independently sourced, then the audit cannot be said to involve independent verification. Wolnizer (1987, p.187) argues this case in the following way, basing his prescriptions on the concept of technical ophelimity or the functional fitness for use of audited information:

> The technical ophelimity of accounting information is not a matter of the personal

integrity or good intentions of auditors. The personal performance of auditors may be the better for their adherence to a strict code of ethics; but without an established technical efficacy, even the most moral and ethical behaviour by auditors cannot produce independently authenticated and reliable accounts. It is the business of the style of accounting and auditing envisaged in this study, to ensure that the periodic accounting by managers for the financial position and progress of firms is corroborable and authenticated independently of them.

In other words, accepting the Wolnizer argument, the assumption to be made about accounting information contained in corporate reports is that not only should it be verifiable, but it should also be independently verifiable if it is to be reliable. This prescription is used throughout this chapter because it relates to a corporate issue present in almost every other chapter. This concerns the ability of corporate management to manipulate its reported accounting calculations within the context of GAAP, and for the corporate auditor to be either a witting or an unwitting party to this contradiction of corporate governance and managerial accountability. In other words, the Wolnizer view of verification and attestation, and therefore of audit evidence and opinion, rescues the corporate audit from the considerable criticism that it is concerned primarily with recalculation and form rather than corroboration and substance.

The assumption of verification and audit evidence

The above remarks about the verifiability of reported accounting information suggest a further feature without which verification would be meaningless. This concerns the need in corporate auditing for evidence with which to judge the quality of reported information. In particular, if such information is assumed to be verifiable, it must also be assumed that there is evidential material with which to conduct the verification processes. This connection is made by a number of writers including Paton and Littleton (1940, p.18); Lee (1972, p.61); Schandl (1978, p.22); Sherer and Kent (1983, p.21); and Flint (1988, p.22).

In summary, these thoughts suggest an independent verification function based on the availability and use of evidential material, and from which evidence can be derived to base the audit judgment about reporting quality. But they also suggest a standard by which such evidence can be compared and to which the auditor can conform (Flint, 1988, p.111). The problem, as suggested in Chapter 9, is the lack of well-defined and accepted standards for this purpose (Flint, 1988, p.111), and therefore the difficulty of successfully completing the audit task which Wolnizer (1987, p.4) describes as quality control – that is, of the fitness of use of corporate financial statements with particular regard to user decisions (pp.6–8).

Each of these thoughts has been postulated earlier in this text in a multifaceted way – that is, corporate accounting information is verifiable; there are no unnecessary restrictions on verification; the corporate auditor is competent to verify; the relevance and reliability of the accounting information can be verified (p.166) and reported meaningfully; and, particularly with respect to this chapter, there is sufficient competent evidential matter for verification and report.

Financial reporting qualities to be evidenced

As indicated in previous chapters of this text, the primary qualities of corporate financial statements which are perceived to be the subject of verification are relevance and reliability within the broad context of decision usefulness for the report user (see FASB, 1980; and ASB, 1991b). And, as particularly mentioned in Chapter 9, verifying these qualities constitutes a significant problem for corporate auditors. They have little formal guidance with which to make their audit judgments as to what is or is not either relevant or reliable in audited financial statements. The remainder of this section investigates this problem in further detail.

Accounting policy-makers not only specify relevance and reliability as the main qualitative characteristics expected of corporate financial statements, but also outline the more detailed properties of accounting information which need to be present if relevance and reliability are to exist. In other words, the corporate auditor would appear to have a duty to evidence the presence of the following criteria.[1]

- **Feedback value and predictive value** (FASB, 1980, para.51; and ASB, 1991b, para.24) To be relevant, the reported information should be capable of confirming or correcting earlier user expectations of corporate performance and position, and assisting predictions of these matters. The corporate auditor is therefore presumably expected to seek and evaluate evidential material to judge the feedback and predictive values of the audited financial statements.

- **Timeliness** (FASB, 1980, para.56; and ASB, 1991b, para.41) The relevance of the reported information is affected by its timeliness in use – the less timely, the less useful it will be. Again, it is presumed that the corporate auditor will require to evidence this point.

- **Representational faithfulness** (FASB, 1980, para.63; and ASB, 1991b, para.28) To be reliable, the reported information should faithfully represent the events and objects it purports to represent, particularly their economic substance (ASB, 1991b, para.30). The corporate auditor requires to identify evidential material which reflects such substance.

- **Precision and uncertainty** (FASB, 1980, para.72; and ASB, 1991b, para.29) The corporate auditor deals with verifiable accounting information which is neither precise or certain but which, nevertheless, can be reliable.

- **Neutrality** (FASB, 1980, paras. 78–9; and ASB, 1991b, paras. 31 and 33) To be reliable, reported accounting information should not be biased to any particular decision or decision outcome, and the corporate auditor needs to verify for this constraint on the overall informational quality expected.

The considerable problem for corporate auditors in each of these cases is that they have to rely on their personal experience and knowledge to judge each reporting situation in terms of these qualities. To date in the UK, no formal guidance has been issued on such matters and, in the US, the FASB (1984) recognition concepts statement does little to clarify matters for the auditor. A fundamental recognition criterion is prescribed as measurability – measuring a relevant attribute of a reportable item with sufficient reliability (FASB, 1984, para.63). Relevance and reliability are defined as in the 1980 statement, and are subject to the cost–benefit constraint (para.63).

recognition concepts statement does little to clarify matters for the auditor. A fundamental recognition criterion is prescribed as measurability – measuring a relevant attribute of a reportable item with sufficient reliability (FASB, 1984, para.63). Relevance and reliability are defined as in the 1980 statement, and are subject to the cost–benefit constraint (para.63).

In other words, the prescriptions and definitions which are available are recursive, and the corporate auditor is faced with an audit task of evidencing, judging and reporting on relevance and reliability with no standard by which to accomplish these processes. Flint (1988, p.111) points out the presumption of such a standard in auditing, and the difficulty of coping with one which is undefined – as in 'a true and fair view'. The situation is identical in the case of standards which are defined with ambiguity and circularity. Indeed, this is not the first time this issue has been recognized in the literature. Chambers (1966, p.149), for example, states that, to be objective, relevant information should not anticipate specific user actions. FASB (1980, para.81) concludes that verification of information contributes little or nothing to its decision relevance. Indeed, FASB (1978, para.8) associates the audit function with reliability only.

Perhaps this is why the function of external financial reporting is deliberately described as general purpose (FASB, 1978, para.28; and ASB, 1991b, para.6). It is the means by which accounting and auditing policy-makers avoid the substantial issue of the corporate auditor being unable to substantiate, judge and report whether or not the verified financial statements are decision-relevant. The situation with reliability is little better. Guidance on relevant attributes which can be reliably measured is distinctly lacking – except for vague generalized statements describing the presumed common interest of report users in the amount, timing and uncertainties of expected cash flows (FASB, 1980, para.25; and ASB, 1991b, para.15). This suggests that, perhaps, the corporate auditor may be evidencing, judging and reporting on information pertinent to these cash-flow effects. But nothing is certain in this matter and, as previously stated and justified, the remainder of this chapter will be based on the assumption that the corporate auditor can evidence, judge and report on relevance and reliability in the context of corporate governance and managerial accountability. The most immediate matter to be examined is the nature and role of evidence and evidential material.

Audit evidence and evidential material

Evidence is typically conceived of as a proof or means of establishing the truth. In corporate auditing, such a view is adapted to the verification function, and evidence is seen as a means of justifying the assertions (or hypotheses) which are inherent in the contents of audited financial statements (Mautz and Sharaf, 1961, p.68). In other words, the accounting numbers (and related words) in the income, cash-flow and financial position statements assert certain events, objects and consequences of corporate activity. Audit evidence is what corporate auditors bring to bear on their judgments concerning the relevance and reliability of these accounting assertions (and, thus, their fair presentation or truth and fairness). It is the means by which the corporate auditor achieves a state of assurance about reporting quality – of knowing rather than just believing in it (Mautz and Sharaf, 1961, p.70). Evidence settles doubts about the audited subject-matter, and it influences the auditor's mind (p.89). Evidence helps to prove what happened in the past by means of evidential material which relates to that past (Toba, 1975, p.9), and it is the ultimate basis for the corporate auditor's opinion on reporting quality (Toba, 1975, p.9; and Flint, 1988, p.104).

In this respect, it is important that the reader distinguish between evidence (the overall basis for audit reporting), and evidential material (the various means by which auditors construct their evidence to support their opinions). Evidential material is the basis for thinking, knowing, acting and constructing facts and assertions in the corporate audit (Toba, 1975, p.8). Its composition depends on individual audit circumstances (Mautz and Sharaf, 1961, p.74), and its audit influence depends on the skills and experience of the corporate auditor (p.89). In other words, each corporate audit contains a unique set of circumstances which determine the nature, mix and quality of the evidential material required, and the latter, when evaluated and judged by corporate auditors, constitute their evidence in support of their opinions.

Auditing standard-setters prescribe audit evidence and evidential material in a relatively consistent way. The primary charge is for a sufficiency of evidence with which to support the audit opinion on the quality of reported financial statements (AICPA, 1991, p.7; and APC, 1980b, para.4). More particularly, the AICPA (1991, pp.7, 121 and 124) in the US describes the evidential material needed as being sufficient and competent to evaluate financial statement assertions. It further defines competent in terms of validity and relevance (p.124); validity as reliability but depending on individual circumstances; sufficiency as persuasive rather than convincing and, again, depending on the circumstances (p.124); and ignores the need to define relevance. The APC (1980b, para.4) in the UK, on the other hand, looks for relevant and reliable evidence in sufficient amount to draw reasonable audit conclusions, but makes no further comment.

Thus, these institutional bodies create a situation in which evidence and evidential material are not only not clearly distinguished, but are also described in terms which are either undefined (as in the UK) or defined in a recursive manner (as in the US). In particular, the terms 'relevance' and 'reliability' are used in both the reporting and auditing prescriptions. This means the corporate auditor is in the very curious and difficult situation of being asked to give an opinion on the relevance and reliability of reported financial statements (without formal guidance or standards), using evidence (and, thus, evidential material) which is relevant and reliable (without formal definition).

Characteristics of evidential material

A review of the literature of audit theory and standard-setting provides a profile of the expected attributes or characteristics of evidential material. This suggests a multi-faceted concept of immense complexity in terms of putting it into practice. The evidential material used in corporate audits is obviously multi-dimensional, and reflects the degree to which corporate auditors must be competent in skills and experience, and the numerous roles they undertake in their audit function (Hogarth, 1991, p.284).

The following are given only briefly as an introduction to these evidential characteristics and, as in much of corporate auditing, there is a preponderance of words, and an absence of definition.

Philosophical characteristics

Several audit theorists attempt to provide a philosophical framework for audit evidence and evidential material. In particular, Mautz and Sharaf (1961, pp.68–9) distinguish evidence which is natural and most persuasive, from that which is either created and sustained by human effort or rational argument based on human observations. In this respect, the corporate audit is seen to be largely dependent on created or argumentative evidential material. Such material is constructed and is subject to human frailties. It can be fabricated and manipulated. It can be 'lost' and 'found'. Unsurprisingly, its general qualities are described as varying from the authoritative to the mystical, and to involve different approaches ranging from deductive reasoning to inspiration, and empiricism to pragmatism to scepticism (Mautz and Sharaf, 1961, pp.91–7; and Flint, 1988, p.114).

Operational characteristics

These criteria are specified as part of the functional operations of the audit. They describe the qualities expected of evidential material and, as such, govern the conduct of the audit – that is, assuming the sequence of evidential material providing the evidence on which to base the audit opinion. Whatever qualities are sought in evidential material will affect the quality of the audit opinion (Flint, 1988, p.106).

The most fundamental criterion for evidential material is utility (Lee, 1986, p.155) – that is, that it is capable of providing evidence with which to test the quality of the accounting assertions being attested. However, although it is the most basic evidential quality, it is also the most ambiguous, and requires to be supplemented by criteria which assist the corporate auditors to practise. The first supporting criterion which can be advocated is 'relevance' (AICPA, 1991, p.124; APC, 1980b, para.4; and Lee, 1986, p.156), a term which is usually prescribed in undefined form but which, for purposes of this text, is taken to mean the capacity of evidential material to influence the audit decision concerned. However, as is the case with its specification in corporate financial reporting, relevance is meaningful only if it is accompanied by reliability (AICPA, 1991, p.124; APC, 1980b, para.4; Lee, 1986, p.156; and Flint, 1988, p.108).

Evidential reliability, however, is also typically prescribed in vague or undefined form. Lee (1986, p.156) and Flint (1988, p.108), for example, advocate it recursively in relation to the reliability of the evidential source; and APC (1980b, para.4) makes no explanation of the term. AICPA (1991, p.124), on the other hand, provides some indication of meaning in terms of the independence of the evidential source, and the effectiveness of internal control both giving the auditor greater assurance of reliability. The independence of evidential material is a main foundation for the thesis of Wolnizer (1987, pp.26–7) that the 'fitness for use' of audited financial statements depends on their content being independently and empirically tested. In turn, this requires evidential material to be independent of management (p.4). If corporate management can manipulate the evidential material which supports the accounting messages of its performance as reported in the audited financial statements, there cannot be confidence that these statements are reliable. Thus, evidential material should be objective – free from any biases of management or other interested parties (Lee, 1986, p.156), and the most objective source is an independent source.[2]

Other evidential qualities specified by audit theorists and policy-makers support the relevance and reliability criteria, and include observability or perceptibility (Toba, 1975, p.9) (the evidential material should be empirically testable, a condition particularly necessary to achieve the quality expected by Wolnizer (1987)); timely (Mautz and Sharaf, 1961, p.78; and Flint, 1988, p.105) (the auditor always works within a time limit which constrains the availability of evidential material); cost (Lee, 1986, p.157; and Flint, 1988, p.105) (the benefits of evidential material require to be weighed against the costs of obtaining it); and sufficiency (AICPA, 1991, p.124; APC, 1980b, para.4; Lee, 1986, p.156; and Flint, 1988, p.104) (in order to come to an opinion on the quality of the financial statements, the auditor requires a sufficient amount of relevant and reliable evidential material to evaluate).

The nature of evidential material

The nature of evidential material in auditing is explained by the AICPA (1991, p.123) in terms of the accounting data contained in the audited financial statements, and of all corroborating information available to the auditor. This approach emphasizes the accounting orientation of the current audit, and its focus on recalculating the accounting representations being verified prior to externally reporting them. The evidential material of an accounting nature includes various accounting records of transactions and adjustments (including cost allocations); and the corroborating material includes accounting documentation, oral responses from company managers and employees, physical inspections, and external confirmations (AICPA, 1991, p.123).

Thus, evidential material can be classified in two ways (Lee, 1986, pp.158–61). The first category is immediately available material which corporate auditors can access relatively easily to conduct their tests. This includes accounting records, documents, calculations, and physically observable processes and objects. As such, it is material which exists within the corporate entity, and is subject to its managerial control. It is therefore observable, empirically testable and potentially relevant. But it lacks the quality of independence which is a necessary part of its reliability. The second category is created evidential material and includes explanations from company managers and employees, assessments of company systems, external confirmations, and external events. In this category, the material is a mixture of dependent and independent factors but, generally, requires more individual input from the corporate auditor than is the case with the other category. In other words, particularly in the case of evidential material which comes from a source external to the company, the independence (and reliability) of the audit evidence process is sustainable.

Judging evidential material in corporate auditing

Evidential material is a necessary part of the corporate audit process because it allows the auditor to reason to a conclusion about the quality of the audited financial statements (Mautz and Sharaf, 1961, p.73). In effect, the corporate auditor gathers relevant and reliable evidential material, evaluates and judges its content, and uses this evidence to formulate an opinion on the statements (Mautz and Sharaf, 1961, p.87; and Wolnizer, 1987, p.27). The more variety of material, the stronger the audit conclusion (Mautz and Sharaf, 1961, p.98; and Flint, 1988, p.105).

What is being described about the corporate audit is a process of expert judgment, in which a series of testable propositions is constructed by corporate auditors, and evidence is sought by them with which to judge the validity of the propositions (Mautz and Sharaf, 1961, p.103; and Toba, 1975, p.9). In the context of this text, the propositions concern the relevance and reliability of the accounting messages contained in the annual financial statements of a reporting company. The corporate auditor's judgment is focused on evidential material which confirms or rejects the existence of these reporting qualities, and much depends on the persuasiveness of this material (Mautz and Sharaf, 1961, p.104; and Flint, 1988, p.108).

The skills of the corporate auditor with respect to evidence are multiple (Hogarth, 1991, p.283) – first, specifying testable accounting propositions; second, identifying and collecting appropriate evidential material to test these propositions; third, evaluating such material in terms of its relevance and reliability; and, fourth, judging the validity of the propositions in light of such evaluating (Mautz and Sharaf, 1961, pp.103–9). What corporate auditors are therefore doing is seeking explanations in evidence which support the reasonableness of the verifiable accounting descriptions of corporate activity. In this respect, it is essential that they obtain sufficient explanation to justify their audit conclusions (Flint, 1988, p.104; see also Heiman, 1990, pp.888–9 for researched evidence of this effect).

The process of audit judgment is a complex matter. Much of the audit activity concerned involves cognitive skills which are difficult to observe (Hogarth, 1991, p.279). The problem is not only one of determining how auditors judge evidential material, but also of how well they do so, and whether they can be assisted to improve their judgments (p.278). Given the multidimensional complexity of the various roles involved in processing evidential material, there is a danger that 'oughts' become 'cans' (p.280), and that suboptimal judgments are regarded as inappropriate (p.282).

In other words, the verification of accounting representations of a highly complex corporate activity is one in which the evidential material, and the judgments of that material, may be less than ideal. The question is how good the corporate auditor's judgment processes need to be to do an effective job (Hogarth, 1991, p.281). The answer is not easy to give. Chapter 8 indicates there are areas and occasions in which corporate auditing has been deficient, and Chapter 9 reveals the difficulties and weaknesses in auditing informational quality. However, as Hogarth (1991, p.284) points out, an effective audit need not necessarily be one in which ideal judgments require to be made at each stage. Instead, the effectiveness may come from a proper co-ordination of individual judgments prior to the giving of the final reported audit opinion. Much research, however, requires to be undertaken to properly explore the nature of the corporate auditor's audit judgment process (see Gray, 1991).

Corporate audit propositions to test

The previous sections in this chapter allude to the presence in the corporate audit function of specified propositions or assertions concerning the accounting content of audited financial statements. These propositions are the basis for testing for the quality required in the accounting (Mautz and Sharaf, 1961, p.79). Indeed, audit standard-setters prescribe their existence for such purposes (AICPA, 1991, pp.122–3). For example, corporate auditors prior to testing assert the existence or otherwise of such matters as physical assets and invisible controls, and shape their search for confirming evidential material accordingly (Mautz and Sharaf, 1961, pp.80–1). They also make testable assertions concerning past events and transactions (p.82) and future phenomena (such as repayments, disposals and maturities).

These assertions can be expressed quantitatively and qualitatively (Mautz and Sharaf, 1961, pp.82–3). Their existence assists corporate auditors in their decisions on gathering and evaluating evidential material which provides the evidence to 'know' rather than merely 'believe' in the quality of attested financial statements (Mautz and Sharaf, 1961, p.70). Toba (1975, p.10) distinguishes audit propositions as elementary (concerned with basic facts and events) and general (regarding reporting generalities). The most generalized of audit propositions is 'present fairly' in the US or 'a true and fair view' in the UK. The more elementary the proposition, the easier it is to judge it in terms of available evidential material. Conversely, the more general the proposition, the less easy to evidence and judge. This is supported in the conceptual arguments of Kissinger (1977, pp.323–6) who points out that financial statements can be fairly presented in the presence of inconsistencies with GAAP or ineffective internal controls, or unfairly presented when consistent with GAAP or with effective internal controls. In each case, the problem relates to the potential for senior corporate management to interfere in the reporting process, which is a major reason for Wolnizer's (1987, p.27) proposal to test audit propositions with independent evidential material from the public domain (such as market prices).

The concept of audit risk

Inherent in much of the above discussion of the corporate audit process and the use of evidential material is the topic of audit risk – that is, the danger which corporate auditors face in an audit situation involving accounting information that they will fail to detect material misstatement of income, cash flow or financial position (Sennetti, 1990, p.103). Indeed, corporate auditors are required to give reasonable assurance of the lack of such misstatement as a result of their audit actions (AICPA, 1991, pp.37 and 266; see also APB, 1991, p.8). Audit risk takes three forms – planned risk in pre-audit when the engagement is assumed by corporate auditors; *ex post* risk in the sense of being unknown to corporate auditors until their work is complete; and estimated risk known to auditors during the audit by their assessment of corporate circumstances (Sennetti, 1990, p.104). In other words, corporate auditors face risk when they enter into an audit contract; some of this risk they will assess and allow for in their work, and the remainder will remain unknown despite their reviews and tests.

By its nature, *ex post* risk cannot be assessed pre-audit. However, the other two categories can be identified and some form of assessment made – generally, the higher the assumed risk, the more stringent the audit action. At the pre-engagement stage, there is evidence of corporate auditors assessing audit risk prior to committing to an audit contract (Huss and Jacobs, 1991). This is a situation in which it is difficult to distinguish audit risk from business risk. Corporate auditors who assess a prospective corporate client with a view to deciding whether or not to enter into an audit contract are essentially assessing the potential audit risk in terms of their business risk – that is, the extent to which the risk of not exposing material misstatement will economically impact their business. This is a further example of the corporate auditor's conflict between serving the public interest and recognizing his or her economic self-interest.

There is also evidence of corporate auditors using sophisticated statistical techniques to asses audit risk at the planning stage (Harper, Strawser and Tang, 1990), This is compatible with specific audit standard-setting prescriptions that auditors should plan for as low a level of audit risk as possible, and design their audit procedures to obtain reasonable assurance that material misstatement will be detected if it is present in the client company's systems (AICPA, 1991, pp.38–40). In other words, the corporate auditor is expected to plan sufficient audit actions to minimize audit risk and maximize misstatement detection.

Audit risk can also be divided into three parts (AICPA, 1991, p.40). These are inherent risk which concerns the probability of misstatement in the absence of adequate controls, control risk which relates to the probability of misstatement despite the presence of controls, and detection risk which exists whether or not controls exist because of the actions of the auditor. From this perspective, audit risk is a combination of factors relating to risks specific to the corporate client and its control systems, and risks specific to the corporate auditor (Gwilliam, 1987, pp.190–1). Thus, it ought not to be thought of as a problem that is client specific. Instead, it also involves corporate auditors and their competency to assess and test for risk.

In this respect, any model of audit risk which corporate auditors may formally or informally use should be comprehensive and consistent in its assessment of the probability of risk, specify the audit risk probabilities determined, allow for the economic costs of audit errors, and assume an audit cost minimization strategy (Gwilliam, 1987, pp.202–6; see also Adams, 1991). It should also take into account the possibility of non-systematic transactions giving a higher incidence of error, and the particular need to identify high risk areas in which there are repeated errors (Houghton and Fogarty, 1991, pp.6–7).

Materiality and the corporate auditor [3]

A subject closely linked with audit risk is materiality – that is, audit risk expressed in terms of the probability of lack of detection of material accounting misstatement (AICPA, 1991, p.37). Thus, a major concern for corporate auditors, when assessing the audit risk they face in the audit engagement, is at what point does a possible misstatement become sufficiently material to affect their audit actions and eventual opinions? There are two related factors at work in this area. First, the risk of accounting misstatement not being detected by auditors (because of factors relating to corporate control and their level of competence); and, second, the question of the quantitative and/or qualitative nature of the misstatement and its effect on the audited financial statements and the audit report.

Materiality should therefore be considered as multidimensional in nature. It is a subject affecting both accounting and auditing – particularly concerning the concept of relevance; what makes a difference to a report user's decision is information which is sufficiently material in terms of its message content to influence the judgment of that user (Lee, 1984, pp.2–3). Materiality thus affects the preparers and users of corporate financial reports as well as their auditor. In particular, the latter professional requires to consider the following factors when judging materiality and audit risk in relation to the accounting matters he or she is verifying.

The nature of the transactions audited

The qualitative nature of a transaction may be sufficient to trigger a materiality decision by the corporate auditor irrespective of the financial magnitude involved (as in the case of a transaction involving an illegal act which has a direct or indirect material effect on audited financial statements (AICPA, 1991, p.68)). Thus, materiality is an audit judgment which considers factors other than the accounting size of transactions. However, conventionally, corporate auditors are required to consider materiality in terms of the accounting effects of corporate actions which they observe in the normal course of the audit (AICPA, 1991, p.70).

The relative materiality effect

The corporate auditor typically judges the materiality of an accountable object or event in terms of relativities. That is, subject to the issue of the nature of the transaction, the financial effect of the item concerned is quantitatively compared to a relevant basis in order to determine whether it would be significant enough to make a difference to a report user. This suggests the use of specified quantitative criteria. To date, audit standard-setters have discussed the issue generally, and concluded that it is difficult to resolve (Lee, 1984, p.18). However, there is some evidence of corporate audit firms using pre-specified relative criteria for this purpose (pp.18–19). The problem with this is the lack of justification of quantified materiality 'trigger-points', and the danger of criteria removing or reducing the need for individual corporate auditors to exercise their expert judgment according to specific circumstances.

The relationship to financial reporting quality

If there is one thing that is clear about the materiality decision in corporate auditing, it is that it directly impacts audit decisions on the quality of reported financial statements (Lee, 1984, pp.22–3). In the context of this text, this means the materiality of a specific transaction or accounting datum needs to be judged by the corporate auditor in terms of its general effect on the fair presentation or truth and fairness of the financial statements. Put more specifically, materiality impacts the relevance and reliability of these statements. It therefore requires to be judged by the corporate auditor in terms of effects on user decisions and actions, representational faithfulness of the underlying phenomena and, most importantly, managerial accountability to shareholders and other interested stakeholders.

However, at the present time and as discussed in Chapter 9, corporate auditors lack adequate guidance on such issues as user decisions and reporting recognition. They are therefore not in a strong position to make materiality judgments (Godsell, 1991, p.60). They do so on the basis of their reviews of individual corporate circumstances, and their cumulative experience and skills. As Gwilliam (1987, p.228) concludes, in this area of audit activity it is difficult to find out how these individual judgments are made, and what form they take. Thus, the importance of continuing research into the cognitive aspects of auditor judgments in the presence of risk can be seen (Hogarth, 1991, pp.277–8).[4]

Verifying evidential material in corporate auditing

Although this text is not intended to describe corporate audit practice in detail, it is pertinent to the reader to outline in broad terms some of the main audit processes. This is done in this section as a background to discussing the conceptual aspects of the corporate auditor's emphasis on such matters as systems reliance and testing, GAAP compliance, analytical review, and opinion reporting.

The fundamental corporate audit process is one of identifying audit objectives, planning audit procedures to meet these objectives, gathering and evaluating evidential material to implement the plan, reviewing the evidence from audit actions, and forming and reporting an appropriate opinion. Each of these distinct stages in corporate auditing needs to be planned, controlled and recorded by auditors (AICPA, 1991, pp.7 and 31–5; APC, 1980b, para.2; and APC, 1980d). In particular, and in order to minimize confusion and lack of understanding of the corporate auditor's role, they can issue an unambiguous communication to corporate management as to what they are or are not going to do during the audit (APC, 1984). In other words, the commencement of the corporate audit process should be with an explicit specification of the audit purpose and procedure.

However, in making and operationalizing this specification, corporate auditors face a number of broad issues which govern the conduct of their audit actions. These relate to the volume of corporate activity, the control procedures used by the corporate client, the technology employed by the company to process auditable information, the regulations which govern corporate reporting, and the reporting responsibility of the auditor. These will be discussed in sequence in the following paragraphs.

Audit testing

With the exception of the smallest corporate organizations, the volume and complexity of business activity over an annual period is such that corporate auditors cannot verify every event and transaction. On the grounds of time, cost and informational redundancy, they therefore audit only a selection from the overall activity. In other words, the well-established audit emphasis is to conduct tests of the corporate informational process to obtain evidence of its efficiency and effectiveness as a basis for the reported financial statements. The quality of these statements is dependent on the quality of the underlying informational process.

In order to assess the quality of the system producing accounting numbers for reporting purposes, corporate auditors require to make expert judgments concerning the nature and size of their tests of it. With respect to each auditable part of the information system, auditors' judgments depend on their prior assessment of the audit risk associated with the area concerned. Such tests involve a number of different audit techniques including inspection, observation, enquiry, computation and review (AICPA, 1991, pp.123–4; and APC, 1980e, para.10).

The two main categories of tests which the corporate auditor conducts are compliance and substantive (APC, 1980e, para.8; see also AICPA, 1991, pp.47–50). Compliance testing is required to assess the strengths of controls inherent in information and related systems, and substantive testing is designed to assess the accuracy of the data processed in these systems. Use is recommended of statistical sampling techniques to conduct the compliance and substantive testing (AICPA, 1991, pp.209–24) – a matter which involves not only the uncertainties of audit risk generally (pp.211–12), but also the sampling risks associated with incorrect audit decisions to accept or reject control strength and informational accuracy (pp.212–13) (see also Manson, 1991).

Assessing internal controls

The audit of a complex volume of corporate business activity on a test basis assumes that the corporate auditor relies to a certain extent on the strengths of the controls which are in place to protect the integrity of the company's informational systems. Thus, an important aspect of the contemporary corporate audit is the auditor's assessment of internal controls. These controls are largely focused on the production of information with which to manage the business and protect its operations, resources and obligations. They therefore include most controls and are not narrowly defined only in terms of accounting (AICPA, 1991, pp.74–6; and APC, 1980f, para.3). When relied on by the corporate auditor, internal controls do not constitute evidential material. Instead, they represent a verifiable proposition which the auditor requires to test (Toba, 1975, p.23) – that is, the internal controls are sufficient (or insufficient) to rely on for purposes of coming to an opinion on the quality of the financial statements on which they are based.

Essentially what the corporate auditor is doing with internal controls is assessing the control risk he or she faces in auditable systems (AICPA, 1991, p.73) – that is, the risk of the company's internal systems lacking sufficient control to provide relevant and reliable information about its operations, resources and obligations. Internal control is corporate management's responsibility (AICPA, 1991, p.76; and APC, 1980f, para.4), and the existence of good internal controls is no guarantee of informational accuracy and freedom from fraud (AICPA, 1991, p.76; APC, 1980f, para.6; and Kissinger, 1977, p.326). However, if corporate auditors rely on the company's internal controls as a basis for determining the quality of its audited financial statements, they are required to obtain an understanding of the controls, and to test compliance with these controls (AICPA, 1991, p.73; and APC, 1980f, para.5). In particular, they are required to obtain sufficient understanding of internal controls to plan and test their compliance and substantiveness (AICPA, 1991, p.76; and APC, 1980f, para.7).

What this means is that, in order to substantiate their opinions on the quality of audited financial statements, corporate auditors assess their audit risk in terms of their reliance on control risk (Sennetti, 1990, p.111). And such reliance requires an understanding of the functional effectiveness of the internal controls of the client company. Thus, they not only have to be skilled at making these assessments, they also have to be knowledgeable about corporate operations and the controls associated with these features (AICPA, 1991, p.77). This point reinforces earlier comments in this text concerning the competency expected of the corporate auditor.[5]

Systems technology and the corporate auditor

So far in this text, and because the discussion is of a theoretical rather than a practical nature, the subject-matter of corporate auditing has been discussed without attention to the information-producing technology which is used by corporate organizations. However, at this point, and in the context of the corporate auditor's responsibilities to assess the quality of the data output from the client company's information system, it is relevant to discuss briefly the audit issues raised by contemporary technologies. The major concern is corporate auditors' competence to assess and judge their audit risk in the context of information systems and controls which are implemented in computerized form.[6]

In Chapter 6, it is postulated that corporate auditors are competent to fulfil their audit tasks. Given computerized information systems, this means that they are assumed to have sufficient information technology (IT) skills to audit these systems (Chambers and Court, 1991, pp.33–6). Whether they have these skills at the present time is debatable. Developments in IT, and the dangers of information manipulation using IT, may be outstripping the ability of the accountancy profession to cope. The problem of computer-based fraud or error impacting the quality of audited financial statements is particularly pertinent (Chambers and Court, 1991, pp.70–82). If the corporate auditors are unable to audit effectively IT systems from which reported financial statements are derived, then their specialist knowledge of GAAP and related regulations will count for little. They must therefore plan their audits within the context of their clients' information systems, including those which are IT-based (see Grant, 1991).

In particular, corporate auditors require not only to have IT skills, but also specialist and diverse IT skills to cope with different audit situations (Chambers and Court, 1991, pp.11–12). They must assess their audit risk according to uncertainties they perceive and can evaluate within an IT context, especially those related to controls (pp.57–69). They should also be able to improve the quality of their audit function in terms of economy, efficiency and effectiveness by using computer-based audit techniques (such as audit enquiry programs and audit-related expert systems) (pp.231–40).

Review of financial statements

As explained in Chapter 9, a major part of the contemporary corporate audit is concerned with the auditor verifying the extent to which the accounting data derived from the company's information systems have been calculated in accordance with GAAP and other regulatory requirements (including those concerned specifically with disclosure). Much of this topic is discussed in detail in Chapter 9 and elsewhere in this text. Consequently, this section is concerned to remind the reader of the audit requirement to verify and report compliance with GAAP (AICPA, 1991, p.233; and APC, 1980g, paras. 6–7); and the relating of these findings to the over-riding reporting quality standard of 'present fairly' in the US (AICPA, 1992), and 'a true and fair view' in the UK (s.226(2), Companies Act, 1985) The audit problems associated with these relationships are discussed fully in Chapter 9.[7]

Analytical review

As well as assessing and testing the company's information systems and related internal controls, and verifying compliance with GAAP and other regulations, corporate auditors typically conduct an overview of their evidence before formulating their audit opinions. This overview is described as analytical review (AICPA, 1991, p.133; and APC, 1988, para.23).[8] Its main objective in the context of this chapter is to reassure corporate auditors about the credibility of their audit evidence *vis-à-vis* their knowledge of the client company and its operations and environment. In other words, analytical review is concerned to review the audited financial results, and identify and seek explanations of any unusual or exceptional variations or inconsistencies with prior knowledge of the business and previous financial results (AICPA, 1991, p.133; and APC, 1988, para.24).

Audit reporting

Having gathered, evaluated and reviewed sufficient evidential material to constitute the evidence required to form an opinion on the quality of the company's financial statements, the corporate auditor reports that opinion to shareholders and others. In doing so, he or she signals an expert message to these corporate constituents about the informational quality for decision-making purposes, and also the appropriateness of the statements for purposes of managerial accountability. The contents of the corporate audit report, however, are described in technical and legal terminology which derives from the prescribed reporting quality over-rides and which, consequently, is difficult if not impossible for report users to interpret except in the most general of terms.

The current corporate audit report requirement in the UK is governed by Companies Act, 1985, s.235, and also by an audit standard (APC, 1989). These provisions basically describe the audit opinion solely in terms of a true and fair view of profitability and financial position. This approach has received criticism in recent times concerning its failure to communicate the nature of the audit task and to use comprehensible language (see, for example, Hatherly and Skuse (1991) regarding the UK position; and Dillard and Jensen (1983) regarding an earlier US experience). In the US this eventually resulted in an auditing standard which requires a considerable technical content, but which does little to address the issue of the use of technical language to a non-accounting audience (AICPA, 1991, pp.266–7).[9]

Recently, the UK position has been reviewed, and a consultative document has been issued (APB, 1991). In it, the audit report content is prescribed in similar fashion to the current US standard (AICPA, 1991, pp.266–8). But it too does not address the issue of user comprehension. This leaves the typical corporate financial report user in a position where he or she has to interpret personally the meaning of the audit actions and opinion briefly and technically outlined in the standardized report. All that appears to have changed in recent times is that a brief but obscure corporate audit report has become an extended but equally obscure document.

The interests of the recipients of such audit reporting are not served well by such exclusion, and the aim of corporate governance and managerial accountability is not being met. The problems of language use in corporate financial reporting (discussed in detail in Chapter 9) apply also to the issue of the corporate audit report. If terms such as 'present fairly' and 'a true and fair view' are given no meaning by legislators, regulators or the accountancy profession, it is difficult to understand their communicative role as the main part of the corporate audit report – other than that they convey perceptions or images of a reporting quality based on preparation and verification functions supported by a claimed body of knowledge.

Qualified audit reports

Not every corporate audit situation will result in an unqualified audit opinion on the quality of audited financial statements. Indeed, there will be situations in which corporate auditors find that, on the basis of their evaluation of the evidential material which is available, they must qualify their opinions. These situations are regulated by audit standard-setters, with specific rules to determine different types of qualification (AICPA, 1991, pp.275–82; and APC, 1980c). Essentially what these regulations prescribe are different opinions for different circumstance – that is, factors ranging from those which are material but not fundamental, to those which are fundamental; and opinions ranging from 'subject to' or 'except for' to those which are adverse or disclaimed. These qualifications are supported by explanatory comment and, thus, are intended to improve the explanatory powers of the corporate audit report. However, as Gwilliam (1987, p.131) reports from a review of the user and market impacts of audit qualifications, there is little evidence to support the view that audit report qualifications have informational value. This tends to support the conclusion expressed in this and the previous chapter that the use of undefined or ambiguous language by accountants and auditors is serving a role of socially constructing the audit profession, rather than serving the specific interests of report users or society generally.

Other audit reporting

As well as reporting their opinions to shareholders and other constituents, corporate auditors can report on their evidence in other ways. The first voluntary report is in the form of a management letter in which constructive advice is given in relation to organizational problems identified by corporate auditors during their audit engagements. In the UK, such reporting is conceived in broad terms, although it is mainly related to perceived weaknesses in internal controls (APC, 1986b, para.3). In the US, the focus is much more narrowly related to internal controls (AICPA, 1991, pp.115–20), although there is a permission to extend such reporting to other areas (p.118). The main point of these reports is assistance to corporate management. They are not a substitute for the corporate auditor's legal duties *vis-à-vis* attesting the quality of the annual financial statements (APC, 1986b, para.2).

The corporate auditor may also report independently to an audit committee comprising executive and non-executive directors of the client company. These committees exist in the largest organizations as part of the process of corporate governance – for example, in the US, all SEC-regulated companies are required to have a committee (AICPA, 1991, p.225; for a review of the UK experience, see Marrian, 1988). The purpose of the corporate auditor reporting to an audit committee is to put it in possession of information from the audit which will assist its governance function (AICPA, 1991. pp.225–6). In particular, the corporate auditor may communicate on issues such as accounting practices and estimates used by corporate management, and material disagreements with management over accounting and related matters (pp.226–8). Again, this type of reporting by corporate auditors should not be construed as a substitute for their legal audit duties.

A review and overall comment

This chapter attempts to provide the reader with a broad appreciation of the procedures and related issues with which corporate auditors deal in their attest function concerned with reporting quality. The fundamental feature is their need for sufficient 'quality' evidence on which to base their opinions. What is sufficient and what is 'quality' are persistent problems to be answered on each audit occasion by the individual auditor.

Providing such answers, however, is a matter of professional judgment, and this chapter more than any other in the text expresses the corporate audit as a judgmental process. The competence of the individual auditor underlies this process, and it is evident that much research is needed to understand better the audit decisions and judgments which the corporate auditor makes at various stages of his or her audit. In this respect, such decisions and judgments do not take place only at the time of forming the final audit opinion. Instead, they are a continuous feature of the entire audit sequence of activities – from pre-engagement to post-audit reporting.

The phenomenon which is the focus/of audit judgment is audit risk – the possibility of audit failure to detect material misstatement. Such a generalized risk factor is considered by corporate auditors at each stage of their audit, and determines what, when and how they audit. In particular, it influences the evidential material they require in order to provide sufficient evidence to support their audit opinions. Such material takes various forms, and requires different skills to evaluate. Evaluating the client company's internal controls is one such skill. Confirming the company's compliance with GAAP is another.

In other words, what this chapter provides the reader with is a broad impression of a complex technical function which demands a wide range of skills and judgmental competence by corporate auditors. No longer are they required to be skilled at recomputing bookkeeping entries. Instead, they have to deal with information systems which are complex and manipulatory. This has always been the case to some extent, but the IT basis for systems accentuates the problem. In particular, the issue of the independence of evidence and evidential material has to be considered.

The advocation by Wolnizer (1987) for such independence has been approved throughout this text at a theoretical level – that is, as an ideal to be aimed for. His specific suggestion for the use of external market prices for accounting valuations has merit in this respect (Wolnizer, 1987, p.58; see also Sterling, 1979, pp.215–16; and Ruud, 1989, pp.133–8 for similar suggestions). But given the dependence of reported accounting numbers on internal systems of controls and procedures which are designated as the responsibility of corporate management, it is difficult to conceive of a truly independent audit. The technical 'invisibility' of many of the control and processing aspects of IT-based information systems increases the problem. Much thought therefore has to be given to the feasibility issue of achieving a corporate audit which, at least from an accounting perspective, is independent in a meaningful way.

The other substantial issue which this chapter identifies is the influence of undefined or recursive financial reporting labels on the corporate audit report. Not only are such labels prescribed and a major interpretative problem for the corporate auditor, but they also present a more serious problem for their recipient. Typically, the latter person is not a professional accountant, and it is perplexing to try to understand what meaning he or she can obtain from a corporate audit report which specifies the audit achievement and result in terms which are undefined and ambiguous. This is a further recursion in corporate reporting which excludes the supposed beneficiaries from appreciating what it is they are benefiting from. Thus, the issue of financial reporting quality labels is not one which should be addressed solely in terms of their users. Instead, it must be addressed principally in terms of their recipients. Unless this is done, the corporate audit function will continue to be an obscure function which attracts critical expectations and increasing financial penalties associated with perceived failures to meet these expectations.

Notes

1. Policy-makers specify other secondary criteria and constraints. For purposes of this text, only the main qualities have been investigated. Not examining these other matters does not invalidate the argument because it affects all criteria in equal measure. These secondary criteria and constraints include conservatism (or prudence) (FASB, 1980, para.92; and ASB, 1991b, para.32); comparability (FASB, 1980, para.111; and ASB, 1991b, para.34); understandability (FASB, 1980, para.41; and ASB, 1991b, para.38); materiality (FASB, 1980, para.123; ASB, 1991b, para.39); and costs and benefits (FASB, 1980, para.133; and ASB, 1991b, para.42). Verifiability (FASB, 1980, 81) is discussed in the previous section.
2. In research into the sensitivity of auditors to the quality of evidential material, Rebele, Heintz and Bryden (1988, p.51) report their subjects were more concerned with the expertise of the evidential source rather than its independence. This finding tends to contradict the prescriptions of Wolnizer (1987) but it may also reflect the conditioning of auditors with respect to the type of audit they have become accustomed to make.
3. The comments made in this section have been taken from a detailed UK *Audit Brief* on accounting and auditing materiality (Lee, 1984).
4. There are other discussable aspects of materiality in relation to the corporate audit function (see, for example, Lee, 1984, pp.20–4). However, those dealt with in this section are specifically germane to the main emphasis of this text.
5. The procedures which corporate auditors follow in relation to planning and testing their corporate clients' internal controls are reasonably standard (see, for example, details in AICPA, 1991, pp.78–9 and 84–6; and APC, 1980f, paras. 11–18). They include suitable planning, reviewing, observing, testing, evaluating and re-evaluating activities (see also Felix and Niles, 1988, pp.45–51), and adequate recording, documenting and reporting of findings.
6. The term 'computer' is defined in this context to include all information technology likely to impact the conduct of the corporate audit. This includes personal and mainframe computers, image processing, smart cards, robotics, expert systems, and various communication and networking systems (Chambers and Court, 1991, pp.9–22).
7. Problems which are prescribed by audit standard-setters include reviewing corporate

events after the financial reporting date, and before the audit reporting date, which may impact the audited financial statements (AICPA, 1991, pp.329–36; and APC, 1982); and assessing the corporate client as a going concern, and the impact of this assessment on reported accounting information (AICPA, 1991, pp.197–202; and APC, 1985).

8. As revealed in prescriptions and guidance for analytical review (AICPA, 1991, p.129; and APC, 1988, para.11), such procedures can be undertaken at any stage of the audit as a means of assisting the auditor to plan, test and report. Analytical review in this chapter, however, relates to the final review by the corporate auditor prior to reporting to shareholders and other stakeholders. For a full discussion of analytical review, see Higson (1991).

9. The contents of the US report include statements of its title, identification of the financial statements audited, the responsibility of management for the contents of the financial statements, the use of prescribed auditing standards, confirmation of auditors' plan to have reasonable assurance of no material misstatement, the use by auditors of audit tests, their assessment of the use made of GAAP, evaluation by auditors of the presentation of financial results, and their opinions of these results (AICPA, 1991, pp.266–7).

Further reading

Y. Toba (1975) A general theory of evidence as the conceptual foundation in auditing theory, *The Accounting Review*, January, pp.7–24 (one of the few attempts to conceptualize on the nature and role of audit evidence).

R.K. Mautz and H.A. Sharaf (1961) *The Philosophy of Auditing*, American Accounting Association, pp.68–110 (a broad review of the nature of audit evidence and its capacity to influence the auditor).

S. Turley and M. Cooper (1991) *Auditing in the United Kingdom*, Institute of Chartered Accountants in England and Wales and Prentice-Hall International (a researched study of the audit methodologies and practices currently used by audit firms).

R.M. Hogarth (1991) A perspective on cognitive research in auditing, *The Accounting Review*, April, pp.277–90 (a critique of research into the judgmental and decision-making aspects of the audit process).

D.J. Hatherly and P.C.B. Skuse (1991) Audit reports, in M. Sherer and S. Turley (eds), *Current Issues in Auditing*, Paul Chapman Publishing, pp.115–30 (a discussion of the limitations and improvements necessary to audit reporting).

Discussion and essay topics

1. What qualities of reported accounting information is the corporate auditor primarily attempting to evidence?
2. Distinguish between evidence and evidential material in the corporate audit process.
3. What are the fundamental criteria governing evidential material used in the corporate audit process?
4. Describe the process of audit judgment.

5. Prepare a critique of the concept of audit risk.
6. The concept of materiality is fundamental to both corporate auditing and accounting. Discuss why it is so important, specifying the various dimensions of the concept.
7. What are the main aspects of the verification process in corporate audit practice?
8. Discuss the nature and significance of corporate audit reporting, pointing out any perceived frailties in the conventional system.

References

Accounting Standards Board (1991a) *Foreword to Accounting Standards*, Accounting Standards Board.

Accounting Standards Board (1991b) The objective of financial statements and the qualitative characteristics of financial information, *Statement of Principles 1 Exposure Draft*, Accounting Standards Board.

Accounting Standards Board (1991c) *Statement of Aims*, Accounting Standards Board.

Accounting Standards Committee (1975) *The Corporate Report*, Accounting Standards Committee.

Accounting Standards Committee (1986) *Explanatory Foreword to Statements of Standard Accounting Practice*, Accounting Standards Committee.

Accounting Standards Committee (1990) Reflecting the substance of transactions in assets and liabilities, *Exposure Draft 49*, Accounting Standards Committee.

Adams, R. (1991) Audit risk, in M. Sherer and S. Turley (eds), *Current Issues in Auditing*, Paul Chapman Publishing, London, pp. 144–62.

Alkhafaji, A.F. (1989) *A Stakeholder Approach to Corporate Governance*, Quorum Books, Westport, CT.

American Accounting Association (1966) *A Statement of Basic Accounting Theory*, American Accounting Association.

American Accounting Association (1973) *A Statement of Basic Auditing Concepts*, American Accounting Association.

American Institute of Certified Public Accountants (1972) Basic concepts and accounting principles underlying financial statements of business enterprises, *Accounting Principles Board Statement 4*, American Institute of Certified Public Accountants.

American Institute of Certified Public Accountants (1973) *Objectives of Financial Statements*, American Institute of Certified Public Accountants.

American Institute of Certified Public Accountants (1975) The adequacy of auditing standards and procedures currently applied in the examination of financial statements, *Report of the Special Committee on Equity Funding*, American Institute of Certified Public Accountants.

American Institute of Certified Public Accountants (1991) *Codification of Statements on Auditing Standards: No.1–64*, American Institute of Certified Public Accountants.

American Institute of Certified Public Accountants (1992) The meaning of 'present fairly in conformity with generally accepted accounting principles' in the independent auditor's report, *Statement on Auditing Standard No.69*, American Institute of Certified Public Accountants.

Antle, R. (1982) The auditor as an economic agent, *Journal of Accounting Research*, Autumn, pp.503–27.

Antle, R. (1984) Auditor independence, *Journal of Accounting Research*, Spring, pp. 1–20.

Armstrong, P. (1991) Contradiction and social dynamics in the capitalist agency relationship, *Accounting, Organisations and Society*, **16**(1), pp.1–26.

Auditing Practices Board (1991) Proposals for an expanded auditors' report, *Consultative Paper*, Auditing Practices Board.

Auditing Practices Committee (1980a) Explanatory foreword, *Auditing Standards and Guidelines*, Auditing Practices Committee (1989).

Auditing Practices Committee (1980b) The auditor's operational standard, *Auditing Standard 101*, Auditing Practices Committee.

Auditing Practices Committee (1980c) The audit report, *Auditing Standard 102*, Auditing Practices Committee.

Auditing Practices Committee (1980d) Planning, controlling and recording, *Auditing Guideline 201*, Auditing Practices Committee.

Auditing Practices Committee (1980e) Audit evidence, *Auditing Guideline 203*, Auditing Practices Committee.

Auditing Practices Committee (1980f) Internal controls, *Auditing Guideline 204*, Auditing Practices Committee.

Auditing Practices Committee (1980g) Review of financial statements, *Auditing Guideline 205*, Auditing Practices Committee.

Auditing Practices Committee (1982) Events after the balance sheet date, *Auditing Guideline 402*, Auditing Practices Committee.

Auditing Practices Committee (1984) Engagement letters, *Auditing Guideline 406*, Auditing Practices Committee.

Auditing Practices Committee (1985) The auditor's considerations in respect of going concern, *Auditing Guideline 410*, Auditing Practices Committee.

Auditing Practices Committee (1986a) Reliance on other specialists, *Auditing Guideline 413*, Auditing Practices Committee.

Auditing Practices Committee (1986b) Reports to management, *Auditing Guideline 414*, Auditing Practices Committee.

Auditing Practices Committee (1988) Analytical review, *Auditing Guideline 417*, Auditing Practices Committee.

Auditing Practices Committee (1989) Reports by auditors under company legislation in the United Kingdom, *Auditing Guideline 503*, Auditing Practices Committee.

Auditing Practices Committee (1990) The auditor's responsibility in relation to fraud, other irregularities and errors, *Auditing Guideline 418*, Auditing Practices Committee.

Ball, R. (1989) Accounting, auditing and the nature of the firm, *Working Paper 89–03*, Managerial Economics Research Centre, University of Rochester.

Beck, G.W. (1973) The role of the auditor in modern society: an empirical appraisal, *Accounting and Business Research*, Spring, pp.117–22.

Bevis, H.W. (1962) The CPA's attest function in modern society, *Journal of Accountancy*, February, pp.28–35.

Bird, P. (1970) The scope of the company audit, *Accounting and Business Research*, Winter, pp.44–9.

Bledstein, B.J. (1976) *The Culture of Professionalism*, W.W. Norton and Co., New York.

Boockholdt, J.L. (1983) A historical perspective on the auditor's role: the early experience of the American railroads, *Accounting Historians Journal*, Spring, pp.69–86.

Bowers, F. (1989) *Linguistic Aspects of Legislative Expression*, University of British Columbia Press.

Brief, R.P. (1975) The accountant's responsibility in historical perspective, *The Accounting Review*, April, pp.285–97.

Briloff, A.J. (1972) *Unaccountable Accounting*, Harper and Row, London.

Briloff, A.J. (1976) *More Debits Than Credits: The Burnt Investor's Guide to Financial Statements*, Harper and Row, London.

Briloff, A.J. (1990) Accountancy and society. a covenant desecrated, *Critical Perspectives on Accounting*, 1(1), pp.5–30.

Bromwich, M., Hopwood, A.G. and Shaw, J. (eds) (1982) *Auditing Research: Issues and Opportunities*, Pitman, London.

Brown, R. (ed.) (1905) *A History of Accounting and Accountants*, T.C. and E.C. Jack, Edinburgh.

Brown, R.G. (1962) Changing audit objectives and techniques, *The Accounting Review*, October, pp.696–703.

Burchell, S., Clubb, C., Hopwood, A., Hughes, J. and Nahapiet, J. (1980) The roles of accounting in organisations and society, *Accounting, Organisations and Society*, 5(1), pp.5–27.

Burke, P. (1992) The fabrication of Louis XIV, *History Today*, February, pp.24–30.

Burton, J.C. and Fairfield, P. (1982) Auditing evolution in a changing environment, *Auditing: A Journal of Practice and Theory*, Winter, pp.1–22.

Byington, S.R. and Sutton, S.G. (1991) The self-regulating profession: an analysis of the political monopoly tendencies of the audit profession, *Critical Perspectives on Accounting*, 2(4), pp.315–30.

Carmichael, D.R. (1988) The auditor's new guide to errors, irregularities and illegal acts, *Journal of Accountancy*, September, pp.40–8.

Carr, E.H. (1987) *What is History?*, Penguin Books, Harmondsworth.

Chambers, A. and Court, J.M. (1991) *Computer Auditing*, Pitman, London.

Chambers, R.J. (1962) Towards a general theory of accounting, *Australian Society of Accountants Annual Lecture*, University of Adelaide.

Chambers, R.J. (1963) Why bother with postulates?, *Journal of Accounting Research*, Spring, pp.3–15.

Chambers, R.J. (1966) *Accounting, Evaluation and Economic Behaviour*, Prentice-Hall, Englewood Cliffs, NJ.

Chambers, R.J. (1989) Time in accounting, *Abacus*, March, pp.7–21.

Chambers, R.J. and Wolnizer, P.W. (1991) A true and fair view of position and results: the historical background, *Accounting, Business and Financial History*, March, pp.197–213.

Chastney, J.G. (1975) True and fair view – history, meaning and impact of the 4th Directive, *Occasional Paper 6*, Institute of Chartered Accountants in England and Wales.

Chatfield, M. (1974) *History of Accounting Thought*, Dryden Press, San Diego, CA.

Chen, R.S. (1975) Social and financial stewardship, *The Accounting Review*, July, pp.533–43.

Clegg, S.R. (1989) *Frameworks of Power*, Sage Publications, London.

Coase, R.H. (1937) The nature of the firm, *Economica*, **4**, pp.386–405.

Collingwood, R.G. (1974) Human nature and human history, in P. Gardiner (ed.), *The Philosophy of History*, Oxford University Press, pp.17–40.

Connor, J.E. (1986) Enhancing public confidence in the accounting profession, *Journal of Accountancy*, July, pp.76–83.

Cooper, D.J. and Hopper, T.M. (1990) Stimulating research in critical accounts, in D.J. Cooper and T.M. Hopper (eds), *Critical Accounts*, Macmillan, London, pp.1–14.

Davies, J.J. (1979) Accountants' third party liability: a history of applied sociological jurisprudence, *Abacus*, December, pp.93–112.

Davies, P.C.W. and Brown, J.R. (1986) *The Ghost in the Atom*, University of Cambridge Press.

DeAngelo, L.E. (1981) Auditor independence, 'low balling,' and disclosure regulation, *Journal of Accounting and Economics*, August, pp.113–27.

Dicksee, L.R. (1892) *Auditing: A Practical Manual for Auditing*, Gee and Co., London.

Dillard, J.R. and Jensen, D.L. (1983) The auditor's report: an analysis of opinion, *The Accounting Review*, October, pp.787–98.

Drummond, A. (1891–3) On the mode of conducting an audit, *Transactions of the CA Students' Society of Edinburgh*, pp.3–16.

Ewen, S. (1988) *All Consuming Images: The Politics of Style in Contemporary Culture*, Basic Books, New York.

Felix, W.L. and Niles, M.S. (1988) Research in internal control evaluation, *Auditing: A Journal of Practice & Theory*, Spring, pp.43–60.

Financial Accounting Standards Board (1978) Objectives of financial reporting by business enterprises, *Statements of Financial Accounting Concepts 1*, Financial Accounting Standards Board.

Financial Accounting Standards Board (1980) Qualitative characteristics of accounting information, *Statements of Financial Accounting Concepts 2*, Financial Accounting Standards Board.

Financial Accounting Standards Board (1984) Recognition and measurement in financial statements of business enterprises, *Statements of Financial Accounting Concepts 5*, Financial Accounting Standards Board.

Financial Accounting Standards Board (1985) Elements of financial statements of business enterprises, *Statements of Financial Accounting Concepts 6*, Financial Accounting Standards Board.

Firth, M. (1980) Perceptions of auditor independence and official ethical guidelines, *The Accounting Review*, July, pp.451–66.

Flesher, T.K. and Flesher, D.L. (1984) The development of the auditor's report in the United States, *Working Paper 45, Working Paper Series, Vol.3*, The Academy of Accounting Historians, pp.58–70.

Flint, D. (1971) The role of the auditor in modern society: an exploratory essay, *Accounting and Business Research*, Autumn, pp.287–93.

Flint, D. (1982) *A True and Fair View in Company Accounts*, Gee and Co., London.

Flint, D. (1988) *Philosophy and Principles of Auditing: An Introduction*, Macmillan, London.

Fogarty, T.J., Heian, J.B. and Knutson, D.L. (1991) The rationality of doing 'nothing': responses to legal liability in an institutionalised environment, *Critical Perspectives on Accounting*, 2(3), pp.201–26.

Foucault, M. (1977) *Discipline and Punish: The Birth of the Prison*, Allen Lane, London.

Fraser, I.A.M. and Nobes, C.W. (1985) The assumed users in three accounting theories, *Accounting and Business Research*, Spring, pp.144–7.

Gaa, J.C. (1991) The expectations game: regulation of auditors by government and the profession, *Critical Perspectives on Accounting*, 2(1), pp.83–108.

Gambling, T. (1977) Magic accounting and morale, *Accounting Organisations and Society*, 2(2), pp.141–52.

Gambling, T. (1978) *Beyond the Conventions of Accounting*, Macmillan, London.

Gambling, T. (1987) Accounting for rituals, *Accounting, Organisations and Society*, 12(4), pp.319–29.

Gambling, T. (1990a) Reality, image and accounting, unpublished paper, University of Birmingham.

Gambling, T. (1990b) Accounting as the sport of kings, unpublished paper, University of Birmingham.

Garner, P. (1966) The development of accounting principles and standards, in P. Garner and K.B. Berg (eds), *Readings in Accounting Theory*, Houghton Mifflin, Boston, MA, pp.95–109.

Gerboth, D. (1987) The accounting game, *Accounting Horizons*, December, pp.96–9.

Godsell, D. (1991) *Auditors' Legal Duties and Liabilities*, Longman, Hardmondsworth.

Goldman, A. and Barlev, B. (1974) The auditor–firm conflict of interests: its implications for independence, *The Accounting Review*, October, pp.707–18.

Goodrich, P. (1987) *Legal Discourse: Studies in Linguistics, Rhetoric and Legal Analysis*, Macmillan, London.

Gower, L.C.B. (1979) *Principles of Modern Company Law*, Stevens & Sons, London.

Grant, J. (1991) Planning for an effective and efficient audit in a computerised environment, in M. Sherer and S. Turley (eds), *Current Issues in Auditing*, Paul Chapman Publishing, London, pp.163–71.

Gray, R. (1990) The greening of accountancy: the profession after Pearce, *Certified Research Report 17*, The Chartered Association of Certified Accountants.

Gray, R. (1991) Evidence and judgment, in M. Sherer and S. Turley (eds), *Current Issues in Auditing*, Paul Chapman Publishing, pp.131–43.

Gray, R. (1992) Book review, *Accounting, Auditing and Accountability Journal*, 5(1), pp.92–3.

Gregory, B. (1988) *Inventing Reality: Physics as a Language*, John Wiley, Chichester.

Griffiths, I. (1986) *Creative Accounting*, Sidgwick and Jackson, London.

Guthrie, S.C. (1968) *Christian Doctrine: Teachings of the Christian Church*, John Knox Press, Louisville, KY.

Guy, D.M. and Sullivan, J.D. (1988) The expectations gap auditing standards, *Journal of Accountancy*, April, pp.36–46.

Gwilliam, D. (1987) *A Survey of Auditing Research*, Prentice-Hall, Englewood Cliffs, NJ.

Gwilliam, D. (1991) The auditor's liability to third parties, in M. Sherer and S. Turley (eds), *Current Issues in Auditing*, Paul Chapman Publishing, London, pp.60–75.

Hain, H.P. (1966) Accounting control in the Zenon Papyri, *The Accounting Review*, October, pp.669–703.

Harper, R.M., Strawser, J.R. and Tang, K. (1990) Establishing investigation thresholds for preliminary analytical procedures, *Auditing: A Journal of Practice & Theory*, Fall, pp.115–33.

Harvey, D. (1989) *The Condition of Modernity*, Basil Blackwell, Oxford.

Hatherly, D. (1992) A case of treating the symptoms?, *Accountancy*, March, p.33.

Hatherly, D.J. and Skuse, P.C.B. (1991) Audit reports, in M. Sherer and S. Turley (eds), *Current Issues in Auditing*, Paul Chapman Publishing, London, pp.115–30.

Heath, L.C. (1987) Accounting communication and the Pygmalion syndrome, *Accounting Horizons*, March, pp.1–8.

Heiman, V.B. (1990) Auditors' assessments of the likelihood of error explanations in analytical review, *The Accounting Review*, October, pp.875–90.

Hein, L.W. (1963) The auditor and the British Companies Acts, *The Accounting Review*, July, pp.508–20.

Hein, L.W. (1978) *The British Companies Acts and the Practice of Accountancy: 1844–1962*, Arno Press, Salem, NH.

Higson, A. (1991) The rise of analytical auditing procedures, in M. Sherer and S. Turley (eds), *Current Issues in Auditing*, Paul Chapman Publishing, London, pp.172–80.

Hines, R.D. (1982) The usefulness of annual reports: the anomaly between the efficient markets hypothesis and shareholder studies, *Accounting and Business Research*, Autumn, pp.296–309.

Hines, R.D. (1988) Financial accounting: in communicating reality, we construct reality, *Accounting, Organisations and Society*, 13(3), pp.256–61.

Hines, R.D. (1989a) The sociopolitical paradigm in financial accounting research, *Accounting, Auditing and Accountability Journal*, 2(1), pp.52–76.

Hines, R.D. (1989b) Financial accounting knowledge, conceptual framework projects and the social construction of the accounting profession, *Accounting, Auditing and Accountability Journal*, 2(2), pp.72–92.

Hogarth, R.M. (1991) A perspective on cognitive research in auditing, *The Accounting Review*, April, pp.277–90.

Holmes, G. (1991) The auditors' 364 days without teeth, *Accountancy*, April, pp.30–1.

Hooks, K.L. (1992) Professionalism and self interest: a critical view of the expectations gap, *Critical Perspectives on Accounting*, **3**(2), pp.109–36.

Hopwood, A.G. (1987) The archaeology of accounting systems, *Accounting, Organisations and Society*, **8**(2/3), pp.207–34.

Hopwood, A.G. (1990) Accounting and organisation change, *Accounting, Auditing and Accountability Journal*, **3**(1), pp.7–17.

Hopwood, A.G. and Johnston, H.T. (1986) Accounting history's claim to legitimacy, *International Journal of Accounting*, Spring, pp.37–46.

Houghton, G.W. and Fogarty, J.A. (1991) Inherent risk, *Auditing: A Journal of Practice & Theory*, Spring, pp.1–21.

Humphrey, C. (1991) Audit expectations, in M. Sherer and S. Turley (eds), *Current Issues in Auditing*, Paul Chapman Publishing, London, pp.3–21.

Humphrey, C., Moizer, P. and Turley, S. (1992a) *The Audit Expectations Gap in the United Kingdom*, Institute of Chartered Accountants in England and Wales.

Humphrey, C., Moizer, P. and Turley, S. (1992b) The audit expectations gap – plus ça change, plus c'est la meme chose?, *Critical Perspectives on Accounting*, **3**(2), pp.137–62.

Huss, H.F. and Jacobs, F.A. (1991) Risk containment: exploring auditor decisions in the engagement process, *Auditing: A Journal of Practice & Theory*, Fall, pp.16–32.

ICAS (1992) Integrity, objectivity and independence, *Statement of Professional Conduct 1*, Institute of Chartered Accountants of Scotland.

ICAS/ICAEW (1989) *Auditing and the Future*, Proceedings of an Auditing Research Conference, Institute of Chartered Accountants of Scotland and Institute of Chartered Accountants in England and Wales.

Ingram, R.W. and Rayburn, F.R. (1989) Representational faithfulness and economic consequences: their roles in accounting policy, *Journal of Accounting and Public Policy*, Spring, pp.57–68.

Jenkinson, M.W. (1913–14) The audit of a public limited company, *The Glasgow CA Students' Society Transactions*, pp.113–26.

Johnson, O. (1992) Business judgment v. audit judgment: why the legal distinction?, *Accounting, Organisations and Society*, **17**(3/4), pp.205–22.

Johnson, T.J. (1972) *Professions and Power*, Macmillan, London.

Johnson, L.T. and Storey, R.K. (1982) *Recognition in Financial Statement: Underlying Concepts and Practical Conventions*, Financial Accounting Standards Board.

Kedslie, M.J.M. (1990) *Firm Foundations: The Development of Professional Accounting in Scotland 1850–1900*, University of Hull Press.

Kissinger, J.N. (1977) A general theory of evidence as the conceptual foundation in auditing theory: some comments and extensions, *The Accounting Review*, April, pp.322–39.

Kitchen, J. (1982) Auditing: past developments and current practice, in A.G. Hopwood, M. Bromwich and J. Shaw (eds), *Auditing Research: Issues and Opportunities*, Pitman, London, pp.25–51.

Knapp, M.C. (1985) Audit conflict: an empirical study of the perceived ability of auditors to resist management pressure, *The Accounting Review*, April, pp.202–11.

Krause, E.A. (1971) *The Sociology of Occupations*, Little, Brown, Boston, MA.

Lacey, J.M. (1986) Issues in the perception of auditor independence, *Research Report 1*, SEC and Financial Reporting Institute.

Langenderfer, H.Q. (1987) Accounting education's history: a 100-year search for identity, *Journal of Accountancy*, May, pp.302–31.

Larson, M.S. (1977) *The Rise of Professionalism: A Sociological Analysis*, University of California Press.

Lavin, D. (1976) Perceptions of the independence of auditors, *The Accounting Review*, January, pp.41–50.

Lee, T.A. (1968) The impact of company legislation on the independence of auditors, *The Accountant's Magazine*, July, pp.363–7.

Lee, T.A. (1970a) A brief history of company audits: 1840–1940, *The Accountant's Magazine*, August, pp.363–8.

Lee, T.A. (1970b) The nature of auditing and its objectives, *Accountancy*, April, pp.292–6.

Lee, T.A. (1971) The historical development of internal control from the earliest times to the end of the seventeenth century, *Journal of Accounting Research*, Spring, pp.150–7.

Lee, T.A. (1972) *Company Auditing: Concepts and Practices*, Institute of Chartered Accountants of Scotland.

Lee, T.A. (1977) The modern audit function: a study of radical change, in B. Carsberg and T. Hope (eds), *Current Issues in Accounting*, Philip Allan, Englewood Cliffs, NJ, pp.87–106.

Lee, T.A. (1982) The will-o'-the-wisp of 'true and fair', *The Accountant*, 15 July, pp.16–18.

Lee, T.A. (1984) Materiality: a review and analysis of its reporting significance and auditing implications, *Audit Brief*, Auditing Practices Committee.

Lee, T.A. (1986) *Company Auditing*, Gee and Co., London.

Lee, T.A. (ed) (1988) *The Evolution of Auditing Thought and Practice*, Garland Publishing, New York.

Lee, T.A. (1992a) Following through on relevance and reliability, *Accountancy*, July, p.90.

Lee, T.A. (1992b) Financial reporting quality labels, image-making and the social construction of the audit profession, Working Paper, University of Alabama.

Lee, T.A. and Tweedie, D.P. (1977) *The Private Shareholder and the Corporate Report*, Institute of Chartered Accountants in England and Wales.

Lee, T.A. and Tweedie, D.P. (1981) *Institutional Use and Understanding of Financial Information*, Institute of Chartered Accountants in England and Wales.

Littleton, A.C. and Zimmerman, V.K. (1962) *Accounting Theory: Continuity and Change*, Prentice-Hall, Englewood Cliffs, NJ.

Lloyd, C. (1986) *Explanation in Social History*, Basil Blackwell, Oxford.

Lyall, D. and Perks, R. (1976) Creating a state auditing board?, *Accountancy*, June, pp.34–6.

Mannix, E.F. (1976) *Professional Negligence*, Butterworths, London.

Manson, S. (1991) Statistical sampling, in M. Sherer and S. Turley (eds), *Current Issues in Auditing*, Paul Chapman Publishing, London, pp.181–98.

Marrian, I.F.Y. (1988) *Audit Committees*, Institute of Chartered Accountants of Scotland.

Marwick, A. (1981) *The Nature of History*, Macmillan, London.

Mattessich, R. (1991) Social reality and the measurement of its phenomena, *Advances in Accounting*, **9**, pp.3–17.

Mautz, R.K. and Sharaf, H.A. (1961) *The Philosophy of Auditing*, American Accounting Association.

McEnroe, J.E. (1991) Attitudes towards the term 'generally accepted accounting principles', *Accounting and Business Research*, Spring, pp.157–62.

McGee, A. (1991) The 'true and fair view' debate: a study in the legal regulation of accounting, *The Modern Law Review*, November, pp.874–88.

McMonnies, P.N. (ed) (1983) *Making Corporate Reports Valuable*, Kogan Page, New York.

McNally, G.M., Eng, L.H. and Hasseldine, C.R. (1982) Corporate financial reporting in New Zealand: an analysis of user preferences, corporate characteristics and disclosure practices for discretionary information, *Accounting and Business Research*, Winter, pp.11–20.

Miller, P. and O'Leary, T. (1987) Accounting and the construction of the governable person, *Accounting, Organisations and Society*, **12**(3), pp.235–65.

Miller, T. (1992) Do we need to consider the individual auditor when discussing auditor independence?, *Accounting, Auditing and Accountability Journal*, **5**(2), pp.74–84.

Mills, S.K. and Bettner, M.S. (1992) Ritual and conflict in the audit profession, *Critical Perspectives on Accounting*, **3**(2), pp.185–200.

Mitchell, A., Puxty, A., Sikka, P. and Willmott, H. (1991) Accounting for change: proposals for reform of audit and accounting, *Discussion Paper 7*, Fabian Society.

Moizer, P. (1991) Independence, in M. Sherer and S. Turley (eds), *Current Issues in Auditing*, Paul Chapman Publishing, London, pp.34–46.

Montagna, P.D. (1974) Public accounting: the dynamics of occupational change, in R.R. Sterling (ed.), *Institutional Issues in Public Accounting*, Scholars Book Co., Houston, TX, pp.3–24.

Montgomery, R.H. (1912) *Auditing Theory and Practice*, The Ronald Press Company, New York.

Moonitz, M. (1961) The basic postulates of accounting, *Accounting Research Study 1*, American Institute of Certified Public Accountants.

Moore, D.C. (1991) Accounting on trial: the critical legal studies movement and its lessons for radical accounting, *Accounting, Organisations and Society*, **16**(8), pp.763–91.

Morgan, G. (1982) Accounting as reality construction: towards a new epistemology for accounting practice, *Accounting, Organisations and Society*, **13**(5), pp.477–85.

Moyer, C.A. (1951) Early developments in American auditing, *The Accounting Review*, January, pp.3–8.

Murphy, A.E. (1943) *The Uses of Reason*, Macmillan, London.

Murphy, R. (1991) Time to rebuild the audit foundations?, *Accountancy*, May, pp.23–4.

Ng, D.S. (1978) An information economics analysis of financial reporting and external auditing, *The Accounting Review*, October, pp.910–20.

Ng, D.S. and Stoeckenius, J. (1979) Auditing: incentives and truthful reporting, *Journal of Accounting Research Supplement*, pp.1–34.

Page, M.J. (1991a) The auditor and the smaller company, in M. Sherer and S. Turley (eds), *Current Issues in Auditing*, Paul Chapman Publishing, London, pp.211–23.

Page, M. (1991b) Now is the time to be more critical, *Accountancy*, October, p.31.

Pany, K. and Reckers, P.M.J. (1980) The effect of gifts, discounts, and client size on perceived auditor independence, *The Accounting Review*, January, pp.50–61.

Parker, J.R.E. (1964) The accounting principles dilemma, *The Canadian Chartered Accountant*, October, pp.271–3.

Parker, R.H. and Nobes, C.W. (1991) 'True and fair': UK auditors' view, *Accounting and Business Research*, Autumn, pp.349–61.

Paton, W.A. and Littleton, A.C. (1947) *An Introduction to Corporate Accounting Standards*, American Accounting Association.

Peel, M.J. (1989) The going-concern qualification debate: some UK evidence, *British Accounting Review*, December, pp.329–50.

Pixley, F.W. (1881) *Auditors: Their Duties and Responsibilities*, Effingham Wilson, London.

Popkin, R.H. (1981) *Philosophy Made Simple*, Heinemann, Oxford.

Popper, K. (1986) *The Poverty of Historicism*, Ark Paperbacks, London.

Power, M. (1991) Auditing and environmental expertise: between protest and professionalisation, *Accounting, Auditing and Accountability Journal*, **4**(3), pp.30–42.

Previts, G.J., Parker, L.D. and Coffman, E.N. (1990) Accounting history: definition and relevance, *Abacus*, March, pp.1–13.

Rebele, J.E., Heintz, J.A. and Briden, G.E. (1988) Independent auditor sensitivity to evidence reliability, *Auditing: A Journal of Practice & Theory*, Fall, pp.43–52.

Richardson, A.J. (1988) Accounting knowledge and professional privilege, *Accounting, Organisations and Society*, **13**(4), pp.381–96.

Robertson, W. (1897) The nature and extent of an auditor's responsibility, *The Accountant*, 26 June, pp.632–8.

Ronen, J. (1974) A user orientated development of accounting information requirements, in J.J. Cramer and G.H. Sorter (eds), *Objectives of Financial Statements*, **2**, American Institute of Certified Public Accountants, pp.80–103.

Ruland, R.G. (1984) Duty, obligation and responsibility in accounting policy making, *Journal of Accounting and Public Policy*, Fall, pp.223–37.

Rutherford, B.A. (1988) The doctrine of substance over form, *Research Report 11*, The Chartered Association of Certified Accountants.

Ruud, T.F. (1989) *Auditing as Verification of Financial Information*, Norwegian University Press.

Ryan, F.J.O. (1967) A true and fair view, *Abacus*, December, pp.95–108.

Schandl, C.W. (1978) *Theory of Auditing: Evaluation, Investigation, and Judgment*, Scholars Book Co., Houston, TX.

Securities and Exchange Commission (1984) Matters relating to independent accountants, *Section 600*, Securities and Exchange Commission.

Sennetti, J.T. (1990) Toward a more consistent model for audit risk, *Auditing: A Journal of Practice & Theory*, Spring, pp.103–12.

Shaw, J.C. (1980) *The Audit Report: What it Says and What it Means*, Gee and Co., London.

Sherer, M. and Kent, D. (1983) *Auditing and Accountability*, Pitman, London.

Sherer, M. and Turley, S. (eds) (1991) *Current Issues in Auditing*, Paul Chapman Publishing, London.

Shockley, R.A. (1981) Perceptions of auditors' independence: an empirical analysis, *The Accounting Review*, October, pp.785–800.

Sikka, P. (1987) Professional education and auditing books: a review article, *The British Accounting Review*, December, pp.291–304.

Sikka, P., Willmott, H. and Lowe, T. (1989) Guardians of knowledge and public interest: evidence and issues of accountability in the UK accountancy profession, *Accounting, Auditing and Accountability Journal*, 2(2), pp.47–71.

Sikka, P., Puxty, T., Willmott, H. and Cooper, C. (1992) Eliminating the expectations gap?, *Certified Research Report 28*, The Chartered Association of Certified Accountants.

Skerratt, L.C.L. (1982) Auditing in the corporate sector: a survey, in A.G. Hopwood and M. Bromwich (eds), *Auditing Research: Issues and Opportunities*, Pitman, London, pp.69–80.

Solomons, D. (1989) *Guidelines for Financial Reporting Standards*, Institute of Chartered Accountants in England and Wales.

Solomons, D. (1991) Accounting and social change: a neutralist view, *Accounting, Organisations and Society*, **16**(3), pp.287–96.

Spacek, L. (1958a) Challenges to public accounting, *Harvard Business Review*, May–June, pp.115–24.

Spacek, L. (1958b) The need for an accounting court, *The Accounting Review*, July, pp.368–79.

Stamp, E. (1970) Reforming accounting principles, in E. Stamp and C. Marley (eds), *Accounting Principles and the City Code: The Case for Reform*, Butterworths, London, pp.63–154.

Stamp, E. (1980) *Corporate Reporting: Its Future Evolution*, Canadian Institute of Chartered Accountants.

Staub, W.A. (1943) Mode of conducting an audit, *The Accounting Review*, (1904), April, pp.91–8.

Staubus, G.J. (1977) *Making Accounting Decisions*, Scholars Book Co., Houston, TX.

Sterling, R.R. (1967) A statement of basic accounting theory: a review article, *Journal of Accounting Research*, Spring, pp.95–112.

Sterling, R.R. (1970a) On theory construction and verification, *The Accounting Review*, July, pp.444–57.

Sterling, R.R. (1970b) *Theory of the Measurement of Enterprise Income*, University Press of Kansas.

Sterling, R.R. (1972) Decision orientated financial accounting, *Accounting and Business Research*, Summer, pp.198–208.

Sterling, R.R. (1977) Accounting in the 1980s, in N.M. Bedford (ed.), *Accountancy in the 1980s – Some Issues*, Council of Arthur Young Professors, University of Illinois, pp.1–44.

Sterling, R.R. (1979) *Toward a Science of Accounting*, Scholars Book Co., Houston, TX.

Sterling, R.R. (1985) *An Essay on Recognition*, University of Sydney Press.

Sterling, R.R. (1981) Costs (historical versus current) versus exit values, *Abacus*, December, pp.93–129.

Sterling, R.R. (1990) Positive accounting: an assessment, *Abacus*, September, pp.97–135.

Stewart, J.C. (1957) Current auditing problems – some reflections and queries, *The Accountant's Magazine*, April, pp.212–39.

Stewart, J.C. (1986) *Pioneers of a Profession, Chartered Accountants to 1879*, Garland Publishing (1977), New York.

Stone, W.E. (1969) Antecedents of the accounting profession, *The Accounting Review*, April, pp.284–91.

Storey, R.K. (1964) *The Search for Accounting Principles: Today's Problems in Perspective*, American Institute of Certified Public Accountants.

Temkin, R.H. and Winters, A.J. (1988) SAS No.55: the auditor's new responsibility for internal control, *Journal of Accountancy*, May, pp.86–98.

Thornton, D.B. (1988) Theory and metaphor in accounting, *Accounting Horizons*, December 1988, pp.1–9.

Thurley, S. (1991) Palaces for a nouveau riche king, *History Today*, June, pp.10–14.

Tietjen, A.C. (1963) Accounting principles, practices and methods, *Journal of Accountancy*, April, pp.65–8.

Tilley, I. (1975) A critique of historical record accounting, *Accounting and Business Research*, Summer, pp.185–97.

Tinker, T. (1985) *Paper Prophets: A Social Critique of Accounting*, Holt, Rinehart and Winston, London.

Tinker, T. (1991) The accountant as partisan, *Accounting, Organisations and Society*, **16**(3), pp.297–310.

Tinker, T. and Neimark, M. (1990) Displacing the corporation with deconstructionism and dialectics, in D.J. Cooper and T.M. Hopper (eds), *Critical Accounts*, Macmillan, London, pp.44–63.

Toba, Y. (1975) A general theory of evidence as the conceptual foundation in auditing theory, *The Accounting Review*, January, pp.7–24.

Toynbee, A. (1972) *A Study of History*, Weathervane Books, Walnut Creek, CA.

Tweedie, D. (1987) Challenges facing the auditor: professional fouls and the expectation gap, *Deloitte Haskins and Sells Lecture*, University College Cardiff.

Tweedie, D.P. (1991) Fraud – managements' and auditors' responsibilities for its prevention and detection, in M. Sherer and S. Turley (eds), *Current Issues in Auditing*, Paul Chapman Publishing, London, pp.22–33.

Tweedie, D.P. and Whittington, G. (1990) Financial reporting: current problems and their implications for systematic reform, *Accounting and Business Research*, Winter, pp.87–102.

Vinten, G. (1991) Modern internal auditing, in M. Sherer and S. Turley (eds), *Current Issues in Auditing*, Paul Chapman Publishing, London, pp.224–39.

Walker, S.P. (1988) *The Society of Accountants in Edinburgh, 1854–1914: A Study of Recruitment to a New Profession*, Garland Publishing, New York.

Wallace, W.A. (1985) 'The Economic Role of the Audit in Free and Regulated Markets,' *Auditing Monograph 1*, Macmillan, London, pp.13–56.

Waterhouse, N. (1934) The liability of auditors, *The Accountant*, 27 January, pp.121–7.

Watts, R. and Zimmerman, J. (1986) *Positive Accounting Theory*, Prentice-Hall, Englewood Cliffs, NJ.

Whittington, G. (1991) Good stewardship and the ASB's objectives, *Accountancy*, November, p.33.

Williams, P.F. (1987) The legitimate concern with fairness, *Accounting, Organisations and Society*, **12**(2), pp.169–92.

Williamson, O.E. (1975) *Markets and Hierarchies: Analysis and Antitrust Implications: A Study in the Economics of Internal Organisation*, Free Press, New York.

Williamson, O.E. (1981) The modern corporation: origins, evolution, attributes, *Journal of Economic Literature*, December 1981, pp.1537–68.

Willmott, H. (1990) Serving the public interest? A critical analysis of a professional claim, in D.J. Cooper and T.M. Hopper (eds), *Critical Accounts*, Macmillan, London, pp.315–31.

Willmott, H. (1991) The auditing game: a question of ownership and control, *Critical Perspectives on Accounting*, 2(1), pp.109–21.

Wolnizer, P.W. (1987) *Auditing as Independent Authentication*, Sydney University Press.

Youkins, E.W. (1983) A history of auditors' independence in the US, *The Accounting Historians Notebook*, Spring, pp.1 and 22–7.

Zeff, S.A. (1972) *Forging Accounting Principles in Five Countries: A History and Analysis of Trends*, Stipes Publishing, Champaign, IL.

Zeff, S.A. (1987) Does the CPA belong to a profession?, *Accounting Horizons*, June, pp.65–8.

Index